S0-AVO-434

THE
LEMON
BOOK

Auto Rights

THE LEMON BOOK

Auto Rights

Ralph Nader
Clarence Ditlow
with
Laura Polacheck
and Tamar Rhode

MOYER BELL LIMITED : MOUNT KISCO, NEW YORK

To all the embittered lemon owners who shared their frustrations
with us, we dedicate this book.

Published by Moyer Bell Limited

Copyright © 1990 by Center for Auto Safety

All rights reserved. No part of this publication may be reproduced
or transmitted in any form or by any means electronic or mechanical, including photocopying, recording or any information re-
trieval system, without permission in writing from Moyer Bell
Limited, Colonial Hill, Mt. Kisco, New York 10549

Third Edition

**LIBRARY OF CONGRESS
CATALOGING-IN-PUBLICATION DATA**

Nader, Ralph.
    The lemon book / Ralph Nader and Clarence Ditlow. —3rd ed.
    p. cm.
    ISBN 1-55921-019-2 : —ISBN 1-55921-020-6 (pbk.) :
    1. Automobiles—Purchasing. I. Ditlow, Clarence.
    II. Title.
TL162.N28 1989
629.222—dc20   89-37111
                                                            CIP

Printed in the United States of America

CONTENTS

CONTENTS

APPENDICES

INTRODUCTION

If the dictionary wished to illustrate the word "frustration," it could not do better than describe the feelings of a new car owner who has landed a lemon. After shelling out sixteen thousand dollars or more for a new car, the consumer reasonably expects to own a vehicle that meets certain standards of quality, performance and reliability.

At the time our first lemon owner's manual was published in 1970, the consumer was effectively shut out of the legal system—most lawyers wouldn't touch a lemon case because of the relatively small amount of money involved when compared to legal fees. The individual who fought a giant auto company in court made the headlines because it was so rare.

When our second lemon book was published in 1980, the system had changed but not enough. More consumers got redress. Many consumers had followed the advice in the first book and obtained refunds for their lemons; others created new strategies in seeking redress that were reported in the second book for buyers to follow. But while customers got more persistent in remedying their lemons, manufacturers got more resistant to replacing them.

While Congress had passed a federal lemon law known as the Magnuson-Moss Warranty Act in 1975, the auto companies exploited loopholes in it to avoid application of the refund/replacement provision for lemons. Regulatory agencies set up to safeguard the buyer had come under the influence of industry lobbyists and failed to carry out their mandates to protect consumers.

Auto manufacturers have not changed since the days of the Model-T, let alone since the 1970 or 1980 *Lemon Books*. When it comes to consumer protection, public health and safety, there's nothing new under the hood—what auto companies can get away with, they will. If the government doesn't require it, and it can be concealed from consumers, the auto companies won't produce it.

The Center for Auto Safety and I still receive tens of thousands of letters from angry motorists each year who were sold lemons. In reading through the torrent of lemon letters, it is obvious that the letter writers are saying something greater and beyond their individual problems. They are saying that even though the law has been improved, it is still inaccessible to their pleas for receiving the automotive value for which they paid. They are marketplace victims with neither effective rights nor remedies.

Many of these letters contain details of the defects and the twisted unresponsive route that the buyer pursued to the dealer and then up the hierarchy of the auto company's bureaucracy. Only a persistent few received justice. The rest were given the corporate straight arm. Anarchy, carefully contrived by the auto industry, still prevails.

During the 1980's, the auto industry dominated the decision-making in Washington more than ever before. From its first days in 1981, the Reagan Administration ignored its duty to enforce the law and, instead, kept its political promise to get the government off the backs of the car companies. Recalls plummeted to record lows as defect investigations were dropped. All rule making ceased and major safety standards were rolled back. The revocation of the bumper standard prohibiting any damage to cars in 5 MPH crashes alone cost consumers $5 billion per year, a hefty portion of which lined the pockets of car companies as consumers were forced to buy replacement bumpers and fenders when they would have previously driven away without a dent.

Only the ceaseless work of consumer and safety activists during this time prevented greater carnage and damage. They took the revocation of the passive restraint standard to the Supreme Court and won a unanimous decision that the revocation was illegal. As a result, every 1990 car will have passive restraints with many having the lifesaving air bag. Other measures such as tread wear ratings for tires and emission recalls were also reinstated by the courts.

It takes no special insight to observe that these failures are correctable with different leadership. Indeed, Congress had given the Department of Transportation, Environmental Protection Agency and

Federal Trade Commission additional and strengthened authority in the 1970's to perform their tasks. What is still needed is the passage of a government official's accountability law and an affirmative program of citizens access and right to sue, with federal funds for needy petitioners. This change would provide avenues of direct public discipline and direction for agencies who now surrender to inappropriate, excessive or unlawful industry and White House pressures.

What **has changed** in the past two decades is the consumer's willingness to fight back. More and more consumers have become less and less willing to tolerate the failure of the auto industry to provide reliable vehicles meeting minimal industry, not to mention higher, standards of quality, durability and performance. When the consumer instead receives a lemon, or an otherwise unsafe and unreliable car, topped off with poor warranty performance by manufacturer and dealer, he or she wants to do something about it; and this greater degree of consumer awareness is reflected in the outpouring of consumer complaints on automobiles.

This increase in consumer resistance and awareness has funneled into a significant consumer strength. Determined consumers are banding together to protect their consumer rights, putting pressure on their lawmakers to provide consumers with a more responsive complaint handling system—improving the lemon owners' chances of obtaining full refunds for their lemons. Many of their success stories are described throughout this book to illustrate the usefulness of the strategies we suggest.

In response to this consumer outcry for greater protection, 45 states and the District of Columbia have passed lemon laws since 1982 to better enable consumers to return their lemons. Even here the auto companies attempted to dilute the effectiveness of state lemon laws by setting up industry-run arbitration boards to decide when to order a refund for a lemon. These industry boards more often resembled kangaroo courts than fair and impartial tribunals. But consumer groups such as Motor Voters and legislators such as John Woodcock of Connecticut fought back to get the auto company fox out of the arbitration chicken coop by setting up independent, state-run boards through revised "lemon law II's" in states such as New York, Connecticut, Minnesota, Vermont and Massachusetts.

With the aid of thousands of letters from lemon owners, we have prepared this volume of material that describes, first, how best to get your vehicle fixed or replaced, and next, how to avoid the lemon experience the next time you buy a car. There are no easy ways to achieve these objectives, and this book does not pretend otherwise. What it does strive to do is offer advice to the embattled car buyer, to educate the legal profession about the viability of these cases, and to push for more basic reforms of the laws and remedies to protect the new car buyer.

Consumers are the key to all of these objectives. Their detailed complaints provide documented examples and reflect the urgent need for reform movements that reach back into the plants and onto the design boards where the defects are born and raised. Their often creative response to manufacturer-dealer obstinacy suggests ways to break the log jams and win.

Individual consumer complaints often lead to recalls of defective vehicles. General Motors's reluctant recall of 6.7 million 1965–69 Chevrolets with defective engine mounts is not only the largest recall in history but also a prime example of the importance of citizen pressure and widespread publicity about safety hazards. This matter first came to light when several citizens complained to me about the nightmarish failure of their cars' engine mounts—a jammed accelerator and gear shift, loss of power braking and steering wheel assist resulting in loss of vehicle control. On investigating the defect, I found that GM had successfully stalled a government investigation by claiming arrogantly that there was no safety defect. More and more complaints were received as news stories were generated about people who had experienced this defective behavior in GM cars. Under intense public pressure, the long dormant investigation of this defect was pulled from the back files of the Department of Transportation where it had been buried by corporate deceit and bureaucratic indifference. Without the tenacity of the media led by Detroit News reporter Robert Irwin who wrote dozens of articles on GM's efforts to cover up the engine mount scandal and concerned owners who complained loudly and persistently about the potentially catastrophic consequences of engine mount failure, this defect might have remained uncorrected.

Consumer organizing and citizen action can bring corporate giants to earth even where the government fails to act. Diane Halferty of Seattle organized Consumers Against General Motors (CAGM) when General Motors sold her the economic lemon of the century, a 1978

Cadillac with a 350 cubic inch diesel engine that was nothing more than a converted gasoline engine. Instead of the legendary 250,000 mile durability of a diesel, the 1.1 million GM diesels scarcely made it to 50,000 miles without a major engine failure. Even worse, the models' resale value plummeted by $3000-6000 as consumers learned of their defects. Rather than be rolled over by GM, Diane Halferty not only organized CAGM but also petitioned the Federal Trade Commission, alerted the national media, filed legal actions and helped organize other GM diesel groups around the country ranging from GMDUDS in Chicago to DOGMAD in San Diego, DDOG in Virginia, Lemon on Wheels in New York and DIESELGATE in Oregon. This concerted consumer action forced GM to drop the diesel in 1985 and reimburse consumers well over a half billion dollars through class action settlements, arbitration, individual legal settlements, extended warranties and free repairs.

More suggestions and more information and more successes are needed for readers, as future editions of this manual will depend heavily on and grow from readers' responses. In effect, the readers have helped to build, piece by piece, an ever more effective handbook of action, which in turn should stimulate the emergence of a just system to resolve complaints quickly and cheaply for all car buyers— new and used. Finally, the more basic objective—better quality automobiles—is more fully attained when the consumer obtains justice in the market- place.

The immense impact of the auto industry on the economy, the environment, and automobile casualties, requires an equally immense consumer alert. The benefits already reaped from auto industry regulations are enormous—motor vehicle safety standards alone have saved over 150,000 lives since 1968, the 55 MPH speed limit saved another 50,000 lives since its imposition in 1974, smog violations decreased by 38% between 1979 and 1986 as tighter statutory auto emission standards took effect, fuel economy standards have reduced oil imports by over 3 billion barrels per day and saved drivers over $40 billion annually in gasoline costs, and more lemons were returned in 1989 than any other year.

But there are still miles to go, lives to saved, air to be cleaned, and lemons to be squeezed before we can say the auto has been tamed. Last year, more than 47,000 lives were lost on the highways and over 2 million more suffered disabling injuries. Safer motor vehicles, utilizing practical and inexpensive safety features, could have prevented well over half of these fatalities and injuries. In 1988, over 100 million Americans lived in areas that still had air pollution violations. Tighter exhaust standards, cleaner fuels, and more use of mass transit could clean the air to healthy levels within the next 10 years in all but the worst areas such as Los Angeles. Doubling fuel economy standards to 55 MPG by the year 2000 would save 1.5 million barrels per day more gasoline and help lead the way to reduce global warming. Strong lemon laws with consumer counsel and independent arbitration mechanisms would make manufacturers, not consumers, pay for lemons.

Your decision to act, along with other buyers, depends on your determination. If you would prefer to suffer silently than develop the know-how to fight and win, this book is not for you. If you crave for justice and see yourself as a spark plug to help achieve it, then read on, my friend, read on.

—R.N.

ACKNOWLEDGMENTS

It is difficult in a brief acknowledgment to express the full appreciation we owe to the many people who contributed their efforts to the production of this book.

For undertaking the initial work in writing a book to help lemon owners, we thank Lowell Dodge and Ralf Hotchkiss, co-authors of *What to Do With Your Bad Car* (Grossman Publishers 1971; Bantam Books 1971).

For her formative legal work on the second edition and doing the groundwork for all the state lemon laws, we thank Joyce Kinnard, co-author of *The Lemon Book* (Caroline House 1980).

For working long hours on hot summer weekends to put the initial manuscript into the computer, we thank Dorrence Andrews.

For his skillful insight and research into safety features, we thank Russell Shew of the Center for Auto Safety.

For her research on the legal rights of lemon owners and on lemon litigation, we thank Allison Fletcher.

For spending countless hours in the library to uncover lemon anecdotes, statistics and references, we thank Alice Peck.

For contributing lemon law success and horror stories, we thank Rosemary Dunlap, President of Motor Voters.

For advice on the legal rights of lemon owners, we thank Mark Steinbach, a former Center staff attorney and current lemon lawyer.

For their support and encouragement, we thank the entire staff of the Center for Auto Safety.

Finally, we thank the thousands of frustrated and angry consumers who shared their problems with us. Their determination to fight for their rights will help future lemon owners seek the relief they deserve.

LIST OF ABBREVIATIONS

A Car Or Our Money Back (ACOMB)
American Automobile Association (AAA)
Audi Victims Network (AVN)
Auto Consumer Action Panel (AUTOCAP)
Automobile Importers of America, Inc. (AIA)
Automobile Manufacturers Association (AMA)
Automobile Protection Association (APA)
Automotive Trade Association Managers (ATAM)
Better Business Bureaus (BBB)
Canadian Automobile Association (CAA)
Center for Auto Safety (CAS)
Consumer Action (CA)
Consumer Education and Protective Association (CEPA)
Consumer Federation of America (CFA)
Consumers Against General Motors (CAGM)
Consumers Organized Against Ford (COAF)
Department of Energy (DOE)
Department of Motor Vehicles (DMV)
Department of Transportation (DOT)
Detroit Auto Dealers Association (DADA)
Disgruntled Owners of General Motors Automotive Diesels (DOGMAD)
Environmental Protection Agency (EPA)
Federal Trade Commission (FTC)
Highway Loss Data Institute (HLDI)
Insurance Institute for Highway Safety (IIHS)
Motor Vehicle Manufacturers Association (MVMA)

National Academy of Science (NAS)
National Automobile Dealers Association (NADA)
National Highway Traffic Safety Administration (NHTSA)
National Institute for Automotive Service Excellence (ASE)
New Car Assessment Program (NCAP)
New York Public Interest Research Group (NYPIRG)
Office of Technology Assessment (OTA)
Public Interest Research Group (PIRG)
Rubber Manufacturer's Association (RMA)

CHAPTER 1

THE LEMON

November 24, 1981

Center for Auto Safety
Washington, DC

Dear Sir:

As of this writing, our car has been in the shop for repair 60 times. That's right, 60 times, and it's a 1981 Renault 18-I which we purchased one year ago this month.

After trying to trade it off, to no avail, as no one is interested in the car at all. . . . The representative from Renault from Dallas was here about two weeks ago still trying to fix things up and stated there are still 10 things needing to be repaired, and as soon as parts came in, they would be back to work on it at their expense. Nice, huh? Knowing the personality of this car, there are probably 20 things wrong with it now.

How unfair to the consumer. We have had the car in the shop almost two months out of twelve and we are a one car family.

Our sense of humor has now disappeared, but I do submit to you the enclosed "expression poem" which I composed when things were a bit funnier; if nothing else, it makes me feel better to put things on paper.

Who can I write to, who will listen to my tale of woe?
Real People? 20-20? That's Incredible? I just don't know.

Who would believe me anyhow, a car so fine you see.
Nothing could have **that** much wrong with it, not in a century.

1

THE LEMON BOOK

Take my word for it, our little car so dear . . .
Our "precious" Renault, of less than a year . . .

Has knocked, grunted, stopped and groaned.
We have smelled gasoline till we feel stoned.

Each time it was worked on, we sighed, "Maybe at last . . ."
And by the time we drove out, the thought disappeared fast.

The dealer has tried to repair the ailments it's true.
But they'd fix one thing, and then we'd have two.

Lights wouldn't work correctly, the horn wouldn't make a sound,
Flashing red lights lit up on the dash . . . most reasons not found.
FIFTY SEVEN visits to the dealer for repair.
FIFTY SEVEN visits . . . most all is despair.

The French may be lovers and can start a flame,
But electricians they ain't and what a shame.

On a trip, 200 miles out, the air conditioner went inferior.
3,000 miles we traveled with a sweaty posterior.

The repairmen that we asked for help to repair,
Just shook their head sadly and blankly did stare.
They tried new bushings, computer center, just to name a few,
Of replacement parts and things they have tried to do.

Why have we not demanded a brand new car?
Because we aren't up to having a COLD CAR WAR.

A sense of humor we pushed to extreme.
Now I write to you, just to let off some steam.

The French and their fashions and pastry so fine,
Can take this French pastry and stick it,
   "Where the Sun Don't Shine!"

Sincerely,
P. Putman
Fort Smith, AR

The Lemon

It's like being rudely awakened from a good dream. You've had your new car for only a day or two, and you've already begun to experience the defects.

But it's nothing to worry about, you hope. The manufacturer will stand behind its product, and the promise is right there in the new car warranty. So, before your first trip back to the dealer, you make a list of the things wrong with your car—nothing too serious, just little things that keep the car from being perfect. You assure yourself they will be fixed without charge under the warranty. True, when you pick up your car, there is little or no charge for the warranty items you listed. But you then discover that most of the defects haven't been touched. Some of them may never be fixed no matter how many times you ask the dealer to fix them.

The defects you found may not have been especially hazardous. However, some common defects are very dangerous, since they are hidden and often undetectable even by a good mechanic. These defects gradually become worse until they suddenly take all control of the car from the driver. After the accident the driver may be cited for reckless driving.

Carbon monoxide leaks are a good example. People often feel a little tired after driving a fair distance and the fatigue is usually attributed to strain and monotony. Herbert Herring of Old Saybrook, Connecticut, wrote: "My wife and I have a Chevrolet . . . and we have always felt tired in the car and didn't know why. They (the Service Department) 'pooh-poohed' the idea of carbon monoxide." Then, "On June 30 we had three valuable dogs pass away in our car in a sleeping position with windows open about six to eight inches as usual." When the Herrings had their car examined by blowing an air hose up the exhaust pipe, the air stream threw a cloud of dust up into the trunk on the right side near the back seat. Had they been in an accident during the two years in which they had always felt tired in the car, chances are the reason for their dulled reflexes would never have been discovered.

Like many owners, you are probably led to believe there is not much chance that your own car has defects that might cause an accident. You should look behind the assuring advertisements. And even if you are fortunate enough to get a car with only minor defects, you can plan on a good bit of work and frustration putting that new car into shape and keeping it that way. Consumers Union, publisher of *Consumer Reports*, buys dozens of new cars from dealers every year without saying they

3

are from *Consumer Reports*. In 1988, its testers found an average of eight defects **in each car**, ranging from minor to serious. Some cars had as many as 17 defects.

What is it that makes a car a lemon? To most, a lemon is a rare occurrence, an infrequent or even freakish assembly line product which just won't run at all. While it is true that most new cars will run, the number which limp along and haunt their owners with fears of unreliability and danger is alarming.

DEFINITION

Lemons come in two basic varieties. The first type is a car with known defects, defects that develop into a perpetual source of frustration for the owner. This type seems to generate a continuing stream of problems, some minor and others more serious, some of which can be fixed and others which can never be satisfactorily repaired.

The second and more pernicious type of lemon has defects which, like Mr. Herring's exhaust leak, are relatively undetectable. This variety of lemon has been called a "risk waiting for an accident to happen." It occurs with a frequency which, unfortunately, is not well known. Rarely are the causes of accidents thoroughly investigated on the scene. Accidents are usually viewed as driver failures rather than as vehicle failures because, with rare exceptions, police and insurance investigators are not equipped to detect and evaluate vehicle failures, or because damage to the car makes the analysis of defects difficult. Most important, the laws and courts have long avoided bringing the vehicle to account, because it is easier to blame the driver.

HOW LEMONS ARE PRODUCED

All lemons, whatever the variety, grow from a common source— sloppy design and assembly by the auto manufacturers or manufacturers of component parts. A defect caused by an erroneous design of the car or its component parts is called a **design** defect. Potential defects are occasionally left in the design in order to save the manufacturer money. A defect in production caused by an assembly line error is called a **manufacturing** defect. Often defects caused by poor quality control on the assembly line go undetected because of faulty inspection and testing performed by the manufacturer and dealer.

Whether due to poor design on the drawing board or poor quality control on the assembly line, either defect can produce a lemon. If the defect was due to an assembly line error, one car or many cars may be defective, depending upon how many cars were misassembled. If the defect was in the design, all cars of that make and model would be defective. Although most cars become more complex every year, there is no excuse for delivering dangerously designed, poorly inspected, wholly untested cars to the public—cars that are unrepairable when they prove defective and cause needless injury when an accident occurs. Lemons serve as tangible evidence that vehicle safety depends as much on the quality of the car's basic design and assembly as on the presence of certain government-required features called safety devices.

In this book, we will show that the manufacturers have the ability to make better cars. We will also suggest ways consumers can help convince the manufacturers of the wisdom of altering their current patterns of irresponsible behavior.

HOW MANY LEMONS ARE SOLD?

There is no way of arriving at an exact figure. The manufacturers do not publicize this information. But we do know that thousands of letters come into the National Highway Traffic Safety Administration (NHTSA) of the U.S. Department of Transportation every year. Ralph Nader and the Center for Auto Safety receive more than 30,000 consumer auto complaints a year. Many more complaints pour into other consumer offices around the country. Major automotive fleet operators considered 10% of all new cars in 1989 to be lemons. The number of lemons bought back through state-run arbitration programs in 1988, when compared with the total number of vehicles sold, yielded at least 15,000 certified lemons sold nationally each year. The total is surely much higher because other lemons are bought back through manufacturer arbitration programs and the courts while still more, sadly, are just traded in.

Almost every national poll taken within the past three years has found that automotive problems were the largest source of consumer complaints. According to the following sources, problems with the purchase and repair of automobiles represent the number one complaint across the country: the White House Office of Consumer Affairs, a Louis Harris national opinion research survey, the Federal Trade Commission, Council of Better Business Bureaus (BBB), a Congressional survey by the U.S. Senate Consumer Subcommittee, and many state consumer protection agencies and consumer groups around the country.

It is clear that there are hundreds of thousands of consumers who are very upset about the quality of their new cars. The Center estimates that the automobile manufacturers produce at least fifty thousand lemons every year. At an average sticker price of $15,000, this comes to $750 million worth of lemons every year. This does not even include those cars that are so difficult to operate or wear out prematurely that they are quickly traded in or junked. Even though an automobile is likely to be the second most expensive investment you will ever make, you cannot rely upon the old adage that you get what you pay for.

BASIC LEMONAIDE: AN OVERVIEW

December 15, 1988

Center for Auto Safety
Washington, DC

Dear Sir and Madam:

In May 1984 I bought a new 1984 Toyota Celica GT from Toyota of Hollywood and had it rustproofed at the dealership. The rustproofing among other things has not worked. After 3 years it began to rust out. I have had the rust damage repaired 2 times since I bought the car new in May 1984 as you can see from the enclosed receipts, and a small dent repaired from backing into a hydrant.

Here is the MAIN REAL PROBLEM! AT 63,000 miles the oil switch went bad causing me to have to get a whole new engine and water pump at a cost of $1912.26 at the dealer. The 5 year warranty had just expired! I wrote to the Toyota distributor in Jacksonville. They were of no help. According to the mechanic at Palm Springs Service, the oil switches on Toyota cars are defective and should be replaced every time the car is tuned up. He is obviously correct.

Since May 1984 I have replaced this whole car with the following items: A new engine, battery, water pump, both headlights, thermostat, and the rust repaired 2 times! See the enclosed receipts.

Are all cars junk nowadays? This is crazy! No one has helped me. . . . I don't want to buy an engine every 3 years. This is expensive. What do I do? Help!

Sincerely,
J. Dodge
Hialeah, FL

Many lemon owners are under the false impression that defects in their cars can be fixed for free only during the original warranty period and that once their written warranty expires they must pay for everything that goes wrong with the car. Actually, car buyers have many rights including those warranties which are created by law at the time of the sale—they simply have to exercise them. Nonetheless, manufacturers and dealers often tell lemon owners that they have no obligations to the owner outside of the written warranty. If the manufacturers and dealers refuse to repair defects in your car voluntarily, outside agencies or organizations of individual self-help tactics may force the manufacturer or dealer to fix the car.

Besides persistence, the foremost key to success in getting a defective car fixed or replaced is documenting everything that goes wrong with the car. Keep a list of the car's problems along with a record of all attempts at getting the car repaired. Whenever you send a letter, always make a copy for your files. Whenever you visit the dealer, always obtain and keep a copy of the repair order (be sure it is legible). By keeping written records of all defects that plague your car and the many attempts to have them repaired (dates and receipts of service), you will have an easier time proving your car is a lemon. Well-kept records documenting that a car is a lemon are invaluable if a lawsuit is necessary.

Resolving an automobile complaint is often tedious and frustrating. If it is a lemon case, the dealer or manufacturer invariably stalls, rejects or otherwise arbitrarily wards off attempts to get the car fixed or replaced. The reason is pure economics. If car manufacturers replaced defective cars like appliance manufacturers replaced defective toasters, it would cost car makers at least $750 million per year. So be prepared for frustration. No one gets a lemon replaced on their first, second or third trip to the dealer or the manufacturer, but unless those trips are made, the lemon will never be replaced nor a total refund given.

WITHIN THE SYSTEM

Every manufacturer has a system to handle consumer complaints, which should be followed even though it may not work in most cases.

Complaint handling mechanisms outside the system require exhaustion of all remedies that the manufacturer provides.

SAFETY PROBLEMS

The first thing to do if your car has a safety problem like stalling or faulty brakes is to call the National Highway Traffic Safety Administration (NHTSA), which is part of the U.S. Department of Transportation. They have an Auto Safety Hotline, which you can call toll-free at 800-424–9393. In Washington, D.C. call 366-0123. Although NHTSA cannot take direct action in resolving individual complaints, your call may generate a recall where the manufacturer has to repair your car and others like it without charge. By reporting your problem to NHTSA, you may be helping other consumers whose cars have not yet experienced that problem. Occasionally, consumers have received favorable treatment from the manufacturer after NHTSA sent a copy of the consumer's complaint to the auto maker.

THE DEALER

When your new car does not work properly while under warranty, the dealer or manufacturer should repair the car without charge. Just exert your rights a step at a time, keeping records all the way. First, give the dealer a chance to fix the car. Go back to the dealership where you purchased the car, if possible. Ask to see the service manager. If you get no results, see the owner of the dealership or the general manager. The higher-ups can always overrule a stubborn or unknowledgeable subordinate and can authorize a free repair to "retain the goodwill of a customer." A dealer who did not sell you the car is less likely to authorize goodwill repairs.

If the dealership refuses or cannot repair the car satisfactorily, pursue the claim through the rest of the manufacturer's system before pursuing legal channels.

THE MANUFACTURER

November 17, 1987

Mr. F. J. McDonald, President
General Motors Corporation
Detroit, MI

Dear Mr. McDonald:

In 1981 I purchased a Diesel powered Cadillac Fleetwood Brougham, Serial 1G6AB69N289220662.

It now has 41,000 miles on it. Within this limited mileage, I have had **three** transmissions in the car. The first replacement transmission was covered under the extended warranty I had purchased along with the car for $500.

For this last transmission, I have had to pay $661.40. Copy of the bill is enclosed. In my opinion, this is a disgraceful reflection on the quality of General Motors products. The transmission expert who replaced the last transmission told me the car had a 200 series, which is totally inadequate for this size car. This certainly shows poor engineering judgment on the part of GM.

I will not bore you with all the other problems I have had with the car, such as broken blocks, etc.

I am 72 years old, and do not drive in a fashion that would cause transmission problems. In my 55 years of driving, this is my first car which has had to have a transmission replaced . . . and in this instance, it has had **three** in 41,000 miles.

The fault, in my opinion, is solely within General Motors, and I trust you will recognize General Motors' responsibility and reimburse me for the cost of this third transmission.

Sincerely,
George D. Clayton
San Luis Rey, CA

Sometimes the reason for the dealership's failure to fix the car is the dealer's service department may not have been able to diagnose the problem. Other times, dealers simply refuse to fix cars for fear that they will not get reimbursed by the manufacturer. Since the manufacturer not only has superior expertise in finding and repairing malfunctions in the car but also has greater authority to order defective cars to be repaired, call in the manufacturer's representative to look at a defective car the dealer cannot or will not repair. Once again, the manufacturer's representative has a "goodwill" budget to repair cars even when they determine the manufacturer is not at fault.

Contact the manufacturer's division (also called regional, district or zone) office in your area. The locations and correct names of district offices and the complaint procedures are often spelled out in the owner's manual. If the manufacturer's representative refuses to see you, contact the regional office or the manufacturer's owner relations office, often located in Detroit.

AFTER THE WARRANTY EXPIRES

If the car is no longer under the manufacturer's warranty but it fails to operate properly because of a defect that was not corrected during the warranty or that appeared after the warranty expired, follow the same procedures with the dealer and manufacturer outlined above for a warranty complaint. You may have a tougher time getting the dealer or manufacturer to cooperate after the car's warranty has expired, but there is a reasonable chance of success if you are persistent.

Sometimes the manufacturer will repair a defect common to many cars of the same model because the manufacturer recognizes its liability and is willing to remedy the defect. Normally this is done through a warranty extension, policy adjustment or secret warranty offered by various manufacturers over the past few years. So frequently does this happen that at any one time, there are hundreds of these warranty programs going on throughout the auto industry. For example, when the front tires wore out at 9000 miles on his 1986 Oldsmobile Cutlass Supreme, Patrick Sipe of Virginia Beach, Virginia complained to his General Motors dealership. Mr. Sipe had already taken his car to the dealer six times for tire wear and alignment problems that began when the car had only 2000 miles on it. This time the dealer replaced both front tires at GM's expense, even though GM does not warrant tires on cars.

But when Linda Feldman of Miami, Florida brought in her 1985 Buick Riviera because the car's tires were worn at 10,000 miles, the dealer said GM would not accept responsibility for premature wear. A few months later, Ms. Feldman read in a newspaper article that GM was in fact secretly paying for replacement of worn-out tires on cars like hers that were misaligned at the factory. When she confronted her dealer's service department with the news report, they admitted that GM was providing free tires but said free replacement would only be made on cars driven fewer than 12,000 miles. Ms. Feldman's Buick had now been driven over 14,000 miles and was no longer covered.

Ms. Feldman's and Mr. Sipe's experiences are shared by millions of owners of late model vehicles containing serious defects which the manufacturer has acknowledged to its dealers but not its customers. Rather than notify owners of the defect and their eligibility for free repairs, the manufacturer only reimburses those owners who complain loudly and persistently; those who put off complaining, or who never complain at all, must pay for the manufacturer's mistakes. Since these defects often show up after the written warranty has expired, nearly all the cost of these manufacturing mistakes and design defects will be absorbed by consumers. Other times, if enough complaints are registered with the NHTSA Auto Safety Hotline on safety defects, the manufacturer is required to repair the defect because of a NHTSA-ordered "recall." The Environmental Protection Agency (EPA) can order similar recalls for emission control system defects. Such emission defects frequently go beyond what is commonly thought of as emission control, to components such as costly-to-repair engine valves.

OUTSIDE THE SYSTEM

October 26, 1988

Roger Smith, Chairman
General Motors Corp.
Detroit, MI

Dear Mr. Smith,

I purchased a Chevrolet Corsica from Valley Motor Center, 6001 Van Nuys Blvd., Van Nuys, CA 91401, in February 1988.

Valley Motor Center has done everything imaginable but repair the necessary items. They have lied to me; ordered parts and sold them; refused to order parts as promised. They let my car sit for days, doing nothing.

This company has pledged their word that my car would be serviced and ready for me 8 times, holding the car over day after day and would still not have it serviced when I came to pick it up. One lie after another; promise after promise broken. Never have I ever had so much deceit by a company representing a national name auto company.

It appears Valley Motor cares very little about customer service or satisfaction. They simply will not complete the necessary service and repairs to keep my car running as required.

I work in Ventura County, and it has placed great hardship and expense on me. Reliable transportation is a must for my job and I do not have it in this car.

I believe they are just passing the time to let my warranty expire.

It is my desire to return this car to General Motors for a refund so I may purchase a new car for reliable transportation. The Lemon Law under the California Civil Code Section 1793 gives me this option.

Please reply within 10 days. The question of my warranty is important.

Sincerely,
J. C. Franklin
Sherman Oaks, CA

CC: R. Burger, GM, Troy, MI
   E. Rodriguez, Valley Motors, Van Nuys, CA
   Ralph Nader, Washington, DC
   Center for Auto Safety
   J. Franklin II, Attorney, Woodland Hills, CA
   H. Caruthers, GM, Thousand Oaks, CA

If the system does not work, the next step is to make enough noise outside the manufacturer's complaint handling system to get results. A strong commitment is necessary to successfully use this procedure, because you will not get results unless you are willing to persistently follow up letters and phone calls. Having followed the procedures "inside the system" outlined above, you should have a thorough documentation of the refusal of the dealer and manufacturer to remedy your defective car. This documentation will make the steps outside the system easy to follow and results more likely to happen.

LETTER WRITING

The first letter can be used as a "basic instrument" in an expanded complaint campaign. Send this basic letter to the manufacturer's Chairman of the Board or President with copies of that letter to others. Type your letter if possible. A surprising number of complaints are ignored at this stage simply because they cannot be read, take too long to read, or are misread. If you cannot type the basic letter, print or write very legibly. Set forth the car's problems clearly and precisely within the letter and refer to the collected documentation of the car's troubles and your attempts to have the car repaired "within the system." There is no need to send every repair order or other piece of documentation with the letter. Instead, list the history of the lemon troubles, giving the nature of the problem, when it first occurred, what was done about it and when, and the results. Include that list as part of the letter. If there are key documents in the car's history such as major repair bills or admissions by the dealers, include copies of those also. Never send out the original of any document.

Send copies to various organizations such as local and national consumer groups, local and state consumer protection agencies, state attorneys general, federal agencies and members of Congress. Even if these agencies or groups cannot act directly on your behalf, they may send complaints on to the manufacturer requesting that the manufacturer take action.

TELEPHONE CONTACTS

After writing a letter and sending copies to various organizations, call local agencies or groups, especially those that do work on a case-by-case basis with consumers. A telephone call to the manufacturer's main office is recommended if it offers a hotline, or if you have access to a WATS line or do not mind spending money on what may be a long shot. Some people have succeeded in getting their cars fixed by using repeated telephone calls as a symbolic form of protest. For example, call the boss (dealer or manufacturer's representative) or the boss's secretary and say, "I am going to call four times a day every day till doomsday or until you fix my car." This complaint procedure works best where the consumer manages to get a direct dial number of the extension for a top executive. Main switchboards do not respond well to this technique.

TOWARD LEGAL ACTION

Even if consumers have met with utter frustration and rejection by the dealers and manufacturers to this point, they have accomplished one major feat. They have laid the groundwork for successful direct legal action. Every defect is now documented as is every trip to the dealer, every day the car was not in working order, every item of extra expense, every contact with the manufacturer. And this is the basis for a successful resolution of the complaint in the next stage.

PICKETING AND LEMON SIGNS

When an unresolved complaint is against the dealer as well as the manufacturer, you can attach large lemon signs to the car and then park the car near the dealer's showroom (BUT NOT ON THE DEALER'S PROPERTY). It helps to list your basic complaints on some of the signs. Many consumers who have used this tactic successfully have encouraged others with similar complaints to organize a "lemoncade" driving slowly around the block where the dealer is located. A few local consumer groups specialize in picketing dealers. But picketing is a controversial tactic, and dealers have occasionally invoked the authority of the courts and the police in attempts to halt its use. The courts are divided in upholding the right of consumers to use lemon signs and picket a dealership. The cases frequently turn on a minor point such as whether the picketers were on dealer property or interfering with consumers trying to enter the dealership.

NEGOTIATION AND ARBITRATION

Many consumers have successfully negotiated with the dealer through the use of a local consumer group. Others have achieved results through a local Auto Consumer Action Panel (AUTOCAP), organized in some states by the local dealers' association to handle auto complaints. You can also try to arbitrate through the manufacturer's own arbitration programs, which have various eligibility requirements. Ford and Chrysler run their own appeals boards, while GM uses the Better Business Bureau (as do several other manufacturers) to arbitrate complaints. The American Automobile Association (AAA) also runs the arbitration programs of several manufacturers. Many small claims courts attempt to informally mediate or settle a claim before hearing the case.

LEGAL ACTION

When you have repeatedly registered your complaints strongly and do not seem to be getting anywhere, your next step may be a lawsuit. But this does not necessarily mean hiring a lawyer.

Lawsuits are like car maintenance and repairs; some are so simple and minor, you can do them yourself. For example, if your complaint involves a defect which would cost $100 to repair, you can have a mechanic at an independent service facility repair the car and then you can go to small claims court to recover the cost of repairing the car (the jurisdictional amounts vary from state to state). The procedure in small claims courts is usually simple and no lawyer is needed.

Before hiring a lawyer, consult with one. He or she can point out deficiencies in your case or indicate whether small claims court might be better. You can appraise the lawyer; whether she or he seems competent and interested in your case. Look for a lawyer who is willing to take the case on a contingency or percentage basis, where payment depends on your winning, or one who will attempt to recover attorney's fees under the federal lemon law, called the Magnuson-Moss Warranty Act. This Act defines your warranty rights for all products, not just automobiles, and includes a section specifically covering the award of attorney's fees for cases brought under its authority. This is a very important provision; otherwise, no matter how strong a case you had, you may be reluctant to go to court if your attorney's fees take most of your recovery.

Traditionally, lawyers have been reluctant to handle lawsuits against giant corporations such as the auto companies, because the attorneys' costs can easily be greater than the judgments awarded to the consumers if they are billed on an hourly basis. But under the Magnuson-Moss Warranty Act, the court may decide to award attorney's fees as a part of the judgment. This provision makes it economically feasible for consumers to pursue remedies against the auto manufacturers in court.

In some situations a class action may be the best approach. In essence, a group of individuals brings a lawsuit against a manufacturer, thus reducing each individual's fee by sharing the costs of hiring an attorney. For instance, a class action may be filed on behalf of all purchasers of the manufacturer's product who suffered in the same way because of a defect in the product. Even if a class action is not possible, you can find other individuals with defective cars like yours and hire an attorney jointly. If one person cannot afford a lawyer, two, four or more might be able to afford one.

THE ULTIMATE WEAPON—RETURNING THE LEMON

January 9, 1989

Ford Consumer Appeals Board
Southfield, MI

To Whom It May Concern:

On November 23, 1987, I purchased a 1988 Ford Bronco serial number 1FMEU15H7JLA28291. Since that time I have had numerous major repairs to stated vehicle. They are as follows:

1. March 10, 1988—mileage 4202. A defective oil ring resulted in major repairs to the transfer case.
2. May 19, 1988—mileage 6772. Smoke and fumes entering vehicle through ventilating system. Cause—leaking oil onto exhaust system.
3. June 13, 1988—mileage 8257. Leaking oil problem not resolved, oil burning fumes still entering vehicle.
4. July 6, 1988—mileage 9306. Leaking oil problem not resolved, oil burning fumes still entering vehicle.
5. August 1, 1988—mileage 10568. Oil pressure erratic, leaking oil problem not resolved, oil burning fumes still entering vehicle.
6. September 14, 1988—mileage 12787. Exhaust leak, engine pinging. Dealer replaces rear main oil seal to cure oil leak.

7. September 15, 1988—mileage 12795. Picked up vehicle after repairs to rear main oil seal. On trip home quit running, and had to be towed back to dealership for repairs. Problem—oil pump failed shearing off distributor gear. After repairs, exhaust still leaking, engine pinging, oil pressure erratic, leaking oil problem not resolved, oil burning fumes still entering vehicle.

8. November 14, 1988—mileage 15082. Exhaust still leaking, engine pinging, oil pressure erratic, leaking oil problem not resolved, oil burning fumes still entering vehicle. Dealer repairs exhaust leak. All other problems unresolved.

9. November 23, 1988—mileage 15504. Engine pinging, oil pressure erratic, leaking oil problem not resolved, oil burning fumes still entering vehicle. Dealer set timing to 9 degrees to stop pinging, replaces oil pressure sending unit.

10. November 28, 1988—called dealer to report progress, oil pressure still erratic, oil burning fumes still entering vehicle. Service manager states "I will call Hotline" to get help.

December 8, 1988 was the last contact with the dealer. It was indicated he would locate a loaner vehicle and for me to leave the Bronco for repairs. To date I have not been contacted.

I purchased this vehicle to use off-roading in the Sierras as well as pulling my travel trailer on vacations with my family. The question of reliability is a very serious one considering these uses. On long trips (45 minutes or longer) myself and passengers experience headaches, and feelings of severe nausea. In warm weather with the windows up the interior has a strong objectionable odor. I have included two letters from people who have traveled in my Bronco and have shared these experiences. From a health position this vehicle is no longer safe to drive. Not to mention the serious question of reliability. I do not feel there is any way to bring this vehicle into proper operating condition. Based on the Song-Beverly Consumer Warranty Act in California, I believe this vehicle to be fundamentally defective. I expect to be reimbursed the price I paid for the vehicle or have the vehicle replaced with a "just like" 1989 model.

Sincerely,
W. C. Foeppel
Sacramento, CA

Some cars, like Mr. Foeppel's, simply cannot be fixed. Usually, resort to the lemon law or legal action is necessary to obtain a refund of the purchase price or a replacement car, since the dealer and manufacturer will almost invariably refuse to take back the car. Why are the auto companies so stubborn in refusing to compensate the lemon owner? Because the automobile manufacturers produced thousands of lemons every year, and a reasonable policy of taking back lemons in exchange for a full refund or replacement (as a manufacturer of toasters may be more willing to do) would cost auto manufacturers hundreds of millions of dollars every year. If auto companies bought back only 50,000 lemons each year at $15,000 per car, a refund policy would take $750 million dollars out of annual industry profits. It is no wonder the manufacturers refuse to compensate the lemon owners who then must pay for the manufacturers' errors.

LEMON LAW

If repeated repair attempts are necessary within the warranty period for the same defect or nonconformity, and this problem continues to substantially impair the use, value, or safety of your car, you most likely qualify for relief under the lemon law. Almost all states have these laws, which provide lemon owners with a full refund of the purchase price or a replacement vehicle if their car meets this description. Although these laws state that you are entitled to relief upon notifying the manufacturer that your car is a lemon, most lemon laws require you to go through arbitration to actually receive any compensation. Even after an arbitration decision in your favor, the manufacturer may try to fight the award, and you may have to bring suit. Though this is very frustrating, an eventual victory is well worth the effort, not only to make the manufacturer eat one of their lemons, but to put pressure on them to take responsibility for their products.

LEMON LITIGATION

Several different legal theories beyond lemon laws have been successfully used in collecting compensation for lemons. None of them are so simple or the dealer and manufacturer so willing to oblige that you can do it without legal assistance. Lemon owners who want to use legal action to get rid of their lemons can follow two general routes. One is to trade the car in and then sue the dealer and manufacturer for damages arising out of the sale of the lemon. The other general strategy is to cancel the ownership of the car, return it to the dealer or manufacturer, and sue for a refund or replacement.

If your state does not have a lemon law or the lemon law is itself a lemon, or you do not qualify for its protection because you are beyond the time limits, you may still be able to obtain a refund of the purchase price or a replacement vehicle by revoking acceptance. Consult a lawyer if you have decided to return the car to the dealer. The legal procedures for revocation of acceptance must be carefully followed in order to cancel your ownership of the car.

If the dealer cannot or will not fix the one or more defects that plague your car within a reasonable amount of time, and the defect is one that "substantially impairs" the value of the car, you have a right to demand a replacement or your money back. Some lemon owners have revoked acceptance of their new car and have received a replacement car or most of the purchase price back from the dealer or manufacturer without having to file a lawsuit. Others have revoked acceptance of their car and have successfully sued in court for the return of their purchase price. Some have obtained even more than the purchase price as compensation for their troubles. To be successful at this point is rare. The reason is not that the manufacturer is always right, but rather that most consumers give up or do not follow the steps listed above. If consumers follow those steps, dealers and manufacturers will be the ones who rarely win.

CHAPTER 3

HOW TO FOLLOW THE MANUFACTURER'S COMPLAINT PROCEDURE

Upon the advice of the Center for Auto Safety, Susan Jacobs of Santa Monica, California contacted the regional office of Toyota regarding a dispute over timing belt repairs, and shortly after wrote to the Center to relate the successful outcome:

> Just wanted to get back to you because a phone conversation with you a few months ago helped me get a reimbursement from Toyota that I would never have otherwise thought of requesting.
> I have a 1986 Camry with 34,000 miles (bought it used at 24,000 miles) and had to replace a timing belt recently. I questioned this with the dealer—no luck there. At your suggestion I contacted the manufacturer–regional office here in California. They sent me some papers regarding arbitration proceedings, but even before I had a chance to fill them out, I got a call from their Customer Relations Dept. offering to pay for my timing belt. They also agreed (without any urging on my part) to reimburse me for replacement of a muffler which I also had to do recently. Note that when I asked about this at the dealer I got absolutely nowhere and they laughed at me.
> I just received a $500+ reimbursement check from Toyota.

Every manufacturer has a system to handle consumer complaints, which should be followed even though it may not work in most cases. The reason to use the system is two-fold: (1) sometimes it works and (2) complaint handling mechanisms outside the system require exhaustion of all reasonable remedies that the manufacturer provides; i.e., that you have done everything within reason to get the car properly repaired by the dealer and manufacturer.

Besides persistence, the foremost key to success in getting a defective car fixed or replaced is documenting everything that goes wrong with the car. There is nothing hard about this; in fact, it is done for you. The dealer, independent garages, and service stations provide the basic documents to make any consumer successful in getting his or her defective car repaired, replaced, or the vehicle's sales price returned. Basically, these documents are the repair orders (RO's) or other service receipts one gets every time a car is taken in for service. Keeping these documents in an organized manner improves a consumer's chance for effective car relief at least three-fold.

For example, DeVaughn Bird of Merritt Island, Florida saved his receipts and correspondence with GM, successfully using them against the manufacturer in an arbitration hearing before the BBB. In reporting his victory to the Center for Auto Safety, he wrote:

> GM's defense was that I had used contaminated fuel and did not change oil regularly. I had my maintenance records to prove otherwise, and the GM representative said that I was supposed to treat the diesel fuel with an additive to prevent a sludge build-up in the diesel tank. I pointed out that this was not in the GM recommended maintenance for the car.

The BBB directed Buick Motor Division to reimburse Mr. Bird $230 for repairs to the fuel injector, $467 for transmission repair, and to buy back his 1981 Buick Park Avenue for $10,400.

One very helpful document is a written checklist of the work to be done on the car every time it is taken in for service. Not only does this cut down the number of trips made to the dealership when they "forget" to correct a problem, but also this documents the appearance and symptoms of the various defects in the vehicle. Place a copy of this list requesting repairs and pointing out problems to the dealer in your record keeping files. Some consumers record all periodic maintenance such as gas consumption and oil added. This is a very organized approach but not essential. If you do not keep a continuous record of all periodic maintenance, save the receipts from each service performed (except possibly gasoline purchases)—and **that** is essential.

A reliable service station or independent garage is usually the best place to have the car's periodic maintenance performed (such as oil change or tune-ups). Independents tend to be more competitive and charge less than an auto dealership for such service.

Manufacturer's Complaint Procedure

The independent specialty shop is frequently the best place to get your car fixed, particularly if the shop has been in business for a long time and the owner is one of the mechanics. If you can't find a good specialty shop, your second choice should be an independent general repair shop in which the owner is one of the mechanics.

The independent garage is . . . best . . . because they don't sell anything but service and they depend on the customer's coming back [where] dealers are not in business to sell service. They are in business to sell cars.

The Great American Auto Repair Robbery, by D.A. Randall & A.P. Glickman, p. 167-68, Charterhouse: New York 1972.

Most surveys show greater consumer satisfaction with the performance of independent shops when compared to dealerships. One survey in Washington found that 88 percent of customers at the average independent shop were satisfied with the way the shops fixed their cars, compared to 65 percent at the average dealership. Large retail outlets such as Sears Roebuck received a 69 percent satisfactory rating.

SAMPLE RECORD KEEPING SYSTEM

Repair and maintenance records should be kept in one place. A spiral notebook or a pad of paper makes a good record keeping tool. A large envelope or folder is another helpful tool in keeping all repair orders and receipts in one spot. Good organization comes easy if a record keeping system is used from the beginning and the records are kept in a convenient place. If you cannot organize anything, just find an empty drawer or box and at least keep the service receipts in that one place as you get them.

Good organization makes it easy to spot and document a defect. Confronting a dealer with a receipt for a broken gear showing that it had been repaired just 2000 miles before will often result in a free repair without further argument. But if a consumer cannot find the bill or receipt, hassles are almost guaranteed.

Good dealers and repair shops will keep an alphabetical file by owner of all repair work performed. Most dealers have computerized records that can give you a printout of your repair history. Ask for one.

When Paula Eisenstein of Chevy Chase, Maryland did, she found that the engine on her brand new BMW had been overhauled before it had been sold to her. Armed with this information, she recovered $1750 from the dealer in small claims court.

RECORD KEEPING: PROBLEM ANALYSIS

If you decide to use a record keeping notebook, staple each service receipt to a separate page and reserve space towards the rear of the book for analysis of the car's problems. For repair records kept in a drawer or box, take and sort them at least once a year or when a defect is suspected. If there is more than one repair bill for the same or similar problem, this indicates that something is wrong. Look through the repair orders and the service requests given to the dealer or garage for all repair work that might relate to the same problem. For example, complaints of stalling on starts, excessive warm-up time required, hesitation or poor acceleration, backfiring, poor gas mileage, and frequent spark plug replacement indicate a defective carburetor.

After gathering all the related repair orders and other service documents, write down the following information in the notebook or on separate paper:

1. The number of trips to the dealer or repair shop and the repair order or bill numbers for a particular problem.
2. Number of days without the vehicle.
3. Whether a loaner car was provided.
4. Other items, such as whether the car broke down on the road, whether a vacation was interrupted, days of work lost, and cost of alternate transportation. This not only helps identify and document defects or other problems but also arms you with the information necessary to tackle the manufacturer's complaint mechanism.

HOW TO COMPLAIN TO THE DEALER

First give the dealer a chance to fix the car. When a vehicle defect shows up, if possible, go to the dealership where you purchased the car. There are several reasons for this. (1) Since the dealer who sold you the car views you as a customer and would like to sell you your next car, he or she is more interested in seeing that your car is fixed properly. The dealer can do this in several fashions: (a) assigning the car to an experienced mechanic for repair, (b) authorizing a goodwill repair, or (c) having the car roadtested before returning it. (2) Since reimbursement to the dealer by the manufacturer for warranty repairs is usually less than that which dealers charge customers for non-warranty repair work, dealers are more reluctant to provide warranty work for cars they did not sell. If it is not possible to return to the original dealership, find a more convenient dealership with a reputable service department. Local consumer groups and government agencies may rate or recommend local dealers.

The dealership is the first resort on almost all questions and complaints. At the dealership, ask to see the service manager. If the service manager does not help you, find out if there is a customer relations office. All but nonexistent ten years ago, offices geared solely towards customer satisfaction are more and more frequent. If the customer relations office does not satisfy the complaint, go to the top person at the dealership (the owner or the general manager). The top person can always overrule subordinates or grant exceptions to general policies and authorize a free repair to "retain the goodwill of the customer."

Even when the problem is one which only the manufacturer's representative can decide, you can sometimes succeed in enlisting the dealer to go to bat for you in the first contact with the manufacturer's zone office. If the dealer does not help and it becomes necessary to contact the manufacturer's representative, you can at least tell the manufacturer that you have exhausted all possibilities with the dealer. This will help avoid one of the manufacturer's favorite ploys—referring you back to the dealer.

If the dealership refuses or cannot repair the car satisfactorily, pursue the claim through the rest of the manufacturer's system. If you immediately go through legal channels and have not given the dealer and manufacturer a reasonable opportunity to repair the car, you will probably lose. So do not stop if the dealer refuses to repair the car—go on to the manufacturer.

THE MANUFACTURER

April 3, 1989

Customer Relations
Chrysler Motors
Detroit, MI

Dear Sirs,

I purchased a 1988 Dodge Dynasty LE from Ourisman Dodge in Alexandria, VA on April 11, 1988. On the day of purchase I indicated to the salesperson that the front passenger power door lock did not operate properly. He assured me the problems would be resolved and scheduled my car for service. I first brought the car in for service correction on 15 April 1988. Since that time I have had to take the car into the Dealer several additional times for the SAME PROBLEM.

Each time the car was brought in for service the dealer-ship assured me the problem had been resolved. However, the problem was not corrected until March 9th, 1989.

Mr. Iacocca has personally assured Chrysler customers of quality service and satisfaction (as noted in his recent advertisement which is attached), I have yet to see his claim borne out. In fact my attitude toward your recent "Quality is First and Customer Bill of Rights" advertising campaign is "SINCE WHEN?" According to your advertising claims it appears my rights to a quality car, friendly treatment, honest service, competent repairs, a safe vehicle and satisfaction have all been violated.

Sincerely
J. Cewe
Lorton, VA

CONTACT THE MANUFACTURER'S REPRESENTATIVE

Most automobiles manufacturers have several different divisions within the corporation, such as Chevrolet Motor Division of General Motors or the Lincoln-Mercury Division of Ford Motor Company. Each division within the corporation is usually represented in various geographical locations across the country by a zone or district office. The zone office locations are often spelled out in the owner's manual that accompanies each vehicle when purchased from the dealership. The zone office acts as a liaison between the main office, the dealer and the consumer. You can insist on arranging an appointment with the manufacturer's representative through the dealer. If the dealer refuses to cooperate, call the representative yourself. Local zone offices are listed in the white pages of telephone books across the country. The manufacturer's representative will usually ask for the following "basic information":

1. owner's name, address, and phone number;
2. make, model and year of the car;
3. selling dealer's name and location;
4. date of purchase and odometer reading (mileage);
5. nature of problem plus attempts dealer made to repair it.

The manufacturer's representative can arrange to inspect the car at either the dealership or another location convenient to the consumer, as the zone offices have traveling service representatives who make regular rounds to all dealers in the zone.

CONTACT THE MAIN OFFICE

Almost all auto manufacturers have a consumer complaint or owner relations office at their corporate headquarters or main office. The real purpose of the manufacturer's complaint handling campaigns is not to provide direct action on each consumer's complaint, but to channel the consumer back into the manufacturer's bureaucratic complaint handling system.

Thus the main office probably will not resolve your complaint, but it can set up an appointment with the zone representative if you could not do so previously, or it may pressure the zone office to reconsider your complaint. It is the zone office and not the main office that actually comes out and looks at the car. Occasionally, manufacturers have a toll-free number available for what is advertised as "a hotline" to expedite consumer complaints. Even when the manufacturer has a toll-free number or hotline, consumers have trouble using it. For example, consumers complain that they are able to get through to the GM hotline to report accidents, but that representatives often fail to ask for their name or address. Rexford Keel of Castro Valley, California wrote to the Chairman of General Motors about headlight failure and noted, "He (his brother) tried calling your toll-free 800 number, but got no response there. His calls were never returned."

M.H. Klaiman of Placentia, California got a similar non-response from Toyota in complaining about her new Toyota. In expressing her frustration she said:

> Subsequently I complained to the below-named Toyota Motor Sales official about this, but got nothing but a colossal runaround. A letter was sent asking me to phone an 800 number, but when I did, a man on that end said they had no record of my complaint. He sounded both unresponsive and moronic throughout the conversation. His disinterested manner conveyed clearer than his words the company's we-don't-give-a-damn attitude on this issue.

Where it is difficult to reach the manufacturer's main office by calling an advertised hotline or where no hotline exists, call the regular telephone number and report your complaint. Later on, after trying everything in the manufacturer's complaint handling system, the main office can be contacted through the use of letters, rather than telephone calls, to follow up the complaint. But for initial efforts to get a defect or lemon corrected when the local dealer and zone representative are irresponsive, telephone calls are the most efficient way of making contact with the manufacturer's main office.

Even though the main office usually puts consumers back in the proper channels, i.e. the dealer or zone office, ask the main office to take direct action on your complaint. If they refuse, what have you lost? But at least get them to put pressure on the zone office to reevaluate your complaint. Provide the main office representative with the "basic information" given to the zone office and the objections to the way the dealer and the zone office representative handled your complaint. Be sure to take notes on all telephone conversations with the manufacturer, including the name and title of everyone with whom you talk along with the dates of the calls.

If the main office decides to review your case or otherwise intervenes, consider yourself lucky. If the main office orders further action to be taken on your case, they will usually have the zone office contact you. Unfortunately, the manufacturer too often approves the previous handling of a complaint and sends the consumer a form letter which fails to address the real problems. An example of this is the form letter Chrysler's Owner Relations Coordinator, M. Bivins, sent Robert O'Malley of Davis, California in July, 1989:

> The personnel assigned to each of our Zone Offices are responsible for making decisions in all matters concerning warranty and service in their area. Unfortunately, circumstances are sometimes such that the type of relief requested by the customer cannot be provided.
> After reviewing the file, we must concur with the decision rendered by our San Francisco Zone Office in this matter.
> Although we are unable to assist you in this particular matter, we trust that you can appreciate our position.

Ford's Detroit District Office took a broader brush-off tack in a September, 1988 letter to Kay Lengemann of Imlay City, Missouri, in which they said no one could help her.

> Thank you for your recent letter concerning the toxicity of your burning car seat. We are certainly sorry to learn of your experience.
> As a Customer Service Department we try to provide every customer with the answer to their questions. However, at times inquiries are beyond the scope of our department. Yours is such a situation.

With the advent of arbitration mechanisms discussed in Chapters 4 and 8, some manufacturers will refer consumers to their own dispute resolution mechanism. Ford and Chrysler each have an arbitration board, known as the Ford Consumer Appeals Board and the Chrysler Customer Arbitration Board. Other companies use industry groups such as the Better Business Bureau and the Automotive Consumer Action Program (AUTOCAP). A complete listing of auto companies and their arbitration mechanisms is found in Appendix A. If you have not received satisfactory results from your dealer, the zone office, or the main office, you may wish to contact the appropriate mechanism and submit an application to have your dispute settled by them. None of these mechanisms will hear cases which are in litigation, where the consumer no longer owns the vehicle, or where the vehicle is used for commercial purposes.

Be alert to the fact that even these arbitration groups and boards can give you the auto company-like runaround. For example, Janet Doremus was told that she did not fall within the jurisdiction of the Pennsauken, New Jersey Ford Board and that her complaint would be forwarded by them to the proper jurisdiction, South Hackensack. She then received this letter from the Hackensack Appeals Board:

> We are unable to review your case because the dealership involved does not fall within this Board's jurisdiction. We are forwarding your Customer Statement to the Ford Consumer Appeals Board at Philadelphia, P.O. Box 618, Pennsauken, New Jersey.

If a consumer has done all of the above, then either his or her car is in good running condition or further negotiation with the dealer or any other representative of the manufacturer is likely to result only in frustration. But the consumer now has the complete documentation of a defective car that the manufacturer refuses to, or cannot, fix. From here on, the consumer must go outside the manufacturer's system to get the defective car fixed, replaced, or the purchase price returned. When going outside the system, one must be careful to watch out for ruffled feathers as the following example shows.

One consumer tried for three months to get his car repaired at the dealership and through the manufacturer's representative, but without satisfaction. Iman Womack of Norman, Oklahoma could stand no more "runaround," so he painted lemons and slogans on his new Chevrolet station wagon. Then he drove around the Murdock Chevrolet showroom. Unfortunately, the owner's son, Cliff Murdock, Jr., physically attacked the dissatisfied customer, and Womack ended up in the hospital for 32 days. The younger Murdock was convicted of assault and battery by a jury. Womack was awarded $3,000 in actual damages and $10,000 in punitive damages in his lawsuit against the dealership.

C H A P T E R 4

HOW TO COMPLAIN:
STRATEGIES
"OUTSIDE THE SYSTEM"

In the fall of 1978, Dorothy Spicer, a 60 year old widow from Latonia, Kentucky crossed the Ohio River to purchase a car from an Ohio dealership. Soon after, she brought the car back for a touch up to the paint job. This and the cost of a rental car were to be covered under the extended warranty she had purchased.

When Mrs. Spicer returned to pick up the car, she was informed that the warranty would not cover the rental car. Disturbed by this news, she made a notation on the service order which was supposed to be submitted to GM, that the $20 charge was for a rental car due to the dealer's defective paint job. When she refused to remove this comment, the dealer refused to let Mrs. Spicer remove her car from the garage. An argument over the switch to the garage door ensued with Mrs. Spicer pushing the switch to open the door and the dealer pushing the switch to close it. Finally, after warning the employees that she would take the door with her, she proceeded to do just that. The dealership swore out a felony warranty for her arrest for damages to the door.

Had she been convicted, Mrs. Spicer could have been sentenced to up to five years in jail and fined $2,500. When she appeared in court, the dealer refused to drop the charges unless she agreed to pay $500 they claimed she owed for the damage to the door and agreed not to sue. Having gone through so much frustration thus far, she did not relent.

On June 8, 1979, Mrs. Spicer appeared before a grand jury and came out triumphant, cleared of all charges against her. This did not end her drive. She was now determined to recover for the emotional stress which had put her in the hospital for two weeks. She brought suit against the dealer joining GM and Oldsmobile as defendants. Although they were dismissed as parties to the case, Mrs. Spicer, victorious once more, accepted a settlement offer of $25,000 from the dealer.

Lemon Times, Fall, 1980

Although some irate consumers use radical solutions, most consumers resolve their complaints without going quite this far. When the manufacturer's complaint handling system does not work, the consumer can often make enough noise through aggressive and innovative complaints to get results. And, of course, it is not necessary to break the law. But a strong commitment is necessary to successfully use these strategies. Having followed the procedures in Chapter 3, "inside the system," you should have thorough documentation of the refusal of the dealer and manufacturer to remedy your defective car. This documentation will make the strategies outside the system easy to follow and results more likely.

THE SIGNIFICANCE OF LETTER WRITING

As a responsible consumer you should communicate your dissatisfaction and impatience with the industry that markets new cars averaging eight defects on delivery in 1989, according to *Consumer Reports*. Through letter writing you should demand to participate in decisions that affect you. As it now stands, whether you get satisfaction when you complain is the company's decision, not yours.

At present, with but a few challenging voices, manufacturers can persist in the comfort of self-deluding circularity: "We make them that way because that's what the consumer buys"; and escape facing the customer's reality: "I have to buy a shoddy and unsafe car because that's all there is on the market." In your letter challenge the manufacturer to respond positively to your request for action or change. At the same time, request a copy of the report which the zone office sends to the corporate or division office after action is taken on your case.

American consumers deserve less defective cars and better repair service when defects appear. They also deserve a complaint-handling process that displays sensitivity to the substance of the customer's complaint and to the constructive aspects of his or her role as a complainer. When letters begin to accumulate from those who, in the past, simply tolerated the defect without thinking of writing a complaint letter, and those who meant to do it, but didn't get around to it, the automobile industry, the government, and the public will be furnished with a more accurate view of the quality of the American automobile. This added disclosure will spur a variety of efforts within industry and government to eliminate excessive defects and callous complaint handling.

THE LETTER

The first letter can be used as a "basic instrument" in an expanded complaint campaign. Send this basic letter to the manufacturer's chairman of the board or president with copies of that letter to others. Type your letter if possible. A surprising number of complaints are ignored at this stage simply because they cannot be read, take too long to read or are misread. If you cannot type the basic letter, print or write very legibly.

SAMPLE COMPLAINT LETTER

Date

Chairman of the Board
Belchfire Industries
(**address**)

Dear (**name**):
(identification of vehicle)

I bought my new (**year**) (**make**) (**model**) from (**dealer's name**) (**address**) on (**date**). The vehicle identification number is ( ).

(what went wrong)
The (**vehicle**) had (**mechanical breakdowns on an average of every two weeks since the date of purchase**). The major problem has been (**malfunctioning brakes**). The car (**leaks oil and stalls frequently**). (**The heater has never worked.**)

(personal losses)

I have lost at least (   ) days from work in order to have the car repaired. In addition, I have spent over (**$300**) on car rentals in order to perform my job as a (**sales representative**). I have been without adequate transportation ever since (**I bought the car**).

(what went wrong at the dealership)

I have received insufficient help from the service department at the dealership when repairs were needed. On several occasions, I had to miss a day of work only to have the dealership fail to properly repair the car.

(detailed records)

Following are times at which repairs were performed at the dealership:

(**date**)   Problem #1 (**transmission**)
        Repair Order(s) #

(**date**)   Problem #2 (**engine**)
        Repair Order(s) #

(documentation)

I am attaching copies of service orders, repair receipts and car rental receipts for your convenience.

(remedy)

I expect to receive either a refund on my purchase price, a replacement car or a personal guarantee from you that my car will be properly repaired within 10 days.

Please reply within 15 days.

Sincerely,
/s/

cc: Dealer
    Zone Office
    Your attorney
    President's Office of Consumer Affairs
    Your U.S. Senators and Representatives
    U.S. Senate Commerce Committee
    U.S. House Energy and Commerce Committee

Department of Transportation
Environmental Protection Agency
Federal Trade Commission
Center for Auto Safety
Consumers Union
Consumer Federation of America
National District Attorneys Association
Action Line
National Automobile Dealers Association
State Attorney General
Local District Attorney
State or Local Dealers Licensing Authority
    or Department of Motor Vehicles
State Senators and Representatives
Better Business Bureau

GENERAL HINTS

Regardless of the nature of your complaint the following suggestions will increase the effectiveness of your letter and, thus, your
chances of ultimate success.

1. Set forth the car's problems clearly and precisely. Refer to the
   collected documentation of the car's troubles and your attempts
   to have the car repaired "within the system." There is no need to
   send every repair order or other piece of documentation with the
   letter. Instead, list the history of the lemon troubles, giving the
   nature of the problem, when it first occurred, what was done
   about it and when, and the results. Include copies of any key
   documents in the car's history such as major repair bills or
   admissions by the dealer.
2. When your car has many defects, eliminate minor complaints
   when registering your major objections. Trivia tend to under-
   mine the impact of the more serious defects and should be
   included only when you want to paint a picture of a complete and
   utter lemon. If you do include minor defects, make sure the major
   ones stand out by underlining, capitalization, or including them
   in a separate section called major defects.
3. Avoid an apologetic tone. If you have a legitimate complaint,
   simply demand action. In our experience, timidity implied in

such statements as "You may think I am some sort of crank, but . . ." or, "This is the first letter like this I have ever written," does little good. On the other extreme, making yourself particularly abrasive is not to your advantage. Let your complaint carry its own weight, and try to communicate it as clearly and forcefully as you can.

4. Your letter should be as concise as possible. It is probably more effective to relate only the principal parts of an involved story. Senators and representatives, whose offices read thousands of letters, particularly appreciate brevity. On the other hand, if your predicament is complex and involved, there may be no escape from a lengthy exposition. A few of the most helpful cases reported to us have included complete logs, with daily insertions.

Mail this basic letter to the manufacturer's Chairman of the Board or President, certified with return receipt requested, so that you have proof it reached its destination. This one letter, alone, may resolve your complaint as happened for Franklyn Arnhoff of Charlottesville, Virginia when he wrote to Mazda's President in Japan.

But first Mr. Arnhoff wrote Mazda's Customer Relations Department in Florida and got a cold brush-off as follows:

Dear Mr. Arnhoff:

Your vehicle has exceeded the extended manufacturer's warranty. This program was instituted by Mazda as a gesture of goodwill towards its customers. There must be limits beyond which financial consideration can no longer be foreseen and this is the case here.

We regret we are unable to assist you in this matter.

Very truly yours,
Customer Relations Department

Mr. Arnhoff then wrote to Mazda's President in Hiroshima saying. "The manner in which I have been treated in attempting to deal with Mazda is insulting and beneath the dignity of the company." Fourteen days after writing to Japan, Mr. Arnhoff received full reimbursement from the same customer relations office for the $733 in repairs for the defective head gasket on his Mazda 626.

Unfortunately, a single letter does not usually work this well. More often the consumer gets an unsatisfactory response or none at all. Randy Feriante of Menlo Park, California expressed her frustration to Chevrolet, in which she stated in part:

> You have failed to respond to certified letters sent 2/16/89 and 3/6/89 demanding refund of the purchase price and all related expenses for the following vehicle. . . .
> There has been no phone call and the only written correspondence has been another "impersonal" customer satisfaction survey.
> The car has repeatedly been represented as repaired when the brake problem has been evident and demonstrated during every single road test.

WHERE TO SEND THE LETTER

Address your complaint letter to the President or to the Chairman of the Board and send copies to the dealer and the zone office if they have failed to help you. Addresses of company officials are included in Appendix B. Zone office addresses are usually included in the owner's manual that comes with a new car, and often listed in local telephone directories.

Writing directly to the top may prevent many delays and avoid the necessity of writing a different letter to each person along the hierarchy—if the letter is not automatically routed to the customer or owner relations department below. Pressure from the top may offset the tendency of others in the hierarchy to subject you to an annoying runaround involving the dealer, and the central, division and zone offices. It will also exert pressure upon whichever official should take action, as it is sometimes difficult to know who in the corporate hierarchy is responsible. Also, people at the top are more sensitive to solving the problems listed in letters that are being sent to various federal, state and local agencies.

The point is illustrated by this interchange of letters: When a dealer did not answer to her satisfaction an inquiry regarding her car, a Washington, D.C. Volkswagen owner wrote to the distributor. After a less than helpful answer to her request he offered this stock closing:

Thank you for providing us with this opportunity to inquire in your behalf. We sincerely appreciate your interest in Volkswagen and take this opportunity to wish you many happy miles of Volkswagen motoring in the future.

She then wrote to Volkswagen of America in Englewood Cliffs, New Jersey, and they concurred: "We agree with you that the reply you received [from the distributor] is inconclusive." A letter initially addressed to Volkswagen of American probably would have insured a better response from the distributor level, and saved her the need to write the second letter.

SEND COPIES OF YOUR COMPLAINT
TO THE WORLD

The number of people outside the automobile industry that you advise of your problem depends on the degree of your outrage, resources, and interest in more responsible consumer protection in the future. In general, notifying appropriate agencies and officials can only be to your advantage. For example, Dana Browdy of University Park, Maryland finally got reimbursed $850 for repairs after a successful letter writing campaign as he related:

> I received my settlement check on the repair charges I paid to repair my THM-200 transmission in Feb. 1982, by going through the Maryland State Consumer Protection Commission, and the Better Business Bureau Consumer Relation Division in Baltimore. Thank you.

When M. Vaught of Denver, Colorado could not get her Chevrolet Camaro repaired properly at the dealership she followed the manufacturer's complaint handling system through step #3—a letter to the Chevrolet Relations Representative stating the nature of her problem. She listed 16 carbon copies at the bottom of the letter. The dealer responded with a letter of apology and an offer to refund the total purchase price. At the bottom of the dealer's letter were listed the same 16 names of individuals, organizations and agencies as were listed in the consumer's letter. The consumer wrote about her success to the Center for Auto Safety:

> I feel that the reason R. Douglas Spedding [president of the dealership] refunded the money was because of my letter being sent to as many people and places as I did. I even received a job offer from Channel 7 (CBS) to work with their "Call for HELP" program.

Send copies of the basic letter to various organizations such as local and national consumer groups, local and state consumer protection agencies, state attorneys general, federal agencies and members of Congress. Some groups which are able to take on individual cases may give direct assistance where others may be able to give good advice on how to proceed further. Some organizations use complaint letters in conjunction with other complaints they receive to generate broad relief such as recalls which benefit not only the complainant but all others similarly affected. Even if these agencies or groups cannot act directly on your behalf, they may send complaints on to the manufacturer requesting that the manufacturer take action. When the manufacturer receives enough complaints from consumers and organizations, it may decide to repair the defective cars as the best means of quieting the uproar.

One example is the action taken by the Center for Auto Safety in response to a large number of consumer complaints on Ford Aerostar vans. Prompted by hundreds of complaints regarding 1986 and 1987 Aerostar minivans, the Center for Auto Safety wrote to Ford Chairman Donald Petersen urging action. Citing the van as being the most unreliable and unsafe of all those manufactured at the time, the Center called for recalls and improvements in the design and manufacturing of the Aerostar, remedies for rear brake lockup, filler neck fuel leaks, fires on tow packages, faulty clutches, and sliding doors falling off. Ford ultimately conducted five recalls and two warranty extensions to correct many of the defects pointed out by the Center.

INFORMING YOUR SENATORS AND REPRESENTATIVES

Together with a cover note, send a copy of your complaint to your representative and to your senators. They were elected to represent you in Congress, so advise them of problems you face which they can help solve. Keeping them informed has a twofold advantage. It may lead, with other letters, to increased concern in Congress, and eventually to action; it may also bring you direct results. Lee Lorenz of Salina, Kansas wrote to his U.S. Senator, Robert Dole, about the problems he was having with his diesel Buick and GM's refusal to grant an arbitration hearing pursuant to their agreement to do so with the Federal Trade Commission. A few months later Mr. Lorenz wrote to the Center for Auto Safety:

> I am glad to report that Buick Division of General Motors finally agreed to a buyback of my 1983 Buick diesel for $7,000 cash. . . . I feel certain that Senator Dole's entrance into this deal had a lot to do with the Buick decision to get me off their back.

INFORMING OTHER GOVERNMENT OFFICIALS

1. The President of the United States

Writing the President makes more sense than most realize, not to take up his time with your personal complaint, but for other reasons. First, addressing your letter to the White House will help it find its way to the most appropriate federal agency when you are not sure where to send it. Once the letter reaches its destination, the White House referral slip attached to it may mean more expeditious handling. In addition, all the officials who see it along the way become exposed to the problem. But most important, you have provided top officials, even the President, with an additional opportunity to learn what problems are affecting people. The result might well be that these top officials, even the President, will decide it is important for them to spend time on widespread consumer problems.

Do not fear that your letter will distract the President or Presidential staff from more important concerns, because there is a part of the President's staff charged with responsibility for handling citizen complaints, to which your letter will be referred. Called the Office of Consumer Affairs, it is part of the Executive Office of the President and is headed by the President's special adviser on consumer affairs. The current director is Bonnie Guiton. She and her staff represent the consumer for the President, draft consumer legislation, and keep the federal government informed on consumer problems. The office advises the President on policies with identifiable consumer components. It has a tiny office with a small staff, but you can make it grow by sending copies of complaint letters you write, whether auto-related or not, to the President, White House, Washington, D.C. 20500.

2. Specific Agencies and Congressional Committees

On the federal level, in addition to writing the President, send a copy of your complaint letter directly to a particular federal official or to a Congressional committee known to be concerned with the special type of problem you are facing. In particular, Congressional committees do not regularly hear from consumers and will benefit from a direct letter. There are other reasons as well.

A lawyer representing a West Coast lemon owner wrote: "When the car company found out that everyone in the country was going to hear about Mr. Hickey's problems, the dealer fixed the car." You will multiply the weight of your complaint letter to the manufacturer by including a list of five or six carefully selected names to whom copies are being directed. The manufacturer then knows its behavior may be studied by government personnel who can use its nonperformance to strengthen a record of consumer dissatisfaction.

A complaint letter may encourage a public official to go to bat for you. With each copy of your letter, include a very brief cover note requesting that the person or agency suggest what you can do to solve your problem or take whatever steps possible to solve it. Most government agencies are not empowered to act on behalf of one person. However, in a recent case detailed later in this chapter, a single complaint from a Volkswagen owner whose steering wheel came off while driving on the highway, initiated the recall of 104,000 vehicles. As exceptions to the general rule, members of Congress can and do act on individual complaints.

Finally, writing decision-makers is a way of participating in decisions that affect you. Although letter writing is hardly the most ideal form of involvement, it can often turn out to be more significant than the act of casting a vote in an election. Large numbers of well-written letters will eventually force the government to create a system for making better use of citizen letters to define and eliminate injustice and abuse. Even under the current system, when a letter is left unanswered or just perfunctorily acknowledged, it nonetheless often has had a strong impact on those who read it, and helps them define problems they are trying to solve.

REGULATORY AGENCIES

There are particular officials or agencies in Washington to contact regarding:

1. Safety-related automobile defects;
2. Complaints on warranty service;
3. Auto repair problems not connected with the warranty;
4. Tire problems;
5. Deception and fraud in the purchase of your automobile;
6. Emission control-related auto defects;

1. Safety-Related Automobile Defects

In 1966 President Johnson signed a bill that created the National Highway Safety Bureau, now the National Highway Traffic Safety Administration (NHTSA), of the Department of Transportation. NHTSA sets safety standards for new cars and enforces them. It is required to investigate safety-related defects in vehicles, equipment, and tires and to order recalls where defects are found. Consumer complaints frequently form the basis for a NHTSA recall order. In the case of the record recall of 15 million Firestone 500 tires, the agency received over 5,000 consumer complaints. In some instances, a single complaint is sufficient.

One recall campaign was initiated on the basis of a single complaint from the owner of a Volkswagen Fox. Vicki Chandler of North Carolina filled out a NHTSA questionnaire regarding an accident she had when the steering wheel of her Volkswagen "came completely off while driving on the highway." An investigation by NHTSA lead to a recall campaign of 104,000 1987-89 Volkswagen Foxes. The defect was attributed to oil or grease inadvertently applied to the steering shaft. The greased shaft destroyed the friction necessary for proper function of the steering wheel.

Address copies of letters detailing safety-related defects to:

Director
Office of Defects Investigation
National Highway Traffic Safety Administration
Washington, DC 20590

Anyone interested in proposing a new safety feature for automobiles or in getting a vehicle recall can petition the NHTSA to establish a new safety rule or to find that a safety-related defect exists. The petition process is little more than a letter sent to:

Administrator
National Highway Traffic Safety Administration
Washington, DC 20590

To be considered a petition, the letter must:

a. be written in the English language;
b. have a heading that includes the word "Petition;" preferably the heading should be in capital letters;
c. state the facts which show NHTSA that action or an order is necessary;
d. give a brief description of the substance of the action or order that should be taken; and
e. contain your name and address.

NHTSA must then either grant your petition and initiate the appropriate rule making or defect determination process, or deny it. The agency has 120 days to respond to your petition.

To obtain safety information from NHTSA, call their Auto Safety Hotline, toll-free. It serves the citizens of every state except Hawaii and Alaska. The number outside of the Washington, D.C. area is 800-424-9393. In Washington, the number is 366-0123. For hearing impaired, the TTY numbers are 800-424-9153 and 755-8919. The Hotline serves four major purposes:

a. Purchasers or owners of vehicles may verify the safety/defect/recall history of their vehicles.
b. Owners can report vehicle defects to generate recalls.
c. Consumers can request a variety of information from the Hotline staff including consumer educational material, equipment Fact Sheets, copies of safety standards and investigatory reports.
d. For vehicle and highway safety problems outside of NHTSA's jurisdiction, the Hotline can refer you to the correct agency or proper source.

Consumers who call the Hotline should be prepared to provide the year, make, and model of their vehicle and its vehicle identification number. If a safety problem is being reported, a brief description of the problem, mileage, and results of the problem also should be provided.

After calling the Hotline, a consumer will receive a form from NHTSA to be filled out and returned. Occasionally, a manufacturer will help the consumer after receiving pressure from NHTSA. Harry Erickson of Binghamton, New York wrote of his success in being reimbursed for power steering repairs on his Oldsmobile after contacting NHTSA.

> I want to express my appreciation to the National Highway Traffic Safety Administration for providing information that allowed me to save approximately $485 in automobile repair costs.
>
> Special thanks are due to Agent No. 5 who handled our call on September 12, 1988, and Mr. Tom Cooper who contacted us on September 13, 1988. Their courtesy, helpful attitude, and useful information they provided are greatly appreciated.

2. Complaints on Warranty Service

The Federal Trade Commission is interested in the quality of customer service under the warranty offered by car makers. Address copies of warranty-related complaints to:

Warranty Project
Bureau of Consumer Protection
Federal Trade Commission
Washington, DC 20580

The FTC does not generally act on the basis of a single complaint, but your letter, together with those from other consumers, may indicate that there is a general warranty abuse requiring action by the Commission.

For example, CAGM (Consumers Against General Motors) was one of several groups organized to represent diesel owners when problems with the GM diesels erupted. CAGM got its start when the Cadillac Seville owned by Peter and Diane Halferty suffered through two replaced engines and a second transmission in 3 years. Their frustration reached its peak when a dealer offered them only 1/3 of the price of a non-diesel Seville. Diane Halferty took out an ad inquiring as to the experience of others, and based upon the responses she received, organized CAGM. A primary part of CAGM's efforts was to spur the FTC to investigate and pursue GM's defective diesels. Eventually, the FTC reached a consent settlement with GM that required the company to arbitrate all engine and transmission complaints regardless of time and mileage until 1992 and to make public service bulletins on defects. Although the FTC consent settlement was not all that CAGM sought, it was more than many people expected. CAGM on its own negotiated many thousands of successful settlements with GM for consumers.

3. Auto Repair Problems Not Connected With the Warranty

Auto repair industry abuses can be found along with warranty problems or entirely separate therefrom. Repair abuses can range from the incompetent mechanic to the downright fraudulent repair shop. Normally repair abuses are better handled on the state and local level but a number of federal agencies and committees are actively investigating the matter. The Senate and House Commerce Committees have conducted hearings on abuses within the auto repair industry. Legislation on problems consumers face with auto repairs is presently being considered. Letters providing additional insight into these problems, particularly those concerning the need for federal regulations, should be directed to:

Consumer Subcommittee
Committee on Commerce, Science, and Transportation
U.S. Senate
Washington, DC 20510

Subcommittee on Telecommunications, Consumer Protection, and Finance
Committee on Energy and Commerce
U.S. House of Representatives
Washington, DC 20515

Director
Division of Consumer Affairs
Department of Transportation
Washington, DC 20590

Director
Office of Consumer Affairs
Department of Health and Human Resources
Washington, DC 20201

Bureau of Consumer Protection
Federal Trade Commission
Washington, DC 20580

Also contact your regional FTC office.

4. Tire problems

Legislation to improve tire safety still leaves many serious tire imperfections unchecked. Tire complaints of all varieties should be sent to both the Senate Commerce Committee and the House Committee on Energy and Commerce.

If the problem relates specifically to tire safety, direct a copy of your letter to:

Administrator
National Highway Traffic Safety Administration
Washington, DC 20590

5. Deception and Fraud in the Purchase of Your Automobile

The Federal Trade Commission is empowered to issue cease-and-desist orders to those individual businesses that are engaged in interstate commerce and found to be practicing deception or fraud on consumers. The FTC issued such an order to an auto dealer in northern Virginia to prevent him from selling used Volkswagens as new and from falsely advertising himself as an authorized Volkswagen dealer.

If you have been the victim of any sort of deception or fraud in purchasing a new car, a copy of your complaint letter should be sent to:

Chairman
Federal Trade Commission
Washington, DC 20580

6. Emission Control-related Auto Defects

In 1970 the Environmental Protection Agency (EPA) was created when Congress passed the Clean Air Amendments. The EPA sets emission standards for new cars and enforces them. It is required to investigate emission-related defects in vehicles and equipment and to order recalls where defects are found. Consumer complaints frequently form the basis for an EPA recall order just as they do for a NHTSA recall order. To complain about defects in the vehicle emission control system, write to:

> Director
> Office of Mobile Sources
> Environmental Protection Agency
> Washington, DC 20460

STATE AND LOCAL AGENCIES

While you may succeed in getting help on your complaint from officials at the federal level, it is also possible to obtain individual assistance at the state and local level.

1. The State Attorney General and Your Local District Attorney

If you have been a victim of deceptive practices or fraud, send a copy of your letter to your state attorney general and to your local district attorney. Include a copy of your letter of complaint to the manufacturer. Many states now have special offices under the attorney general that deal specifically with consumer protection.

The attorney general's office of your state may file a class action lawsuit on behalf of you and other similarly situated consumers. For example, Ohio Attorney General, Anthony J. Celebrezze and his consumer protection staff conducted an investigation into preparation fees being charged by a Columbus dealer. New car purchasers were led to believe that charges added on to an agreed upon price were costs paid by the dealer to prepare a car for sale when actually the dealer had been paid by the manufacturer for these services.

State and local officials can take action only if specific laws have been broken. The district attorney and the attorney general are both public prosecutors. It is up to them to decide whether to prosecute after they receive a complaint. If they do take your case to court, charges will be pressed by the state; any conviction will usually result in a fine or imprisonment for the guilty company or company official. A Birmingham, Alabama dealer was sentenced to three years in prison and fined $235,000 for rolling back odometers on demonstrator cars. Following a 2½ week long trial, a jury convicted him of mail fraud, odometer fraud and conspiracy.

In Clearwater, Florida, the Consumer Fraud Division of the state attorney's office filed criminal charges against a Pontiac dealership for false advertising. A customer had apparently tried to purchase a car at a special advertised price. When told by a sales representative that the car the customer was considering (a 4 door, fully equipped version) was not available at the price he had seen advertised, he arranged to have the more expensive model suspended from a crane over the dealership, draped with a banner reflecting the more reasonable advertised price.

The attorney general also has broad powers to initiate hearings on consumer protection and safety. For instance, in 1966 the Attorney General of Iowa held hearings on poor design for safety in automobiles that were instrumental in getting federal safety legislation passed. In 1987, Attorney General Bronson LaFollete of Wisconsin held hearings on problems in BBB arbitration that led to improvements in the system and better decisions for consumers.

2. Dealer Licensing Agency / Department of Motor Vehicles

Most states and some cities license automobile dealers. Licensing agencies have the power to initiate proceedings to terminate the license of a dealer. Dealers are generally anxious to settle any complaints brought to the attention of the local licensing authority as quickly as possible. Rarely are licenses revoked, but a rash of complaints against any one dealer may cause that dealer serious trouble.

The Departments of Motor Vehicles (DMV) or Transportation (DOT) of your state may have the authority to cancel a dealer or repair shop's registration or even file suit against a business after an investigation. When the Wisconsin DOT received complaints about an Eau Claire recreational vehicle dealer, it launched an investigation that resulted in a May 1989 suspension of the dealer's license and refunds and payments totaling $26,000.

The California Bureau of Automotive Repair also takes an aggressive stand to protect consumers from automotive repair abuses. The Bureau of Automotive Repair, established by the California Automotive Repair Act, began operating in 1972. It was the first state agency of its kind to file court or administrative actions against hundreds of repairmen and dealers. The major enforcement tool of the Bureau is its power to take away the registration of a dealer, thus prohibiting him or her from doing business in California. Besides licensing and regulating auto repair shops, the Bureau administers the official lamp, brake and smog device programs for the state.

The Bureau accepts and processes complaints at various offices throughout the state. Bureau staff attempt to resolve the complaint by contacting the dealer. If no agreement is reached, the complaint is referred to a field investigator who meets with the consumer and dealer. In some cases, the investigator examines the repair work in question and makes sure that the provisions of the state law have been followed. In cases where no illegal activity has occurred, the Bureau may act as a moderator between the consumer and the repair shop. When the Bureau determines that state law has been violated, it may take administrative or criminal action against the violator. From July, 1987 to June, 1988 the Bureau received a total of 64,605 complaints, 45% of which it settled. In what they refer to as the Citation Program, the Bureau sends defective automobiles to inspection stations. If the auto passes inspection, the Bureau issues a citation to the station owner, the inspector, and the mechanic. The number of stations that were cited under this program neared 1,500. If a station continues this practice, the Bureau will seek action to revoke its license. Twenty-three such actions were initiated last year. Civil or criminal action will be brought against a station if they are operating unlicensed, fraudulently, or negligently.

3. State Senators and Representatives

Elected state officials do their best consumer protection by enacting legislation such as lemon laws when they are alerted to abuses by constituents. John Woodcock of Connecticut and Sally Tanner of California led the effort to get lemon laws in their states which then spread to the rest of the nation. Both held hearings at which consumers testified on their lemon experiences.

By writing to your state representatives, you will keep them informed of auto abuses and build a record for corrective legislation.

Include copies of complaint letters you have written to automobile manufacturers. If you do not know the name of your state representative, check at your local library for a copy of your state's current legislative handbook, which lists the names of all representatives. If your state does not have a good auto consumer agency like that of California, your letters can help create one.

4. Local Consumer Protection Agencies

New York City has one of the most effective Departments of Consumer Affairs. In operation since 1968, the department has resolved an average of 15,000 complaints a year. Its powers and activism include wide-ranging investigative, licensing, and regulatory authority. The department actively intervenes on behalf of consumers. Cities establishing such agencies, or citizens seeking ways to strengthen their local consumer protection agencies, may benefit from writing:

Commissioner
Department of Consumer Affairs
80 Lafayette Street
New York, New York 10013

Ask specifically for copies of the legislation under which the department operates.

Another city cracking down on motor vehicle repair fraud is Dallas, Texas. The Dallas Motor Vehicle Repair Ordinance is enforced by an investigative staff of the Dallas Department of Consumer Affairs, which boasts over $150,000 in recoveries for consumers. The Texas Motor Vehicle Commission has been active in enforcing state advertisement regulations and recently took action against a new car dealership, charging that they had failed to honor advertisements offering new vehicles for sale at or below the "factory invoice price." During the 1987-1988 fiscal year, the Department investigated 2,084 complaints, issued 414 violation notices, and recovered $153,169 for consumers.

Montgomery County, Maryland also has an active consumer protection agency. The Office of Consumer Affairs handles approximately 5,000 complaints annually. It is authorized to initiate investigations, subpoena documents, negotiate settlements which are legally binding, and revoke licenses. Not only can the office bring suit, it has done so successfully on several occasions. For instance, backed by the state Motor Vehicle Association and Consumer Protection Division, the county successfully brought suit against the owner of two local dealerships for 13 counts of deceptive practices involving pricing, repairs, and selling used cars as new. The charges resulted in court ordered revocation of the dealer's license to own, operate, manage, or be employed by any auto dealership in the county for 10 years and a $2.6 million fine.

OTHER PLACES TO SEEK HELP

ACTION LINE

In most large cities, a newspaper, or radio or television station operates a quick action citizen complaint service, sometimes referred to as "Action Line," or "Hotline." If your problem is (a) simple, (b) susceptible to brief description, and (c) loaded with a relatively high level of injustice, your chances of interesting a reporter or investigator in your problems are good. Using the thinly veiled promise of negative publicity, they can often negotiate a victory for you. Usually Action Lines are more effective against local operators than against corporate giants like the auto makers. However, one Los Angeles consumer got favorable action in a timely manner upon exposing his woes to four area TV stations. After having his engine rebuilt, he had his friend (he was blind) bring the car to a Firestone service center for an oil change. Following a trip to Louisiana, the friend discovered that the engine had burned out because it had lost all its oil. A Louisiana Firestone service center denied Firestone's liability. After complaining to the media that Firestone had left him broke and homeless, leaving him no choice but to sleep outdoors, Firestone paid the complete cost for his engine repair and, in addition, for his overnight stay at a hotel.

Another consumer relayed his story to a local newspaper in Crosby, Texas in reference to the customized Chevrolet Astro van he purchased in August, 1988, "I bought it on a Friday, I took it back to the dealer for repairs the following Monday." After accomplishing nothing by contacting GM and the BBB, David Miles had his daughter make signs for the van claiming "Chevrolet—the Heartburn of America." This was, of course, a take-off on their advertisement "Chevrolet—The

Heartbeat of America." The signs attracted the attention not only of motorists, but the media as well. A television consumer advocate, after a 45-minute interview, promised some research into the state lemon laws. A final meeting in January, 1989 with BBB arbitrators turned out positive results. GM was instructed to buy back the lemon.

THE BETTER BUSINESS BUREAU

The BBB's in most communities are financed by member businesses and exist to serve the interests of the business community. Their main task is to keep fly-by-nights out of town. Few are any use to individual consumers, and little effort should be expended trying to get them to act in your behalf. Some BBB's may write a letter of inquiry if your complaint is against a local dealer; others may give you access to a tally kept on the number of complaints against various dealers and repair establishments. One value of complaining to a BBB is that consumer groups frequently use BBB complaint totals in evaluating the quality of auto dealer and repair shops. Unless consumers complain to BBB's a dishonest dealer or shop may get a good rating and continue to victimize consumers.

INDUSTRY PUBLIC RELATIONS GROUPS

The automobile and tire industries are well organized into trade associations, foundations, and councils to advance the interests of member companies through joint lobbying and public relations efforts. These groups are insulated from company-consumer relations and often profess ignorance of serious consumer dissatisfaction. To enlighten them we suggest you direct any surplus copies of your complaint letter their way.

The major trade groups for the tire and auto industries are:

Motor Vehicle Manufacturers Association (MVMA)
7430 Second Avenue, Suite 300
Detroit, MI 48202

As the domestic automobile industry's trade association, the MVMA primarily looks after the interests of the "Big Three." The MVMA fosters industry unanimity on many consumer issues, feeding the press with calculated answers to soften the effect of the Big Three's anti-consumer positions. The MVMA publishes "Motor Vehicle Facts and Figures" annually.

Automobile Importers of America, Inc. (AIA)
1725 Jefferson Davis Highway, Suite 1002
Arlington, VA 22202

The AIA represents the major automobile importing companies, including certain parts suppliers and overseas associations. The Association keeps its members up-to-date on U.S. federal, state and local laws and regulations that affect the manufacture and sale of imported automobiles and parts.

Tire Industry Safety Council
844 National Press Building
Washington, DC 20045

This organization was effectively formed to serve as a lobby against new tire safety standards and legislation. It protects the tire industry's slipping image by heading off disclosures in Washington which are unfavorable to tire companies. Despite its title, it has little to do with advancing improvement in tire safety. It once described its purpose as providing "a medium through which constructive suggestions and information can be fed back to the tire industry."

Rubber Manufacturers' Association (RMA)
1400 K Street NW
Washington, DC 20005

The RMA represents 200 member companies which manufacture tires, tubes, mechanical and industry products, sporting goods and other rubber products. The Association provides monthly and annual statistics on consumption, production and inventory of rubber products.

National Automobile Dealers Association (NADA)
8400 Westpark Drive
McLean, VA 22101

The automobile dealers are organized nationally into the National Automobile Dealers Association (NADA). If your complaint is primarily against a dealer send NADA a copy. NADA can also tell you whether there is an AUTOCAP (Automotive Consumer Action Program) organized in your area by the local auto dealers association to handle auto complaints. (AUTOCAPS are explained later in this chapter.)

INSURANCE-RELATED SAFETY ORGANIZATION

Insurance Institute for Highway Safety (IIHS)
1005 N. Glebe Road, Suite 800
Arlington, VA 22001

IIHS is not a trade association although it is funded by major insurance companies. It is a nonprofit organization, active in the fields of auto safety and damage reduction. IIHS is a scientific and educational organization, dedicated to reducing the losses which result from crashes on the nation's highways. IIHS has been a leader in advocating measures in U.S. laws and regulations to prevent auto-related deaths, injuries and property damage.

NATIONAL AND LOCAL CONSUMER GROUPS

Send copies of your original letter of complaint to national and local consumer groups which may use your complaint to help you directly or indirectly. See Chapter 5 for more information on consumer groups. The following are national consumer organizations which should be alerted to any complaints which affect large groups of consumers:

Consumers Union
256 Washington Street
Mount Vernon, NY 10553

Consumers Union is a nonprofit organization, nationally recognized for its magazine, *Consumer Reports*, which is unique in that it accepts no advertising. Its product reports and ratings are thus protected from possible commercial incentives and advertiser interference. The April issue is its annual report on automobiles.

Center for Auto Safety
2001 S Street NW, Suite 410
Washington, DC 20009

The Center for Auto Safety is a nonprofit public interest advocacy group organized in 1970 by Ralph Nader and Consumers Union but now independent of both. The Center bases much of its research priorities on consumer complaints. Each letter is most useful in determining patterns of defects or other problems to be investigated. The Center seeks general remedies such as vehicle recalls that will aid large numbers of similarly situated customers. This is the primary way that the Center is able to help the tens of thousands of individuals who directly seek its assistance each year or who are referred to it by Ralph Nader.

Consumer Federation of America (CFA)
1424 16th Street NW, Suite 604
Washington, DC 20036

See Chapter 5 for information on the CFA.

A Car Or Our Money Back (ACOMB)
Melvin Redman, Chairman
2078 Second Avenue
New York, NY 10028

ACOMB is organized to assist consumers who have purchased GM cars with defective V-6 engines.

SUMMARY

Send copies of your original letter of complaint to those who may be able to assist. For different types of complaints, the list of persons receiving copies will vary somewhat.

See the "cc" list in the "Sample Complaint Letter" earlier in this chapter for a letter to the manufacturer complaining about the refusal of a dealer to make repairs under the warranty.

WHAT THE MANUFACTURERS DO WITH COMPLAINT LETTERS

When they choose, the manufacturers can turn the complaint-handling process into an exercise in consumer futility or, in some cases, even an engine of consumer harassment. Their tactics range from complete silence to evading your complaint by means of a time-consuming run-around between the central office, zone representative, and the dealer. Stephanie Kaetz of Birmingham, Alabama wrote to General Motors President Robert Stempel about mistreatment by the dealer and Pontiac Division:

> When I requested the names and addresses of the officers of General Motors and the Pontiac Division so that I could write, that information was supplied only after repeated requests and I was told that it was pointless to write any of the officers as my letter would only be referred back to Customer Service and that they could not help me.

In most cases you are at the complete mercy of these devices, but by understanding them you can avoid delay, prevent additional losses, score a point or two, or even win a just settlement. It is clear that your letter is digested by a system with glaring deficiencies as detailed below.

1. Low Level Concern

Complaint letters, even when addressed to chief executives, are often routed to customer or owner relations departments, staffed by persons whose prime qualification, judging from their pronouncements, is that they go by the book, i.e., they are proficient at form letters.

The ritual of the system bothered Betty Lear of Hamden, Connecticut, who wrote to the Office of Consumer Relations for Cadillac:

> Not only am I a number, but this is certainly a sad commentary on our society today. Passing the "buck," not caring what happens to a customer much less a human being or even potential future business.

Cadillac obviously doesn't need my business and couldn't care less. It is also a put down to be written to by a consumer representative when I have written to one of the chairmen of General Motors.

2. No Consumer Participation

Once the investigation of the zone office is initiated there is little or no opportunity for the customer to participate. Decisions costing consumers hundreds of dollars are made sometimes without consulting the owner, sometimes without even inspecting the vehicle in question. J.L. Althoff of Crystal Lake, Illinois wrote to Ford Motor Company to notify them that his car had left the factory without properly installed rear struts. After receiving no answer, he phoned Ford's 800 number, was assigned a case number and promised a return phone call. When no one called, he again called the 800 number. This time he was told that since the dealer had said everything was o.k., his case had been closed.

D. Short of Alexandria, Virginia, whose new Chevrolet engine failed, specifically requested to be present at the dealer's when the zone service representative came to inspect his engine. When he called a week later to check, he was told the zone representative had completed his visit. He was, therefore, deprived of an opportunity to present his case.

3. Inaccurate Reporting

General Motors states that 85% of the complaints were resolved to the satisfaction of the owner. They do not say, however, whether this figure is based on zone representative reports or on checks with complaining owners. The owner has no way of knowing whether the zone representative has accurately reported the outcome of the matter. Particularly in cases where the decision is against the consumer, as for instance where warranty coverage is denied, the owner should be informed in detail of the reasons for rejecting his request. Providing owners as a matter of course with a copy of the zone representative's reports to the Central Office (excluding, of course, comments on dealer performance intended for internal consumption) would add immeasurable legitimacy to the system.

4. Wearing You Down to the Point of Exhaustion

On October 28, 1987, Lois Sarver of Miami, Florida sent the following letter to Ralph Nader:

> I enclose a copy of my letters to the Chairman of the Board and Vice Chairman of Ford Motor.
>
> It is a disgrace what we consumers are subjected to and must (try) to tolerate.
>
> I have lost countless hours of worktime, not to mention the stress and distress, trying to get my problem solved. I just can't take it any more.
>
> Please do what you can to help me.

Once you recognize that the goal of the manufacturer is to send you through their maze, do not give up. Give them a deadline as Bonnie Brockstein of Rockville Centre, New York did in this letter to Pontiac:

> I have recently been advised that as a matter of Federal law, I may have a right of action against GM for a replacement or a refund, plus attorneys' fees, for your failure to correct the defects after a reasonable number of attempts. (Reasonable up to four attempts.)
>
> If I don't receive total satisfaction within a month from the date of this writing, I intend to pursue all legal remedies that I may have.

Sometimes manufacturers add insult to injury in their form responses as did General Motors in the following response to J. J. Mautner, Jr., of Mamaroneck, New York:

> This is with reference to your letter directed to our Detroit office concerning your Chevrolet.
>
> Certain high standards have been developed over the period of years of manufacturing automobiles, and such standards are the basis of any decision made pertaining to a purchase of a product by a consumer or the judging of it by the purchaser.
>
> As explained to you, your Chevrolet can be considered normal and falling within the established standards for it.

Mr. Mautner wrote to Ralph Nader that "I cannot imagine getting such a letter, but seeing is believing. I guess they just don't care about us little guys."

5. Passing the Buck to the Dealer

Dr. Robert Zuch of Philadelphia contacted the main office of Pontiac regarding electrical problems with his 1982 Pontiac Firebird. A customer services representative bounced him back to the dealer in this letter declining Pontiac's inability to intervene:

> We regret the occurrence of the situation you report. Pontiac dealers are independent businessmen who operate on their own capital. For that reason, we do not attempt to regulate the details of their daily operations; however, we do expect them to operate in a professional manner. This we know is the goal of all Pontiac dealers.

Saab-Scania of America sent a similar letter to June Glover of Williamson, West Virginia after she contacted them for more information about the danger posed by potential engine fires which had resulted in a recall. Failing to pay attention to the point of her letter, Saab replied:

> In reference to your letter of February 22, 1989, I am sorry to read that you are having difficulty scheduling Recall service with your dealer, but that is a matter that will have to be resolved at dealership level.

The manufacturer went on to cite the dealer's function as an independent business, thus absolving itself of responsibility.

M. Donnelly of Elizabeth, New Jersey, was told by Chrysler's Pennsylvania zone office representative after four months of correspondence that "Chrysler is not a third party to a retail transaction involving Chrysler cars purchased from a Chrysler dealer and that Chrysler is in no way at all responsible for the business ethics of their dealers, that they are independent businessmen, on and on." As Mr. Donnelly explained his reaction in a letter to Ralph Nader:

> I have not even gotten a dirty Kleenex from Vittori [Chrysler-Plymouth dealer, Salem, N.J.] and nothing from Detroit. . . . After all my correspondence, this entire spectrum of so called customer relations is like the false fronts of buildings in old western movies. You think it's there, but in reality it amounts to

nothing. Zielke, using usual Chrysler techniques, states in his only letter that both N.Y. and Valley Forge offices have made countless tries to contact me, etc. This is an absolute lie.

What these consumers realize well is that manufacturers describe dealers as "independent" only when dealers are needed to insulate the manufacturers from their own mistakes.

6. Telling a Simple Lie

It is not unusual to hear every excuse as to why assistance cannot be given to a customer for his particular problem. Outright denials of responsibility and lies are often reported by consumers.

Mary Pat Herrmann of Johnstown, Colorado had taken her new Eagle Medallion back to the purchasing dealer several times for repairs. Finally she filed a claim with Chrysler's Customer Arbitration Board. A copy of the zone office's statement to the board claiming they had spoken to Ms. Herrmann and that there were no longer any outstanding warranty issues, prompted her to send this angry note:

> In response to your last statement to me as your customer (Statement to the Customer Arbitration Board), I would like to express to whomever wrote the verbage, "WE HAVE TALKED TO THE OWNER." **WHEN**??? This is a FALSE STATEMENT. I have not spoken to anyone, since my letter dated March 3rd, 1989, regarding this situation.

Norman Voelzow described to the Center for Auto Safety his troubles with General Motors and their failure to replace tires that made a noise "much like you would expect while driving a Pickup Truck having snow tires." General Tires, the tire manufacturer for his 1988 Chevrolet Caprice showed Mr. Voelzow a Chevrolet technical service bulletin regarding their tire warranty and suggested that he contact Chevrolet. He brought his car to one Chevy dealer who sent him to another dealer, who in turn told him to call Chevrolet's 800 number. Incredibly, Chevrolet sent him back to the second dealer, who—what else—sent him to General Tire.

When J. Donovan of Washington, D.C., whose school buses carried the children of prominent Republicans to and from private schools each day, complained about gas leaks from three of his school buses, the General Motors representative checked them, but blamed the error on the builder of the school bus body in North Carolina. When Mr. Donovan called the body builder, he was told that the gas tanks were installed by GMC in Pontiac, Michigan. Informed of this, the GMC representative admitted he had made a "mistake" about the gas tank. GMC, he said, did make and install them.

The gas leak problem rose again. General Motors attributed it this time to a faulty tank neck extension which, they told Mr. Donovan, was made in North Carolina and not by GM. This time the *Washington Post*, which was investigating Mr. Donovan's problems, called North Carolina, and again it turned out that General Motors had to admit a "mistake."

7. Promises and Silence

Many owners indicate even if they receive an initial acknowledgement letter, usually from Detroit, the promise of a follow-up from a local zone representative is never kept.

Mr. Gilbert Caballero was distraught with the sudden jerking that would occur while driving his 1987 Ford Bronco II. A log of the phone calls made to resolve his problem illuminated the manufacturer's poor responsiveness. Following each entry was the reply he was given indicating by whom and at what time his call would be returned and the words "No call was ever received." At one point, some two months later, he was even assigned a new case number. This did not, however, result in a call back.

8. Cost

The absurdity of corporate complaint handling procedures is not at all diminished by the fact that the costs of customer relations are passed on to the car buyer, who is, therefore, made to pay for his own harassment. A less callous approach would lead the manufacturers to decide marginal and minor cases on the side of the consumer, save the time and expense of runaround letters, and recoup the cost of fixing the cars in future repeat sales.

AND STILL NO SATISFACTION

Retaliation through further communication with the manufacturer through normal channels, as suggested in this chapter, is of limited value. It relies on the presumption that a reasonable request, reframed and repeated, will appeal to the corporate conscience. Now and then it may work. But to overcome the monumental indifference of the complaint handling system in the larger number of cases, devices are required which creatively seek out points of vulnerability in corporate defenses, or which mount a more credible challenge than can be posed by an isolated consumer.

Ways of seeking weak points in corporate armor and organizing with other consumers are discussed in Chapter 5. Ways of mounting a credible challenge through a lawsuit follow in Chapter 6.

INDUSTRY COMPLAINT BUREAUS

Finally awakened by the mounting consumer complaints on automobiles, the auto industry is taking a few initial steps in setting up complaint resolution mechanisms. But rather than being enthusiastic efforts to resolve consumer complaints, they are aimed at warding off more effective independent complaint bureaus under state lemon laws. The following are some of these efforts.

AUTOCAP

In 1974, the U.S. Office of Consumer Affairs encouraged the Automotive Trade Association Managers (ATAM) and the National Automobile Dealers Association (NADA) to set up the Automotive Consumer Action Program (AUTOCAP). AUTOCAPS exist in 26 states primarily in large metropolitan areas. (See Appendix A for list of participating states.) Where one exists, the local AUTOCAP may help you and the dealer settle the complaint. As a result of this first step, only 20 percent of all cases go to a panel. If the parties cannot agree, the case goes before the panel—usually without your having to appear in person. If the consumer does not attend a panel meeting, the dealer is not permitted to and the panel makes a recommendation on the basis of written information alone. Decisions by the panel are not legally binding for either the dealer or the consumer, however the program has experienced a fairly high compliance rate on the part of dealers when a recommendation is made that is not in their favor.

The average panel has nine members: six "consumer representatives" and three dealers. As of 1989 approximately 13,500 dealers had given their support to AUTOCAP. This method of resolving auto complaints will resolve some complaints. But the panels will not resolve the worst cases or the genuine lemon and not all manufacturers endorse AUTOCAP as their dispute resolution mechanism, relying instead on a self-monitoring device such as Ford's Consumer Appeals Board.

DETROIT AUTO DEALERS ASSOCIATION

A program begun in 1974 to handle consumer complaints against Detroit area new car dealers resolved almost 2,000 complaints in its first three years of operation. The Detroit Auto Dealers Association (DADA) organized and operates the following complaint handling program. According to DADA, when complaints are made to local consumer groups or the news media, the letters are often passed on to the association. DADA officials mail the complaint to the dealership owner who contacts the consumer. If the problem is resolved, the dealership makes a written report within 30 days to DADA, describing action taken to solve the consumer's complaint. If the dealer does not respond within 30 days, DADA sends a second letter asking for the report. If another 30 days pass without a response, DADA sends a registered letter informing the dealer that the complaint will be sent to the state attorney general's office. Copies of the consumer's letter and the dealer's letter, if written, are sent to the newspaper or agency which was first contacted.

FORD CONSUMER APPEALS BOARD

In September 1977, Ford Motor Co. began a program to help resolve its consumer service complaints: a five-member consumer complaint panel, called the Consumer Appeals Board. The Board meets on a local level once a month, without presentation from the dealer or consumer involved. Unlike the AUTOCAP program, any decision by the Ford board will be binding on the company and the dealer. But decisions of the board are not binding on the consumer who is free to take further action if he or she so desires. The boards are usually made up of two dealers, a state official, a vocational educator and a "consumer advocate." It is important to note that the Board will not hear complaints where the consumer no longer owns the vehicle, is currently in litigation over the vehicle, or complaints involving personal or property damage, or sales and delivery problems.

BETTER BUSINESS BUREAU ARBITRATION

The Better Business Bureau (BBB) conducts an Auto Line arbitration program which is used by eight auto companies: General Motors, American Motors, Nissan, Volkswagen/Audi, Porsche, Honda/Acura, Rolls Royce, Subaru, and Saab. Consumers who submit to BBB are given a list of arbitrators and may rank them according to preference. You also have a choice of having your case decided through written submissions, a hearing conducted over the telephone, or an oral hearing, where both you and the auto manufacturer's representative appear in person. The decision made by the arbitrator is binding on the manufacturer but not the consumer, who may reject it and pursue other remedies. This program also operates at no cost to the consumer.

CHRYSLER CUSTOMER ARBITRATION BOARD

The CCAB is also a third party body established to resolve consumer complaints free of charge. Like the Ford Board, the CCAB does not hear disputes regarding the sale of new or used cars, the design of a vehicle or its components, or a case in litigation. Although the dealer is bound by any decision, the consumer is free to pursue other means of recourse. The Board is composed of three voting members: a local consumer advocate, an independent technical representative certified by the National Institute of Automotive Service Excellence, and a representative from the general public. The Board promises that a written decision will be issued within 40 days.

AAA AUTOSOLVE

Autosolve is a pilot program recently created to hear consumer disputes with Hyundai, Mazda and Toyota. Like the Chrysler and Ford Boards, a decision is binding only on the manufacturer/dealer, not the consumer. The car cannot be over 5 years or 50,000 miles, cannot be company owned, or out of the possession of the complainant. Although it is not necessary to be the original owner, the five years begins with the original owner. The panel consists of three AAA employees: an ASE certified mechanic, a traffic safety specialist, and a lemon law expert. Consumers interested in pursuing arbitration may fill out the form provided in the owner's manual or by the manufacturer.

CHAPTER 5

THE LEVERAGE OF GROUP ORGANIZATIONS

"When Consumer Federation of America talks, Congressmen listen . . . Consumers are a powerful constituency."
—*Wall Street Journal*

False Odometer Statement
Potamkin Drops 24,000 Miles

Coolidge Walthall bought a 1985 Ford Taurus from Potamkin Mitsubishi of Springfield, PA in August 1988. Including financing, he paid $15,850 for the Taurus. While this may seem to be a very high price, Mr. Walthall was assured that the car was practically new, with only 4,200 miles on it. As required by Federal and State law, Potamkin gave Mr. Walthall a written statement showing the odometer at 4,232 miles. Feeling reassured by this, he bought the car. He paid $1,000 cash down and traded in his 1982 Oldsmobile.

After the sale, Potamkin tried to register the title of the Taurus in Mr. Walthall's name. However, the Department of Motor Vehicles rejected the registration because the odometer reading was false or inaccurate. Potamkin contacted Mr. Walthall and said that they had made a "mistake" with the odometer reading. They offered him several options which he rejected. Mr. Walthall joined CEPA for help in resolving this problem.

Looking into the matter, CEPA found that, in fact, Potamkin had not made a "mistake." The previous owner had given Potamkin an odometer statement that there was an extra 24,000 miles which the odometer did not show. The Taurus had actually been driven over 28,000 miles, not 4,232. Even though they had been told the true mileage, Potamkin gave Mr. Walthall an odometer statement saying the Taurus only had 4,232 miles on it.

CEPA began negotiating with Potamkin to arrive at a settlement. While Mr. Walthall asked to return the Taurus and get his money back, Potamkin said he could return the car, but they would give him only $77. After the down-payment, trade-in, and first loan payment, Mr. Walthall has already put $2,073 into the Taurus. By offering $77, Potamkin was asking him to take a $2,000 loss. Their excuse was Mr. Walthall's trade-in was worth $2,000 less than what they gave him!

That offer was soundly rejected and Potamkin made another one. They offered to let Mr. Walthall keep the Taurus and deduct $1,000 from its purchase price. Since the reduction did not cover the extra 24,000 miles, the offer was rejected. Any loss for Mr. Walthall was unacceptable since Potamkin created the problem.

CEPA took Mr. Walthall's case to the streets and picketed Potamkin to let other consumers know. On January 3, 1989, Mr. Walthall's case was over when Potamkin took back the Taurus and refunded all of Mr. Walthall's money.

Consumers Voice, Vol. 24, No. 1 (1989).

EXPANDING YOUR ARSENAL

No matter how dedicated, intelligent, clever or persistent you may be, it is difficult to have a lasting impact on the auto industry by yourself or even with an attorney. With organizations behind you, a wide range of additional strategies can be invoked, many of them aimed at changing the system which generates these abuses, as well as solving your own lemon problem. So seek out consumer groups in your area (or if no suitable groups exist, start one along the lines suggested later in this chapter), and consider these group-action devices:

CONTACT THE STATE ATTORNEY GENERAL

In the spring of 1977, more than 90 Wisconsin Ford owners experienced similar problems with their four- and six-cylinder engine 1974-77 models. They banded together and formed a group called Consumers Organized Against Ford (COAF). COAF filed its complaints with the Wisconsin Attorney General's office in an action which eventually led to nationwide relief.

Before contacting the Wisconsin Attorney General's office to intervene on their behalf, the irate Ford and Mercury owners had complained to Ford that a cost-cutting step taken by the manufacturer (elimination of the oil feed holes that lubricate cylinder walls) had caused serious scuffing of the cylinder walls, leaving car owners with costly engine repairs. COAF wanted Ford Motor Co. to install new engines in their cars or to compensate owners for costs already incurred. The group also tried to find out if the problem with Ford's four- and six-cylinder engines was nationwide. COAF contacted newspapers throughout the country in search of Ford and Mercury owners who were having the same problem. They received about 200 responses.

Based on its complaints and research, COAF petitioned the Wisconsin Attorney General's office for assistance. The Wisconsin Department of Justice investigated these "piston scuffing" complaints and reached an agreement with the manufacturer. Ford offered free repairs for four- and six-cylinder engines which experienced piston scuffing within 36 months or 36,000 miles, whichever came first. The manufacturer also agreed to reimburse consumers for repairs already performed which were caused by the defect. Ford reached similar agreements with Minnesota and Massachusetts. Then Ford quietly notified its dealers nationwide of a policy adjustment plan to pay for correcting engine damage caused by piston scuffing. However, Ford failed to announce publicly its new plan to offer what amounted to an extended warranty on these cars nationwide.

This action alerted other consumer groups and the Federal Trade Commission (FTC) which had been looking into such unpublicized "goodwill" or secret warranty policies established by auto manufacturers. Under secret warranties, auto makers repair certain defects for consumers who complain, even though the normal warranty has expired. But the manufacturers failed to disclose the extended warranty to all owners. Thus many consumers end up paying for repairs on their own. As a result of its investigation, the FTC issued a complaint against Ford for violating the law by failing to inform all 2.7 million car owners of the design flaw. Shortly thereafter, Ford capitulated and agreed to tell all affected owners about the secret warranty.

All this happened because one group of consumers decided to stand up to a giant automaker.

Consumer groups can also be instrumental in joining car owners who share pernicious problems with their vehicles, and require drastic action. In 1986, when the rate of sudden acceleration accidents in the Audi 5000 grew to one in 400, it was clear a deadly defect in these cars needed to be uncovered. Two years earlier, Alice Weinstein of Woodbury, Long Island was one consumer who understood too well how terrifying this phenomenon can be. In her first sudden acceleration accident, the car plowed into a snowbank after taking off, averting serious consequences. No one believed her when she described what had happened. In the **second** accident a year later, the car ran across her neighbor's lawn into a tree, injuring her and her daughter.

After sharing these incidents with others, she learned she was not alone. Another Audi 5000 owner, Marion Weisfelner, also of Long Island, New York shared her fear and concern. They soon learned of others who had the same horror stories. Ms. Weinstein and Ms. Weisfelner organized fellow Audi 5000 owners whose car had "a mind of its own" to form the Audi Victims Network (AVN), an organization that grew to 1000 members.

Escalating incidents of sudden acceleration in the Audi 5000 and the continued advocacy efforts of AVN grabbed the attention of federal legislators and state attorneys general. Statistics compiled from the Center for Auto Safety and the National Highway Traffic Safety Administration (NHTSA) showed that the Audi 5000 had a sudden acceleration rate ten times that of the car of the **next** highest rate of this phenomenon.

New York Attorney General Robert Abrams, who called Audi's blaming of the driver for sudden acceleration a "shameless effort," joined the Center for Auto Safety and the New York Public Interest Research Group (NYPIRG) in a 1986 petition to NHTSA to investigate and recall Audi 5000s because of the alarming number of runaway incidents. This petition was granted, and in the wake of growing criticism Audi issued a voluntary recall. Its "fix" of the problem, however, in spite of the growing injury and death toll, was to install a shift lock device on the gear shifting mechanism. This allegedly prevented the car from shifting out of park into reverse or drive unless the driver's foot was on the brake. Yet incidents of sudden acceleration were still reported even after this purported cure.

Public attention and concern over this defect exploded. The CBS weekly newsmagazine "60 Minutes" featured a segment on runaway Audi vehicles. The Attorney General of Illinois, Neil Hartigan, wrote a letter to every state attorney general in the country sharply criticizing Audi for its failure to recall the car and its inadequate shift lock remedy. In his letter, he stated:

> Currently under consideration by my staff are two possible courses of action. The first would involve promoting public dialogue and awareness, possibly through a public hearing mechanism. The second would entail litigation such as a mandamus action against NHTSA to force that agency to correctly implement vehicle defect notification procedures, (49 CFR Sec. 577) and/or to issue a mandatory safety defect recall order to the manufacturer. Another litigation possibility is an injunction and restitution action against the manufacturer on behalf of the State and consumers. One such suit has already been filed by a private plaintiff. That suit, a class action instituted on behalf of individual owners and a leasing company, seeks damages for the diminution in resale value in Audi 5000's as a result of runaway reports.

Numerous individual and class action lawsuits have been filed because of sudden acceleration in the Audi 5000, an automobile defect that became a matter of nationwide concern. And it was consumers-turned-activists like the members of AVN who helped bring this tragedy to the national spotlight.

PICKET DEALERS OR REPAIR SHOPS

Picketing by groups of consumers has proved to be a very successful tactic. Few people have had as much success with picketing as Rosemary Dunlap, founder and president of Motor Voters, an all-volunteer consumer organization dedicated to auto safety. Her crusade began while she was living in San Diego, California, after a Volkswagen dealer took three months to fix her car. When the job was finally completed, it was repaired so poorly she refused to take the car home, fearing for her safety. She decided other people should know how she had been treated so they could avoid such shabby treatment, and began a one-woman picket line. She also started protesting with signs calling for state legislation to assist consumers in getting good service from dealers, which created the impetus of the drive for California's lemon law. Soon, she gained support from her community, and others joined her to picket the dealership. Five months later, the dealer settled her complaint by paying her $10,410 which covered the cost of her 1978 VW Dasher and then some.

Buoyed by this victory and educated with a greater understanding of consumer rights, she successfully led the drive for a lemon law in California, and was appointed by then Governor Jerry Brown to a four year term on the state's Bureau of Automotive Repair Advisory Board. Later, after a move to Washington, D.C., she served on the Congressional Advisory Committee on Consumer Protection and Transportation Safety for California Representative Jim Bates. She has gained the attention and respect of both the consumer and auto industry, and has conducted countless radio, television, magazine, and newspaper interviews in the name of auto safety. According to the *Detroit Free Press*, January 11, 1987:

> Auto company lobbyists here in Washington not only know who Dunlap is, they acknowledge that she does her homework. Auto makers are reluctant to discuss Dunlap, but during the past year, they have begun to gripe informally that she knows all too well how to draw national attention to air bags. . . . In sum, says a Toyota Motor Corp. lobbyist, "She has everything it takes to cause this industry many headaches for many years."

Ms. Dunlap's latest picket was of the auto maker Peugeot for its failure to offer air bags, the first of many such protests of manufacturers who do not offer this protection. In this effort, she enlisted the support of the Public Interest Research Group (PIRG) in Connecticut to picket Peugeot in that state. Sales of Peugeot have plummeted far below their own low expectations. And all of this began because a dealer wouldn't fix her 1978 Dasher.

Some success stories require less effort. When James Adams of Oceanside, California traded in his Volkswagen van for a GM Pontiac Catalina diesel station wagon, he thought he had traded "up" for a more fuel efficient, longer lasting car. The diesel engine, paid for at a premium, was so highly touted by GM as an engineering breakthrough he had no warning it would be one of the worst lemons ever devised. Within the next 18 months, the car had three new engine blocks. It consumed one quart of oil every twenty miles. It was in need of such chronic repair that the car was in the shop a total of 87 days within the first year-and-one half!

Finally fed up with the lack of satisfaction he was getting from GM, Mr. Adams joined Disgruntled Owners of General Motors Automotive Diesels (DOGMAD), a group of angry GM diesel owners as its name so well implied. DOGMAD picketed GM dealerships to bring attention to their problems and to compel them to take responsibility for their product. Mr. Adams eventually got relief through the Better Business Bureau and small claims court. Other diesel owners have followed this route, largely because the Federal Trade Commission ordered GM to arbitrate all diesel claims, regardless of age or mileage, until 1992.

Picketing is so successful that sometimes just the threat of this action is enough to resolve a complaint. For example, a few months after E. Spears of Philadelphia bought a Mercury station wagon from Kardon Motors in Mt. Holly, New Jersey he found that the whole floor of the car was covered with rust and holes. The dealer had attempted to conceal the rust with newspaper and carpeting. Mrs. Spears contacted the Philadelphia branch of CEPA. The dealer would not negotiate. As soon as a picket was scheduled, the dealer decided it was time to reach some kind of agreement. The picket was called off, and a delegation was set up. After negotiations Kardon agreed to take the car back and give the consumer a $791 refund. See Chapter 11 for a more complete description of this strategy and examples of its use in auto cases.

GROUP EFFORTS IMPROVE CHANCE OF SUCCESSFUL LEGAL ACTION

Groups of individuals who band together can usually invoke certain legal strategies better than if each individual had acted alone. For example, consumers joined forces against British Leyland Imports when the manufacturer failed to repair their Jaguars, Triumphs, and MGB's in accordance with the cars' written and implied warranties. Led by a Baltimore dentist, 16 plaintiffs jointly filed a suit brought by attorney Barbara Brewer, which alleged misrepresentation in the failure to reveal the cars' defects in addition to the warranty claims. Ultimately, more than 30 lemon British luxury car owners joined the suit with almost every one recovering their purchase price, incidental damages, and attorney's fees.

Another legal strategy successfully used by groups is the delicensing approach. For example, if many consumers were misled by a dealer's or manufacturer's deceptive advertising, they can persuade state licensing authorities to open delicensing proceedings against the offending dealer or manufacturer. It is unlikely that a state licensing authority would suspend or revoke a dealer's or manufacturer's privilege to sell cars in the entire state on the strength of a single consumer complaint. A consumer group might lend enough weight by complaining on behalf of all consumers misled.

Although a single complaint can arouse the attention of a state authority, it will generally take many complaints from other consumers with the same or different problems to bring the authority to take action against the dealer. Here consumer organization is invaluable.

Some organizations can even offer individual help, instead of trying to get a manufacturer to recall a defective model or change a policy. Motor Voters, a consumer group originally formed to advocate California's lemon law which now supports the gamut of auto safety concerns, helped put people in touch with such groups through its newsletter:

> Got a licensing problem? Want assistance with the DMV? Thinking of going to small claims court because of a sour auto deal?
>
> There's a new group in San Diego called "Lemon-Aides" which helps vehicle owners with many of the complexities which can arise.
>
> Recently, Lemon-Aide Louise Price aided a consumer in small claims court. The client and her husband had bought a car "AS IS." Almost immediately, it needed a major transmission job. Cost: $700. The "AS IS" clause normally means the buyer must bear all repair costs, and no warranty is provided. However, using a provision in the California law that applies to all consumer goods—the implied warranty of merchantability—Ms. Price (as an expert witness) helped convince a judge to award the woman half the repair costs.
>
> Reprinted from the *Motor Voter Press*, 1985.

Motor Voters is also instrumental in getting people buybacks for their lemons, both by providing assistance in preparing for arbitration and by arranging experts to testify on consumers' behalf. For example, after Elizabeth and Walter Boone of National City, California brought their 1983 AMC Concord into the dealer for repairs because the brakes failed in a rainstorm, he kept the car for awhile and then told them the needed repairs had been made. However, another incident occurred—this time with their children in the car—which upset the Boones greatly. More repairs were attempted, but the car continued to fishtail in hard braking situations. The Boones contacted an attorney, but negotiations stalled, so they turned to Motor Voters. The group found evidence of a pattern of these complaints, and also put the Boones in touch with an automotive expert, who examined the car and wrote up the braking defect he discovered. After continued publicity about this very dangerous problem by Motor Voters, the dealer refunded the Boones' money, to their great relief.

BRING A CLASS ACTION SUIT AGAINST THE MANUFACTURER

Having an organized auto consumer group will facilitate the identification of abuses and problems that are widespread and affect enough consumers to make a class action suit appropriate. Diane and Peter Halferty were furious when their $20,000 diesel Cadillac Seville needed three engines in three years, the last repair costing $4,500 because the car was out of warranty. They had paid a premium price for the diesel, and now were stuck with a premium lemon. When they tried to trade the car in just 30 months after they purchased it, they were offered only $3,500 because the car had a diesel; the Kelley Blue Book value of a non-diesel was $14,000. Convinced other diesel owners experienced the same dilemma, Diane Halferty placed an ad in the newspaper asking other consumers with diesel woes to contact her.

The GM diesel was the genesis of many consumer groups who brought legal action against the giant auto maker for the diesel powered vehicles. The Center for Auto Safety termed these cars the economic lemons of the century because they cost consumers several billion dollars in excess depreciation and repairs. The Halfertys helped found Consumers Against General Motors (CAGM), a consumer group with 800 initial members that grew to many thousands. In

Oregon, 300 angry diesel owners formed DieselGate. In Virginia, 2,000 diesel owners founded DOGMAD. In New York, angry diesel owners founded Lemon on Wheels and in Chicago they founded GMDUDS. In fact, General Motors did more for grass roots consumer organizing by introducing the lemon 350 CID V8 diesel than anyone since Ralph Nader.

GM denied their claims as meritless, but they could not deny the growing evidence against their diesel engine. According to *The Heartbreak of America*, a 1988 Cadillac report written by James Musselman of Essential Information, Inc., a former GM engineer stated that in numerous tests, the diesel engine had crankshaft, engine block, head gasket, and fuel pump problems. The cars failed to pass California emissions tests, so were banned for sale in the state. The FTC was preparing to file a complaint against GM for the injury to consumers caused by the diesel engine, but instead settled the case and ordered them to arbitrate claims. In spite of this activity, consumers did not receive meaningful retribution against GM until they filed a class action suit against the company. One of the diesel class action lawsuits (for owners of 1978–80 diesels) was settled in 1984 for $22.5 million. Another class action for 1981–85 V-8 diesels is pending, a suit which focuses on the cars' loss of resale value. By helping to find the widespread pattern of defects in GM diesel engines, the Halfertys and CAGM were able to help thousands of consumers gain relief. (See Chapter 6 for a more complete description of how class actions work.)

OTHER EFFORTS

One possible value of organizing consumer discontent into a cohesive force is the added muscle it can bring to bear on resolving the complaints of member-consumers. Other efforts, possible only through organization, may also help you and others:

a. Investigations and reports, with press coverage of exposures;
b. Boycotts of offending dealers or even certain makes found to be unsafe or unreliable;
c. Lemoncades (as well as picketing) against dealers, repair shops, or finance companies which have victimized consumers (see Chapter 11);

d. Lobbying for changes in laws affecting consumer rights and for programs to reduce the enormous dependence of urban and suburban residents on the automobile;
e. Enlisting attorneys to develop test cases and auto mechanics to assist in diagnosis and negotiation;
f. Contacts with industry insiders to help place the responsibility where it belongs.

These are some of the levers of lasting change.

Even when the manufacturer itself recognizes a defect, it often takes consumer action to find a solution. When the 1984 Pontiac Fiero developed chronic overheating and engine fire problems, General Motors set up a "Fiero Thermal Distress Task Force" within the company in an unsuccessful effort to cure the car's defective design. When Lisa Lima of Kankakee, Illinois experienced an engine fire that destroyed her 1984 Fiero, she founded the "Fiero Fire Fighters," a network of owners who became fed up with the car's overheating and engine fire problems. The group has been exploring various avenues of legal action against GM, including a class action lawsuit. (GM has discontinued the Fiero line.)

A consumer group can also function as a clearinghouse on a particular topic. For example, when the Center for Auto Safety received numerous consumer letters complaining of automatic transmission problems in General Motors automobiles caused by faulty transmission fluid, the group mailed out information on how to proceed to many thousands of frustrated consumers. One consumer, F.A. Rosscoe of Richmondville, New York, wrote the Center about what happened after he got the Center's information which included a copy of the GM service bulletin referred to in the form letter. Although GM had announced it would pay for a transmission overhaul regardless of mileage, GM had not been honoring its promise in many cases, including Rosscoe's. After sending GM a copy of the information on GM's own service bulletin along with the repair bill, Rosscoe received a refund for the cost of repairs with GM's full apology. In his letter to the Center, Rosscoe stated, "Once again I thank you for all your help in supplying the needed information that had to be used, even though it took almost two years to culminate in success."

Occasionally, just the threat of an investigation by a consumer group will bring success. For example, the Center for Auto Safety received a disturbing complaint from J. Kaufmann, Jr., of Richfield, Minnesota. His Kawasaki motorcycle had a severe shaking of the front fork and wheel upon deceleration or when one hand was removed from the handlebars. Kaufmann could not obtain proper service on his motorcycle which was purchased new from Bloomington Kawasaki, Bloomington, Minnesota. Kaufmann described his attempt to get his bike repaired as follows:

> The service manager at Bloomington Kawasaki where I purchased the bike told me that this problem was due to a factory design defect and it could not be cleared up. He said to me, "you've got a lemon and you'll have to live with it."

Kaufmann wrote Kawasaki for an explanation of the service manager's comment. After four letters to Kawasaki over a ten month period, he still had no reply. Being a persistent consumer, Kaufmann called 10 different Kawasaki offices or agents. A Lincoln, Nebraska Kawasaki agent told him that the problem with his bike was very common for that model Kawasaki and year. Undoubtedly, as a result of his efforts to shake up the Kawasaki bureaucracy, the consumer received a telephone call from Kawasaki of California the day after speaking with Lincoln Kawasaki and learning about the high frequency of this safety problem in 1976 Kawasaki motorcycles. The California office told Kaufmann that the Lincoln office had given him incorrect information and that there was no basis for his claim about a safety hazard in this particular bike.

At that point, Kaufmann wrote the Center which in turn wrote a letter to the manufacturer. The Center explained the situation to Kawasaki Motors Corp., stating that it was thinking of beginning an investigation into Kawasaki's complaint handling procedures and possible safety hazards in models like Kaufmann's.

Shortly thereafter, the Center received a letter from Kawasaki Motors Corp. executive Sid Saito. He denied the existence of any safety related defect on Kaufmann's bike, but wrote "because the product does not meet his [Kaufmann's] general expectations" and "our failure to adequately control the handling of some customer contacts," Kawasaki will agree to repurchase the motorcycle at no cost to him.

Kaufmann responded to the Center that:

> Regardless of what Kawasaki said wasn't wrong with the bike, there was a very serious problem with that particular vehicle.
>
> In regard to your very kind assistance with my motorcycle problem, I could not be happier about the way it was resolved. Kawasaki did buy back my motorcycle with no questions asked. I would like to say that your strategy in this situation worked just perfectly.

CONSUMER GROUPS

The advantages of having an organized consumer group, as shown above, are many. Of course, a large degree of effort and skill is needed to launch a hard-hitting consumer action group. But examples of successful organizations are numerous, and information on them is available to those who wish to start groups where none exist. Seven organizations, described here, illustrate varying approaches to organizing around consumer issues. Further information on these organizations is available in most cases from the organization itself or from the:

> Center for Auto Safety
> 2001 S Street NW, Suite 410
> Washington, DC 20009

The Center will also consult directly with new and developing consumer groups.

> 1. Consumer Federation of America (CFA)
>   1424 16th Street NW
>   Washington, DC 20036

CFA is a federation of over 500 national, state and local organizations which have joined together. CFA helps affect public policy as it is formulated by Congress, the President, regulatory agencies, the courts and industry. Established in 1968, "CFA is organized for and dedicated to advancing the consumer viewpoint through its lobbying efforts and its informational and educational services."

Although CFA does not take direct action on auto complaints, the organization is instrumental in supporting those laws and policies which protect the rights of auto consumers and efforts by other groups. CFA publishes a Directory of State and Local Organizations (nongovernmental), available for $5.00 from CFA.

2. Automobile Protection Association (APA)
   P.O. Box 117
   Station E
   Montreal 151
   Quebec, Canada

An imaginative and resourceful group of automobile owners banded together in Quebec to form the Automotive Protection Association, also known as Association pour la Protection des Automobilistes. It is an ombudsman-like organization handling "everyday grass-roots complaints of motorists, while at the same time rewarding industry personnel who are competent and honest." APA takes complaints on auto insurance, auto dealer-consumer problems, gas stations and auto repair gripes. It develops dossiers to back up charges and confronts industry spokespersons. If complaints or abuses remain unsettled, the offending organization may find itself exposed on the media and picketed at its main office. Says APA Counselor Vladimir Cekota: "We are a small, lean and mean group while the Canadian Automobile Association (CAA) is quite large."

In addition to picketing and taking complaints, every Friday at 8 p.m. cable viewers can tune into the Lemon Aid show, a talk show devoted solely to car talk. Counselors advise inquiring consumers as to what cars to buy, holding nothing back when it comes to praising or criticizing performance or safety. They handle anywhere from 20–30 telephone complaints a day. These calls and incoming letters serve the basis for their annual rating of automobiles.

3. Consumer Education and Protective Association (CEPA)
   6048 Ogontz Avenue
   Philadelphia, PA 19141

CEPA is an organization of consumers, started in 1965 by Max Weiner, who is the Education Director. Through ingenious organizational devices and its achievement of an almost unbroken string of victories over those who would defraud local consumers, CEPA remains a strong and growing organization.

CEPA's strength comes from its organizing philosophy. It will not lend its organizational backing to aid a single victimized consumer until the consumer first joins CEPA or a CEPA branch and participates in the solution of the problems of other members whose problems have come up for action. The CEPA branches in Philadelphia are autonomous strike forces, each covering a separate geographical area.

CEPA has considerable organizational weight to offer. When a branch decides to take action, the plan moves through several stages. CEPA first sends a letter outlining the complaint to the offending auto dealer. (A copy of CEPA's form complaint is found in Appendix C.) If the letter does not lead to a solution, the branch throws an "information" picket line in front of the dealership premises. A negotiating team accompanies the pickets and if progress is not made in the initial negotiations, the team joins the picket line. The picket continues until an agreement acceptable to CEPA is reached, often within an hour.

The central office of CEPA stores picketing placards on racks for easy access. The office coordinates the picketing schedule of the branches, assists on strategy when a new type of abuse is encountered, and is on hand to take photographs. CEPA pickets focus on educating passers-by rather than disrupting business. The central office informs the local police department in advance of each picket. CEPA's wise policy is to obey court injunctions obtained by local merchants in state court against their picketing. CEPA has been very successful, however, in winning in federal court the dissolution of the state court injunctions.

CEPA's successes are innumerable, many of them against auto repair shops, used car lots, and established automobile dealers. For example, a salesperson at Crisconi Oldsmobile in Philadelphia was fired when CEPA pointed out to the owner that the salesperson had induced a CEPA member to sign a contract in blank and then had proceeded to add $1200 in fictitious charges. CEPA also secured a revised contract for the member.

Reports of CEPA's activities, pictures of pickets displaying signs, photocopies of refund checks, and fraudulent or misleading contracts are published regularly in its monthly newspaper, CONSUMERS VOICE.

CEPA is now a national organization with branches in 40 cities including Cleveland, San Francisco, Fort Wayne, and Milwaukee. CONSUMERS VOICE has received inquiries and subscriptions from Japan, Sweden, India, and Puerto Rico. The organization is supported in part by its members, who pay an annual fee of $15.

4. Consumer Action (CA)
   26 Seventh Avenue
   San Francisco, CA 94103

Consumer Action gives this self-portrait:

> At Consumer Action we believe that **every** consumer should stand up for his or her rights whenever the victim of shoddy products or unfair business practices. Yet we understand all too well that a consumer alone can be nearly helpless: consumer laws are poorly enforced; individual consumer losses are often too small to justify the hiring of a lawyer; and a complaining consumer must be prepared to out-wait a runaround from the merchant that may last one year or more.
>
> Consumer Action exists to even up the odds in the battle for consumer justice in the marketplace. We are a non-profit, community organization. Formed in 1971, our goal is to help consumers achieve greater control over their lives and a stronger voice in the decisions of government and business that affect us all. We are part of a growing, nationwide movement of consumers who believe that by working together we can correct many of our nation's problems. Consumer Action works through research and publication, and through the Complaint Resolution Committee method of grievance handling.

5. Automobile Club of Missouri
   201 Progress Parkway
   Maryland Heights, MO 63040

While the Automobile Club of Missouri, a chapter of the American Automobile Association (AAA), is not itself a consumer group, this Auto Club is one of the most innovative auto clubs in the country. The Club was one of the first to set up an auto diagnostic inspection center for the use of its members. As a result, they have a computerized data bank on defects in various makes and models, plus extensive files on repair practices. One of its most valuable, and consumer-like functions, is to arbitrate complaints for members who have gone through their diagnostic inspection and then had repair problems.

      6. Motor Voters
         1350 Beverly Road
         McLean, VA 22101

Motor Voters is an all-volunteer consumer organization dedicated to promoting auto safety through its advocacy of air bags, improved safety standards for motor vehicles, increased consumer awareness on the crashworthiness of cars they are buying, and the passing and strengthening of lemon laws across the country. Founded in 1979 by its current president, Rosemary Dunlap, it was formerly located in San Diego, where the group was credited with leading the crusade for passage of California's lemon law.

Motor Voters is an active participant in state and federal auto safety legislation, and is frequently called upon to provide testimony in hearings before Congress and state legislatures on these issues, as well as at safety symposiums across the country. The group has been featured in newspaper, television, and radio interviews for its advocacy of consumer protection.

It gains its support primarily from its membership, which requires a $15 contribution. In return, members receive a copy of *The Car Book* by Jack Gillis and a subscription to the semi-annual newsletter, the *Motor Voter Press*.

ORGANIZING DIRECT ACTION CONSUMER GROUPS

If there is no consumer group in your community, organize your own. Consumer groups are valuable tools in resolving car complaints and saving you money. The group can be organized around only one issue, such as Consumers Organized Against General Motors, aimed at resolving GM diesel complaints. It can concentrate on many types of auto ripoffs as Motor Voters does. Or it can handle everything from auto complaints to problems with furniture, televisions or health care as CEPA does. Depending on the purposes of the group, you may or may not need letterhead stationery, legal advice, or a charter. Many helpful guidebooks and organizing manuals exist, including "A Nader Guide for Establishing Local Consumer Auto Complaint Organizations," to help you work out these details. (See Appendix D for a list of titles and where they can be obtained.)

Consumer action will have more lasting impact and benefit a wider number of consumers if a major share of the effort is put into organizing action groups. Imaginative efforts on your part may solve your own problem, but will do nothing to insure that you will not run into the same set of problems with your next car.

The Center for Auto Safety serves as a clearinghouse for persons and groups developing new consumer tactics and forming new organizations particularly in the areas of highway and mobile home safety and any aspect of the automobile. Send questions and success stories to us:

Center for Auto Safety
2001 S Street NW, Suite 410
Washington, DC 20009

C H A P T E R   6

YOUR LEGAL RIGHTS

January 17, 1989

Lincoln Mercury Service Division
Southfield, MI

Gentlemen:

On December 2, I wrote to Ford by certified letter regarding a Continental I purchased on November 30, 1988. The letter advised that the factory had neglected to fasten the struts that keep the rear wheels in place. With only 71 miles on the car, it was only by the grace of God that a serious mishap was avoided.

Upon receiving no reply, I called your 800 number and was assigned Case #002703–743 on December 15, 1988. The person who assigned the case number said someone would contact me the following day, and of course, no one did.

After waiting ten days, I again called and was told that the case was closed. I asked how that could be and they advised that the dealer said everything was o.k. I immediately contacted the dealer and he had no knowledge of the conversation.

On December 23 I again wrote to you by certified mail. Your company signed for the letter on December 27, 1988, and I, again, have had no reply. If this is your "commitment to quality and service" you most certainly are going to have problems.

At this time my wife is still reluctant to ride in the car and feels that if they forgot to bolt on the rear wheels, God knows what else they forgot. With or without your cooperation, I am going to dispose of the car. If I have to file suit against Ford, so be it. It is certainly becoming obvious you don't care one way or another.

Sincerely,
J. L. Althoff
Crystal Lake, IL.

When the manufacturer's complaint-handling procedure does not work, the consumer can often turn to a lawyer for help. As will be discussed in Chapter 10, it is not always necessary to hire a lawyer to enforce one's legal rights, but, in any event, it is wise to investigate your rights. Consumers who know their legal rights are almost always more successful with their complaints than those who do not know their rights. Some legal rights arise from the manufacturer's written warranty. Other rights arise from applicable laws, both federal and state. One important right, freedom of speech, is guaranteed in the U.S. Constitution.

THE MANUFACTURER'S WARRANTY: OVERVIEW

The written warranty that comes with a new car is a sales tool. The new car warranty "reassures" the buyer that the car is guaranteed against defects within a given time period, usually 12 months or 12,000 miles, whichever comes first.

In reality the new car warranty is designed not so much to protect your interests as it is to limit the manufacturer's liability. The written warranty does not promise you a working car, does not promise to replace the car if there are serious defects, and does not accept liability for any loss or damage as a result of defects. But the law favors you, and you may be able to get these remedies!

The essential consumer right under the written warranty is that the dealer must replace or repair parts which to the dealer's "reasonable satisfaction" are defective in workmanship or materials. The buyer has certain obligations under the warranty. The principal one is following a specified service or maintenance schedule, which can be performed by the dealer or an independent garage or service station. Keep the invoices for such service in order to show that the manufacturer's required maintenance was done.

Beyond this central right, the language of the warranty makes it clear that the manufacturer is limiting its liability. An example is the Chevrolet Motor Division Limited Warranty on New 1990 Chevrolets. The warranty says: "Chevrolet does not authorize any person to create for it any other obligation or liability in connection with these cars." This means that advertising claims or promises which are not in the written warranty made by the dealer's salespeople will not be upheld by the manufacturer.

Beware of spoken explanations of the warranty by the salesperson. What the dealership **says** about the warranty may not count when it comes time for warranty service. Check what is **written** in the manufacturer's warranty. These are your undisputed rights. If the dealership makes claims in an advertisement or gives you a **written** explanation or addition to the manufacturer's warranty, then it is the dealership and not the manufacturer who may be obligated to those additional promises.

The warranty makes clear that "loss of time, inconvenience, loss of use of the vehicle or other matters not specifically included are not covered." If a consumer's car is tied up for 3 weeks at the dealership for repairs and a rental car costs $300, the manufacturer will not voluntarily pay you back. As we will see later, this and other attempts to limit the manufacturer's warranty liability may be voided or modified by state law.

YOUR WARRANTY RIGHTS

There are other warranties besides the manufacturers' skimpy written ones which protect the new car buyer. The most important of these are **express** warranties and **implied** warranties that arise under state law. These apply to your car both during and after the manufacturer's written warranty period. In addition, certain vehicle components such as parts of the emission control system may have federal or state mandated warranties. Beyond the mandated federal emission control warranty, federal and state law may set requirements on how the manufacturers limit or honor their warranties.

In sum, your car may have a total of four warranties: **written** warranties, other **express** warranties, **implied** warranties and **federal** or **state mandated** warranties. Warranty problems are often the first and most frustrating problems faced by new car owners. Knowing that you are protected in the following ways will encourage you, the owner, to enforce your warranty rights.

WRITTEN WARRANTIES

All automobile manufacturers provide written warranties with the cars they sell. Most of those warranties are limited to specific parts and expire after a certain period of time and mileage. The average warranty covers major components such as steering, transmission, drivetrain and brakes. Some companies limit the warranty on paint defects to the first few days, claiming that such defects in paint, trim or other appearance items are normally noted and corrected during new vehicle inspection. The manufacturer suggests that any paint or appearance defects be called to the attention of the dealer without delay, since normal deterioration due to use and exposure is not covered by the warranty. (See Appendix E for an example of an actual new car warranty and Appendix F for a comparative table of the warranty coverages of major auto companies.) Manufacturers often offer longer warranties on some components, such as the drivetrain, than on the rest of the car. Tires are frequently warranted by the tire manufacturer under a separate warranty included with the owner information brochures supplied with the vehicle. Many new car dealers have service agreements with tire manufacturers to handle warranty problems with tires.

In order to regulate written warranties on consumer products, Congress passed the Magnuson-Moss Warranty Act of 1975. The purpose of the Act was to make it easier for consumers to get defective cars repaired, total lemons replaced, and to successfully sue the auto companies. According to then Federal Trade Commission Chairman Michael Pertschuk:

> The Act established a rational scheme for warranty disclosures in advertising and marketing, and prevented the use of warranties as a means of decreasing consumers' rights.

For detailed information from the Federal Trade Commission on this law, read "Warranties: There Ought To Be A Law," which can be obtained by writing: Consumer Information Center, Pueblo, Colorado 81009.

THE MAGNUSON-MOSS WARRANTY ACT

Although the Act has many deficiencies, it does provide remedies for consumers whose car warranties are not honored and makes it easier for lemon owners to find attorneys to represent them in breach of warranty lawsuits. The Act includes a "lemon" provision which, in some situations, entitles a lemon owner to his or her choice of a full refund or a new replacement car if the manufacturer/dealer fails to remedy defects after a "reasonable number of attempts" to repair the car.

State lemon laws, which are discussed in detail in Chapter 7, were derived from the replacement/refund protection provisions offered under this Act. Consumers in those states which do not yet have a lemon law are given lemon remedies under this federal law.

Under the Magnuson-Moss Act, all **written** warranties must be easy to read and understand. They must be written in ordinary language, not "legalese." Fine print is not allowed. The warranty must disclose the following in simple and readily understood language:

1. **Who** is covered by the written warranty. May only the first buyer enforce it or a subsequent buyer as well?
2. **Which parts** of the car the warranty does and does not cover.
3. **What** the seller or manufacturer will and will not do in the case of a defect or breakdown. At whose expense?
4. **When** the warranty period begins and ends. How long will the car be covered? Although the written warranty on a new car will invariably read that any implied warranty is good only for the length of the written warranty, this clause is invalid in some states and should be invalid in all. See the following sections on *Disclaimer of Warranties* for further information on this.
5. What you must do in order to get the manufacturer to meet its obligations. A **step-by-step** explanation of the procedure which the consumer should follow in order to obtain performance of any warranty obligation. What are your responsibilities under the warranty? Who is authorized to perform warranty work? The selling dealer or any franchised dealer? This information must include the name of the manufacturer and an address or title of a representative responsible for the warranty performance. A toll-free number to use to contact the manufacturer or service person may take the place of an address.
6. If any informal dispute settlement procedures are available through the manufacturer, information about them must be provided. It may be necessary for you to utilize this program before going to court under the Magnuson-Moss Act or your

state's lemon law, if this is so stated in the written warranty and the program follows certain minimum standards.

7. Any limitations or disclaimers on your right to recover consequential or incidental damages—such as the cost of rental cars when your car breaks down. Once again, such conditions are invalid in some states, meaning you may have a right to collect these damages despite the limitation to the contrary in your car's written warranty. See the section below on *Limitations on Remedies* for the states.

8. The manufacturer's warranty must contain the following statements telling consumers of additional rights beyond what is in the written warranty:

This warranty gives you specific legal rights, and you may also have other rights which vary from state to state. Some states do not allow limitations on how long an implied warranty will last or the exclusion of limitation of incidental or consequential damages, so the above limitations or exclusions may not apply to you.

If the warranty does not include all of the above information, complain to the dealer and manufacturer. Write to the Federal Trade Commission, Bureau of Consumer Protection, 6th & Pennsylvania Avenue NW, Washington, D.C. 20580. Send a copy to the Center for Auto Safety.

"FULL" WARRANTIES

The Magnuson-Moss Act requires all written warranties to be labeled as either **full** or **limited** warranties. A "full" warranty is far better than a "limited" warranty in imposing specific obligations on the manufacturer and dealer as well as giving consumers specific rights against them.

The label "full" on a warranty means:

1. A defective car or part must be fixed or replaced for free.
2. A defective car or part must be fixed within a reasonable period of time after you complain.
3. A consumer cannot be required to do anything unreasonable to get warranty service, such as taking the car to the factory 600 miles away.

4. The warranty must cover anyone who owns the car during the warranty period.
5. If the car cannot be or has not been fixed after a reasonable number of attempts, you get a choice of a new replacement car or your money back. This is the so-called "lemon provision."

There is one thing the word "full" does not promise. A full warranty does not have to cover the whole car. It may cover only selected components or systems such as the engine or drivetrain.

"LIMITED" WARRANTIES

The loophole in the Magnuson-Moss Act is that auto companies are not required to give a "full" warranty. All other written warranties are "limited" and do not have to meet any federal standards, including the all-important lemon provision. A warranty must be labeled "limited" if it gives you anything less than what a "full" warranty gives. A car may have both a full and limited warranty. For example, it can have a "full" warranty on the engine and a "limited" warranty on the tires.

Because of this loophole, many consumer groups, members of Congress and government agencies advocate amending the Magnuson-Moss Act to require all written warranties for new motor vehicles to meet the federal minimum standards for warranty; i.e., be "full" warranties. To avoid a new loophole, the manufacturers should be required to give a written warranty on all new vehicles sold. Otherwise, they may opt out of warranties entirely.

But even the "limited" warranty gives the consumer certain rights. For example, General Motors' 1990 Chevrolet "limited" warranty gives the new car owner the following rights:

1. **REPAIRS COVERED** This warranty covers repairs to correct any defect in material or workmanship during the WARRANTY PERIOD. New or remanufactured parts will be used.
2. **WARRANTY PERIOD** The WARRANTY PERIOD for all coverages begins on the date the car is first delivered or put in use and ends at the expiration of the COMPLETE CAR COVERAGE or other COVERAGE shown below.
(The warranty applies to all owners of the car during the warranty period.)

3. **COMPLETE CAR COVERAGE** The complete vehicle (except those items listed under "WHAT IS NOT COVERED") is covered for 3 Years or 50,000 miles, whichever comes first. After the first year or 12,000 miles, whichever comes first, repairs are subject to a $100 deductible per repair visit. The sealed refrigerant portion of the factory-installed air conditioning system has no deductible the first year, regardless of mileage.

4. **SUPPLEMENTAL INFLATABLE RESTRAINT COVERAGE** The Supplemental Inflatable Restraint System (if equipped in your vehicle) is covered for 3 Years, regardless of mileage (with no deductible).

5. **CORROSION (RUST-THROUGH) COVERAGES** Any body sheet metal panel that Rust-Through due to corrosion is covered for 6 Years or 100,000 miles, whichever comes first (with no deductible). Sheet metal panels may be repaired or replaced.

6. **OBTAINING REPAIRS** To obtain warranty repairs, take the car to a Chevrolet dealership within the WARRANTY PERIOD and request the needed repairs or adjustments. A reasonable time must be allowed for the dealership to perform the necessary repairs.

7. **TOWING** Towing is covered to the nearest Chevrolet dealership, if your vehicle cannot be driven because of a warranted defect.

8. **NO CHARGE** Warranty repairs, including TOWING, labor and parts, will be made at no charge (except for applicable $100 deductible per repair visit after 1 Year or 12,000 miles, whichever comes first).

9. **WARRANTY APPLIES** This warranty is for GM cars registered in the United States and normally operated in the United States or Canada. Although other sections of this written warranty do limit the manufacturer's liability to the owner, the owner still gets at least the legal rights outlined above. Everything that the manufacturer promises in its written warranty is **your legal right**; i.e., the manufacturer is legally obligated to carry out the specific promises it makes.

IMPLIED WARRANTIES

Implied warranties are legal rights created by state law, not by the seller. To the extent they exist, implied warranties create legal rights above and beyond what is in the written warranty. Implied warranties can give consumers the right to get free repair, replacement, or refund if the car is defective and does not work in the ordinary way a car is expected, provided the consumer takes the right steps. Thus, state law gives consumers rights which are similar to the rights given to car owners with a "full" warranty under federal law.

There are two kinds of implied warranties: an implied warranty of **merchantability** and an implied warranty of **fitness for a particular purpose.**

The most common implied warranty is the warranty of merchantability. This means that the car must be fit for its reasonable and ordinary uses, which include safe, efficient and comfortable transportation from one place to another. If it does not, you have a legal right to get a refund or replacement.

For example, after having driven 7/10's of a mile from the dealer's showroom, Mrs. A.J. Smith's new Chevrolet stalled at a traffic light. It stalled again within another 15 feet and again thereafter each time the vehicle was required to stop. When halfway home, about 2-1/2 miles from the showroom, the car could not be driven in "drive" gear at all. Mrs. Smith had to drive in "low" gear at a rate of about 5 to 10 miles per hour. After Mrs. Smith finally arrived home, her husband immediately called the bank to stop payment on his check, and telephoned the dealer to inform him that the sale was canceled. The dealer sent a wrecker to the consumer's home, brought the vehicle in and replaced the transmission. But Mr. Smith refused acceptance of the new car. Then the dealer sued Mr. Smith for the purchase price. The court in *Zabriskie Chevrolet v. Smith*, 240 A.2d 195, 99 N.J. Super. Ct. 441 (1968) agreed with the consumer that the vehicle was substantially defective, that there was a breach of the implied warranty of merchantability, and upheld the Smiths' refusal to take and pay for the car. Despite this victory, an attorney should always be consulted before stopping a check. As happened in this case, the dealer may sue for payment on the check.

Implied warranties are not just applicable to the car as a whole, but to individual components; for example, even though your car may have 80,000 miles on it, if the transmission fails, you should be covered by the implied warranty if the system was built to last up to 100,000 miles. Your owner's manual should indicate how long certain parts should last, even if they are not explicitly warranted to do so. This creates grounds for claim of an implied warranty.

One situation where implied warranties are especially valuable is if you buy a used car, as the manufacturer's warranty will likely be no longer valid. While Lisa Norred was on a test drive of a 1984 Datsun from Auburn Ford in Alabama, she noticed the car was "idling high" and missing. The dealer told her not to worry about it, as the motor had just been washed and he could perform any repairs, if needed. She bought an extended warranty on the car, however, to protect herself from future problems. After she took the car home, it continued to act up, even after eight repair attempts. She was not charged for these repairs, and was given a loaner car on three occasions, but when the car finally stopped running altogether, the dealer refused to work on it unless she paid him for it. She took the car over to a neighboring dealership, where the repairs came to $600.

Not willing to be saddled with this used lemon, she sued Auburn Ford for fraud, breach of contract, and breach of implied warranty. The jury awarded her $7000 in compensatory damages and $40,000 in punitive damages, which the dealer appealed. The Supreme Court of Alabama found that the dealer had neglected to post a "Buyer's Guide" on the car window, a federal requirement under the Federal Trade Commission's "Used Car Rule" and an Alabama state law. This obligates dealers to place a window sticker on any used car offered for sale which fully explains known defects in the car. Under Alabama Code 1975, Section 6-5-102:

> Suppression of a material fact which the party is under an obligation to communicate constitutes fraud.

The dealer then tried to argue Ms. Norred's claim for breach of implied warranty was invalid, as the car was sold "as is," meaning this warranty was waived. The court found that because she bought a service contract, however, the dealer was forbidden to disclaim or modify the implied warranty. Her award was upheld in its entirety. [See *Auburn Ford-Lincoln Mercury v. Norred*, 541 So.2d 1077 (Ala. 1989)]

The other implied warranty, which is less common, is the warranty of fitness for a particular purpose. This occurs when a consumer buys a vehicle for a particular purpose such as hauling a large trailer. This warranty requires the consumer to inform the sales-person of the special use and the salesperson to state that the particular model car will be good for that kind of use. When the consumer buys that model in reliance on the salesperson's advice, an implied warranty of fitness for a particular purpose is created. If the vehicle cannot then perform the job for which it was bought, the consumer is entitled to a refund or replacement.

Implied warranties come automatically with every sale even though they are not in writing or the dealer says nothing about them.

EXPRESS WARRANTIES

The manufacturer's written warranty that comes with a new vehicle is one form of an "express" warranty. However, there may be other express warranties which are not in writing that can apply to the sale of both a new or used car by a dealer. Like "implied" warranties, "express" warranties are also created by state law and the representations of the manufacturer or dealer about the car.

Under state law, express warranties may be created by the seller (manufacturer or dealer) through oral promises, advertisements, brochures, or other media. Any (1) **affirmation** of fact of (2) **promise** made by the seller, (3) **description**, (4) **sample** or (5) **model**, which becomes part of the "basis of the bargain" creates an **express** warranty that the vehicle will conform to the affirmation, promise, description, sample or model. No specific intention to make a warranty is necessary if **any** of these factors is made part of the basis of the bargain. Thus, even where the seller does not use formal words such as "warrant" or "guarantee," an express warranty may still be given. But the seller's statements in which he is "puffing his wares" is not sufficient, i.e., an affirmation merely of the **value** of the vehicle (and not of **fact**) or a statement purporting to be merely the seller's opinion or commendation of the vehicle does not create a warranty. For example, the dealer who states that you are getting "a great little car" has not created an express warranty as to the condition of the car. But the dealer who tells you "this car should run without any problems for at least 20,000 miles" has created an express warranty. To best preserve your ability to enforce such an express oral warranty, always ask the dealer to put the warranty in writing.

When Jumel Allen went to buy a truck from National Truck from Superior Trucks in Houston, Texas, he told the salesperson he needed it to start a hauling business. The salesperson told him he was very familiar with that kind of work, and knew just what he needed. Finding a truck that was suitable for hauling was crucial to Mr. Allen's buying decision, so he relied upon the salesperson's word.

His business was going well, but after seven weeks of using the truck, it collapsed while Mr. Allen was hauling a load, hitting his head and breaking a plate in his mouth. He was lucky to escape without more critical injuries, as he was barely able to steer off the road to safety; the brakes were crushed and the fuel tank was ruptured because of the collapse. Contrary to the salesperson's representation, the truck was not suited for hauling because the frame had been welded instead of bolted. In addition, the truck was not a 1973 model as the dealer advertised but was a 1969 model.

Mr. Allen sued Superior Trucks for breach of express warranties, misrepresentation, personal injury claims, and lost profits. He won at trial, but the dealer appealed. In *Superior Trucks v. Allen,* 644 SW2d 136 (Texas App. 1983), the court upheld the trial court's finding of $22,068 in compensatory damages, which included $8,568 for lost profits, $5,000 in personal injury claims, and $8,500 based on breach of express warranties. However, the appellate court **tripled** this amount under Texas's Deceptive Trade Practices Act, bringing the total recovery to $66,206.

LIMITATIONS AND DISCLAIMERS OF WARRANTIES

Manufacturers and dealers have always tried to limit their warranty liabilities as much as possible. In the past, manufacturers commonly attempted to disclaim both implied and express warranties. With a disclaimer, the manufacturer would assert that although the law may recognize an implied or an express warranty, the manufacturer would not. Today, the manufacturers can validly limit their warranty obligations, but only if certain requirements are met.

DISCLAIMER OF EXPRESS WARRANTIES

Despite what the manufacturer's written warranty may say about "other" warranties, state law gives you "express" warranty rights under certain circumstances, as discussed above. If the car does not live up to the claims made by the manufacturer, the consumer can sue for breach of warranty. For example, S. Lastovich of Hibbing, Minnesota saw a Ford Motor Company television commercial showing pickup trucks dashing over rough terrain and sailing through the air. He based his purchase of a Ford four-wheel-drive truck on claims made in that commercial. After his truck was badly dented during a rough trip through mud and sand, he sued Ford for the $500 cost of repairs. Lastovich argued that Ford's ads constituted an express warranty on his pickup. Even though Ford stated in its written warranty that "there is no other express warranty on this vehicle," a jury agreed with Lastovich and ordered Ford to pay the $500 in actual damages plus $175 in costs.

S. Lastovich described the trial in a letter to the Center for Auto Safety:

> Mr. [Ken] Peterson [his attorney] gave a very brilliant summation and the judge instructed the jury. The point of law on which their discussion rested was one of "express warranties" as outlined in your first "Lemon Book." Indeed, the jury ruled in effect that brochures I had read, TV ads I had seen, promises made to me by the salesperson and impressions I received from demonstrations of similar trucks as mine (on TV) influenced me to purchase the vehicle. By allowing such an excessive amount of flex in their 4-wheel drive truck frames so as to cause damage from box/cab contact Ford was held liable to make repairs for this damage.

Some cases have held that advertisements may create express warranties even where there was no reliance by the buyer; i.e., the consumer did not have to prove he or she actually saw the ad in question, just that it was used in an effort to induce purchases of the car.

LIMITATIONS ON IMPLIED WARRANTIES

Under the Magnuson-Moss Act, if a written warranty is given, then the implied warranties may not be disclaimed. The only limitation of an implied warranty allowed (only in "limited" but not "full" warranties) is a limit on its duration (how long it lasts). The **implied** warranty can be limited in duration only to the **duration** of the **written** warranty; e.g., if you have a one-year **written** warranty, the **implied** warranties cannot be limited in duration to less than one year. Such limitation must be "conscionable," which means that it cannot be extremely unfair or harsh. Federal law also requires such limitation to be "set forth in clear and unmistakable language and prominently displayed on the face of the warranty."

Most manufacturers do limit the duration of the **implied** warranties to the duration of the **written** warranty. That means that when the **written** warranty expires after, say, 12,000 miles or 12 months, the **implied** warranties expire along with it. Since most auto warranties are, in fact, "limited," most consumers will find themselves in this situation.

There is one important requirement on limitations of implied warranties under the Magnuson-Moss Act that may help a consumer who takes his or her lemon case to court: the "conscionability" argument. Usually an "unconscionable" act is one that is totally unfair or harsh to one party or is done in bad faith. If the court agrees that the consumer, as a new car buyer, has been "unconscionably" treated by the manufacturer's warranty provisions, it may declare the warranty limitations "unconscionable" and therefore of no validity. Thus, if the dealer refuses to repair a substantial defect that exists after the written warranty has expired, the consumer should claim in court that the manufacturer has breached the implied warranty and any limitation of the implied warranty was "unconscionable."

When Barry Thomas bought a used 1976 Corvette, he asked whether a wavy patch of paint meant the car had been in a wreck. The salesperson told him he did not know, but he did not think so. In fact, it had been in a collision. When Mr. Thomas questioned why the price was so far above the Kelley Blue Book value of the car, the dealer told him it was because the car was in "top condition." On the purchase order, Thomas signed a blanket disclaimer of all warranties, but was told by the salesperson that this was to protect the dealer from complaints of engine problems from the punishing kind of driving expected from buyers of high performance cars like the Corvette.

After taking the car home, the consumer noticed a severe vibration and drift in its performance, as well as excessive tire wear that impaired its safety. He garaged the car for six months, and then decided to try it out again. It immediately broke down. The mechanic who serviced it noticed suspicious welding in the frame and severe misalignments which indicated the car had been in a collision. Thomas confronted the dealer, who claimed that GM cars were susceptible to excessive tire wear, and offered to have the frame examined but did not offer to repair it. Thomas rejected this offer and sued for rescission and a refund of his purchase price.

First, the court held that Thomas was fully entitled to revoke acceptance of the car and cancel his contract with the dealer, as the value of the Corvette was substantially impaired and he accepted it without knowledge of its nonconformity. But then the court had to decide whether the waiver he signed would prevent him from rescinding the contract under the implied warranty of merchantability. They found that the waiver of his warranty rights was ineffective, since the dealer:

> . . . neither negotiated the warranty nor informed Thomas correctly as to the qualities and characteristics intended to be excluded by the disclaimer. On the contrary, he was told that the disclaimer referred only to engine wear that might occur through his misuse of the vehicle.

The court went on to conclude the Corvette was not merchantable since the goods must at least pass without objection in the trade—a wrecked and repaired car does not pass this test, nor does it provide safe and reasonably reliable transportation as required by the implied warranty. The consumer was awarded return of his purchase price, reimbursement for repair expenses, and compensation for tire replacements. [*Thomas v. Ruddell Lease-Sales*, 716 P.2d. 911 (Wash. App. 1986)]

State law under the Uniform Commercial Code (UCC) which has been adopted by all states except Louisiana requires that a valid disclaimer of an implied warranty of **merchantability** must actually mention the word "merchantability." If the merchantability disclaimer is in writing, which it usually is in the case of auto warranties, it must be conspicuous or visible to the average reader. A valid disclaimer of an implied warranty of **fitness** must be in writing and must be conspicuous. A disclaimer of all implied warranties of **fitness** is valid if it states, for example, that "there are no warranties which extend beyond the description on the face hereof." But this alone could not validly disclaim the implied warranty of **merchantability** because it does not mention the word "merchantability."

A seller can also disclaim the implied warranty of **merchantability** by simply adding the words "as is" or "with all faults" to the sales contract. Watch out for this tactic when buying a used car. Some jurisdictions, such as the District of Columbia and Maryland, forbid a car to be sold "as is" until it is six years old or has 60,000 miles on it.

Even where a manufacturer has attempted to limit the duration of an implied warranty, implied warranty rights are still good if you bought the car in a state which does not allow **any** limitations on the duration of implied warranties. These states include Connecticut, District of Columbia, Kansas, Maine, Maryland, Massachusetts, Mississippi, Vermont and West Virginia, which have specifically modified their state statute or laws so that implied warranties cannot be limited to a specific time period. More states are modifying their laws in this manner, so check with your State Attorney General and local consumer group or agency to see whether your state has joined the above list.

LIMITATIONS ON REMEDIES

The manufacturers and dealers try to limit not only their warranty liabilities and obligations, but the consumer's rights to a remedy, as well. A remedy is a legal tool a consumer can use for the redress of a complaint. One remedy usually limited by auto manufacturers is the right to incidental or consequential damages such as hotel bills when your car breaks down.

State law (the Uniform Commercial Code or UCC) protects the consumer from "unconscionable" limitations or exclusions on consequential damages. The UCC Section 2–719 provides that a "limitation of consequential damages for injury to the person in the case of consumer goods is prima facie unconscionable, but limitation of damages where the loss is commercial is not." Thus, if a consumer loses a week's pay because the defective car is being repaired, the manufacturer may be able to avoid liability if consequential damages had been excluded.

Where the manufacturer has attempted to unreasonably limit a consumer's legal remedies, the Uniform Commercial Code again comes in to aid the consumer in stating:

> Where circumstances cause an exclusive or limited remedy to fail of its essential purpose, remedy may be had as provided in this Act. [Sec. 2–719]

For example, one consumer revoked acceptance of his new Saab after the car kept stalling and was plagued by a series of annoying minor defects. He had been properly following the manufacturer's remedy, which provided that the dealer would repair the car under warranty for such defects. But the repeated stalling which began five months after purchase was never remedied, despite several attempted repairs by the dealer. Also, a defective muffler, a recurrent rattle under the dashboard and the repeated malfunctioning of the seat belt warning buzzer were never repaired properly. When the consumer revoked acceptance, the manufacturer argued in part that the warranty limits a purchaser's remedies to repair or replacement of defective parts, and nothing more.

When the consumer sued in this case, the Supreme Court of Minnesota in *Durfee v. Rod Baxter Imports*, 262 N.W.2d 349 (1977), held that revocation of acceptance and cancellation of the contract was a remedy available to the purchaser. The lower court had found that the Saab "apparently could not, or would not, be placed in reasonably good operating condition" by the distributor or its agents or dealers. The Minnesota Supreme Court stated:

> An exclusive remedy fails of its essential purpose if circumstances arise to deprive the limiting clause of its meaning or one party of the substantial value of its bargain. So long as the seller repairs the goods each time a defect arises, a repair-and-replacement clause does not fail of its essential purpose. If repairs are not successfully undertaken within a reasonable time, the buyer may be deprived of the benefits of the exclusive remedy. Commendable effort and considerable expense alone do not relieve a seller of his obligation to repair.

FEDERAL OR STATE MANDATED WARRANTIES

Certain components of the car such as parts of the emission control system may have federal or state mandated warranties. For example, Section 207(a) of the Clean Air Act requires the auto manufacturers to warrant for the first 5 years or 50,000 miles that vehicle emission control systems be free from defects in materials and workmanship which cause the vehicle to exceed the emission standards. Section 207(b) requires the manufacturer to warrant any component that causes the vehicle to fail an emission test during the first 24,000 miles and any major component such as the catalyst for 50,000 miles. This warranty helps attain clean air while it protects the consumer's pocketbook. This emissions warranty appears on the manufacturer's written warranty because of Clean Air Act requirements. For example, General Motors's 1990 "Limited" warranty gives the Chevrolet car owner the following rights: the Chevrolet Division warrants that the vehicle (1) was designed, built, and equipped so as to conform at the time of sale with applicable regulations of the U.S. Environmental Protection Agency and the California Air Resources Board, and (2) is free from defects in materials and workmanship which cause the car to fail to conform with those regulations for a period of use of 50,000 miles or 5 years, whichever occurs first.

A recent case illustrates how the emissions recall and warranty provisions can work to clean the air and protect the consumer's pocketbook. In July, 1989 Ford had to recall 1.3 million 1985–87 cars with 4-cylinder engines with faulty throttle-body fuel injectors that violated the carbon monoxide and hydrocarbon emission standards. In addition to replacing the fuel injector, Ford had to inspect and replace any catalyst and electronic engine control processor found faulty for free. The recall repairs saved each owner hundreds of dollars. Consumers who already paid to do an emission recall repair can obtain reimbursement after getting the recall notice.

The Clean Air Act makes it a crime for any manufacturer or dealer to refuse to honor a valid emission control warranty claim. If either the dealer or manufacturer refuses to make a warranty repair on the emission control system, remind them that there is a potential fine of $10,000 and then inform the Environmental Protection Agency, Office of Mobile Sources, Washington, D.C. 20460, of the violation. EPA often contacts the manufacturer on behalf of the consumer to have the warranty honored.

HOW TO ENFORCE YOUR WARRANTY RIGHTS

When a car is defective and needs repair, begin with the manufacturer's complaint-handling procedures, described in Chapter 3. If something goes wrong with the car, you usually must give the dealer a "reasonable" number of chances to repair it, whether or not you will eventually invoke the lemon law.

In most cases, where the defect has not caused major damage, the dealer will be allowed to repair or replace the defective part. This is where the written service records discussed in Chapter 3 prove invaluable. They will show the dealer had many opportunities to "cure" (repair) the defect. After the dealer does not or cannot repair the car and the manufacturer refuses to make good on the warranty, you have a right to demand a replacement or your money back if the defect is one that "substantially impairs" the value of the car. In some cases, especially where the defect has damaged the car, or where the car is nearly new, the buyer may be able to return the car without giving the dealer a chance to fix the defect.

For example, in *Zabriskie Chevrolet v. Smith,* discussed above, the court permitted return of the car and refund of the purchaser's payment without allowing the dealer and manufacturer an opportunity to repair the defects. The court rejected offers made by the dealer to cure the defect under the manufacturer's warranty. The court stated that the attempted cure, a substituted transmission, was "ineffective," because it would not conform to what Mr. Smith had ordered. The court said:

> For a majority of people, the purchase of a new car is a major investment, rationalized by the peace of mind that flows from its dependability and safety. **Once their faith is shaken,** the vehicle loses not only real value in their eyes, but becomes an instrument whose integrity is substantially impaired and whose operation is fraught with apprehension. The attempted cure in the present case was ineffective. [Emphasis added]

"TOTAL LEMON" STRATEGIES

If you are stuck with a lemon, a lawyer may help. Legal action is almost always necessary to obtain a refund of the purchase price or a replacement car, since the dealer and manufacturer will almost invariably refuse to take back the car.

Lemon owners who want to get rid of their lemons can follow three general routes. One is to invoke the lemon law, a strategy which is discussed in detail in Chapter 7. Another is to trade the car in and then sue the dealer and manufacturer for damages out of resale of the lemon. Yet another strategy is to revoke acceptance of the car, return it to the dealer or manufacturer and sue for a refund or replacement. A related strategy, "rejection," applies to cases where something major goes wrong during the first few miles, and is sometimes called the "shaken faith" doctrine. As in *Zabriskie* where the car broke down only a few minutes after leaving the dealership, the consumer should "reject" the car immediately.

REVOCATION OF ACCEPTANCE

Revocation of acceptance is usually the key to getting a refund or replacement of a lemon, apart from using the lemon law, which encompasses this strategy. The legal procedures for revocation of acceptance must be followed carefully. Acceptance must be revoked within a reasonable time after the defect is discovered and usually after the dealer has had reasonable opportunity to fix the car. Of course, there are exceptions; see *Tiger Motor* below, where the consumer revoked acceptance on a one-year-old lemon. A "reasonable time" is usually within 90 days after delivery. After returning the car, confirm with the dealer **in writing** that you are revoking acceptance of the car. Certified mail with return receipt requested helps prove that you gave such notice.

To revoke acceptance, deliver the car and the keys to the dealer. Take off the license plates. Do not remove original equipment (factory or dealer-installed) from the car, like the radio. The car must be returned without "substantial change." Normal wear and tear is no problem. Give the dealer something in **writing** at that time notifying him of your intention to revoke acceptance, listing the specific reasons you are returning the car and stating that you are also canceling your insurance and registration. Note the odometer reading at this time. A substantial increase in mileage on the odometer is evidence that the dealer accepted your revocation of acceptance—that he no longer considered you the owner of the car.

Some consumers have used revocation of acceptance successfully, without hiring an attorney. If the dealer or manufacturer is close to taking the lemon back, this device may help. However, if the dealer does not respond favorably, tell him that you will be retaining a lawyer to pursue your complaint. Often hiring an attorney and filing a lawsuit are necessary in order to revoke acceptance successfully; i.e., receiving the return of the purchase price or a new car.

In *Tiger Motor Co. v. McMurtry*, 224 So.2d. 638 (Ala. 1969), Thomas McMurtry had returned his new Ford station wagon to the dealer for repairs on at least 30 occasions. The Ford remained in the custody of

Tiger for repair during one period for a total of about 50 days. Yet Tiger failed to remedy all the defects. The new car was using so much oil that McMurtry was forced to purchase it by the case. The car got approximately 8 miles per gallon, and required a new fuel pump, new carburetor, new piston rings, and a new engine block. Thereafter, the auto continued to skip or misfire and to use oil by the case.

After McMurtry had enough of this lemon, he decided to revoke acceptance. He returned the one-year-old station wagon to the dealer, removed the license plates and canceled his insurance. Then he sued the dealer for a refund of the down payment, the value of his trade-in and all of his monthly payments. He won. The Alabama Court ruled in the consumer's favor, finding a "substantial impairment of value" to McMurtry of the lemon car. Even though McMurtry waited a year before revoking acceptance, the court held that revocation was made within a "reasonable time."

> The evidence supports the conclusion that Tiger Motor Company warranted that it would remedy all defects for the first 24,000 miles, or 24 months after purchase, whichever comes first. In the instant case, the buyer was in almost constant touch with the seller concerning the condition of the vehicle. Repeated attempts at adjustment having failed, we hold the buyer revoked his acceptance of the auto within a reasonable time.

Consult a lawyer if you have decided to return the car to the dealer. Revocation of acceptance is to be used as a last resort, only when you do not want ever to see your car again. This procedure is often the first step in a lawsuit since you may have to sue to get your money back, as in *Tiger v. McMurty*, discussed above. Many consumers have been successful in using this strategy.

Another consumer who revoked acceptance was Angelo Asciolla of Tilton, New Hampshire, whose new Oldsmobile Delta 88 was a lemon. The day after he picked up his car, Asciolla and his wife drove to Wisconsin to visit their daughter. With only 1,390 miles on the odometer, the car broke down. The car had rust in the brakes, drive shaft, exhaust pipe and underbody, ice in the transmission and water in the trunk within one month of purchase. Asciolla was told that the car appeared to have been flooded or submerged. Upon finding this out, the lemon owner immediately informed the dealer that he was not satisfied with the car and wanted it exchanged for a new one. The dealer refused to supply a new vehicle, but offered either to install a new transmission with a 12-month warranty or to extend the present warranties 12 months from the date of repairs. The dealer maintained that the car had never been flooded.

Asciolla's attorney, Willard G. Martin, Jr., filed suit against the dealer and General Motors Corporation. Martin contended that Asciolla's immediate notification of his dissatisfaction to the dealer upon discovery of defects constituted a "revocation of his acceptance" of the automobile under applicable state law. The New Hampshire Supreme Court, in a unanimous decision, found that the buyer was entitled to revoke his acceptance and receive a new car. The Court ordered GM to pay Asciolla $6,148 in legal and storage costs and $100 for every day's delay in delivering a new Oldsmobile Delta 88.

In *Asciolla v. Manter Oldsmobile-Pontiac*, 370 A.2d 270 (New Hampshire 1977), Justice Charles Douglas cited the *Zabriskie Chevrolet* case, holding that:

> The purchaser of a major consumer item such as an automobile may revoke his acceptance of a product when it possesses a defect which, in view of the particular needs and circumstances of the buyer, substantially impairs the value of the item to him. . . . The buyer assumed what every new car buyer has a right to assume and, indeed, had been led to assume by the high powered advertising techniques of the auto industry—that his new car would be mechanically new and factory-furnished, operate perfectly, and be free of substantial defects.

This case also illustrates an exception adopted by a growing number of jurisdictions to the general rule that a car buyer must return the car to the dealership in order to revoke acceptance. Here, Asciolla kept the car in his garage after informing the dealer that he was not satisfied with the car and wanted it exchanged for a new one. The consumer's notification of his dissatisfaction to the dealer immediately upon discovery of the defects coupled with placing the car in the garage (i.e., not driving the car) was enough.

Some courts have held that you can revoke acceptance even after you have had substantial use of the car, if the dealer's assurances that he would be able to fix it delayed the time of revocation. In *Vista Chevrolet v. Lewis*, 704 S.W.2d 363 (Tex. App. 1985), the Lewis's revoked acceptance of their 1981 Chevrolet Monte Carlo almost two years after they took delivery. Ten weeks after they bought the car it would not start if it sat idle over the weekend. Over the next 16 months, the car continued to refuse to start. The dealer made ten futile repair attempts to fix the car. The Lewis's attorney sent a demand letter to Vista Chevrolet and GM threatening revocation, but the dealer just asked for one more chance to fix it. They took the car in, but the problem resurfaced immediately. Finally, when the car had 22,200 miles on it, the Lewis's revoked acceptance, but would not return the car and continued to use it up to the time of the trial, when it had 40,000 miles on it. The court awarded a refund of their purchase price, less an allowance for the Lewis's use and benefit of the car. The court stated that:

> The mere fact that the continued use of a motor vehicle increases the mileage placed on the vehicle does not bar the buyer from revoking acceptance of the vehicle for substantial impairment of the value of the vehicle to the buyer . . .
>
> Also, the mere fact that the motor vehicle was used extensively does not prevent the jury from concluding that there was a breach of implied warranty of merchantability which substantially impaired the value of goods to the buyer.

In signing the final release or settlement in any litigation make sure all items for which you are seeking reimbursement are included in the agreement. Any omissions are likely to be unfavorable to you, though there are isolated cases when the manufacturer loses out. In *BMW of North America v. Krathen*, 471 So.2d 585 (Fl. App. 1985) the Krathens sued for breach of express and implied warranties on their $26,500 automobile which had a front end shimmy that could not be corrected. BMW mailed them an offer to settle the case, which stated that the Krathens could "take judgment against them in the amount of Twenty Thousand Five Hundred ($20,500), plus reasonable attorneys fees and costs heretofore accrued." The Krathens quickly mailed in their acceptance of the offer "as written." BMW filed it with the court, which entered judgment against them pursuant to the settlement. BMW later filed a motion to vacate the judgment, however, when it realized return of the car was not a condition of the agreement. The court ruled that BMW's failure to include this condition was due to its own inexcusable lack of care in drafting the settlement. BMW's motion was denied, and the Krathen's have both the car and a check for over $20,000.

WITHHOLDING PAYMENTS

In some cases, it may be easier to withhold payments on the car rather than revoking acceptance. For example, if the car is not a total lemon and probably can be fixed, but the dealer has been giving you the runaround, stopping payments may be a good incentive to get the dealer to finally repair the defects. It may help to take the car to an independent mechanic to verify that the defects can indeed be fixed and that the car is worth keeping. Show the dealer the independent mechanic's diagnosis before stopping payments to bolster your case. Consult a lawyer before withholding payments. If you do stop paying, the bank will probably **sue you** for the balance on the loan. Thus, the decision to stop paying should be made with a lawyer's advice. Stopping payments is a last resort; it is not something you do every time a small problem occurs.

Where acceptance is revoked, payments may be able to be withheld. If you financed the car through the dealer, contact the bank or finance company where you are making payments. Inform them that you have revoked ownership of the car and that you will not be making further payments. Tell them the dealer is responsible for the note since the car is back at the dealership. In some instances, the dealer will then take the loan back from the bank, leaving the dispute between you and the dealer.

You cannot withhold payments if you obtained the loan **directly** at a lending institution without the dealer's assistance. If acceptance is revoked, tell them what has happened, but continue to make payments on the car. In the first instance, where you financed the car through the dealer, you are legally protected if the dealer or bank sues you for the balance. In the second case, where you got your loan **directly** at a bank or credit union, you are not legally protected if the bank or credit union sues for the balance.

HOLDER-IN-DUE-COURSE RULE

Car loans have traditionally been governed by the "Holder-in-Due-Course" legal doctrine which effectively required consumers to continue car payments on even the world's worst lemon. A rule issued by the Federal Trade Commission (FTC) substantially improves the consumer's position by permitting the consumer who stops making payments to prove that the car is a lemon. You can preserve your credit rating by filing an explanation with the Credit Bureau of why you are withholding payments on your loan. Since you are invoking a form of protection given to you by federal law, you should not be denied credit in any way by exerting this right; otherwise, the law would be effective in theory but not in practice.

The FTC rule is commonly called the "Holder-in-Due-Course Rule." Where the dealer arranges the loan for the consumer on a car that is a lemon, the FTC rule protects the consumer who stops making payments.

The FTC rule protecting the withholding of payments does not protect the consumer who got a loan **directly** from a bank or credit union. It applies only to loans that fall into certain categories. These include where the dealer "refers" buyers to a lender **or** the dealer is "affiliated" with the lender or creditor. "Affiliation" may be created by "contract" or "business arrangement." The arrangement need not be formal in any legal sense, but it must be ongoing and clearly related to the dealer's sales and sales financing. "Referral" means that the dealer cooperates with a lender to channel consumers to that credit source on a continuing basis. Unlike an "affiliation," a referral relationship arises from a pattern of cooperative activity between the dealer and lender, directly relating to the arranging of credit. The fact that a dealer suggests credit sources or provides information to his customers does not alone invoke the FTC rule.

The FTC rule requires dealers, among other sellers, to include this notice in all installment-sales contracts and loans they handle for consumers:

NOTICE
ANY HOLDER OF THIS CONSUMER CREDIT CONTRACT IS SUBJECT TO ALL CLAIMS AND DEFENSES WHICH THE DEBTOR COULD ASSERT AGAINST THE SELLER OF GOODS OR SERVICES OBTAINED PURSUANT HEREOF. RECOVERY HEREUNDER BY THE DEBTOR SHALL BE LIMITED TO AMOUNTS PAID BY THE DEBTOR HEREUNDER.

This mean that consumers can legally invoke the lemon defense against the bank as if the bank had been the seller/dealer. Where the rule applies, the buyer's right to stop making payments on defective goods is protected.

Withholding payments can lead to enforcement of several rights concerning revocation of a lemon. One week after Stanley Jankowitz bought a new 1981 Cadillac from Potamkin Cadillac in New York, the cruise control failed to operate, and the engine and transmission warning lights on his dashboard flashed on intermittently. He took the car in for repair of the electronic control module, but after 9 attempts to correct the problem, he had had enough. With 2,700 miles on it, he told Potamkin to take the car back, and left it in front of his house, never to use it again. He stopped making payments on his GMAC loan after revoking acceptance. When GMAC sued him for failure to make payments, he countersued them, and filed a complaint against Potamkin and GM for breach of warranty, fraud, misrepresentation, negligence, breach of contract, and compensatory and punitive damages. [*General Motors Acceptance Corp. v. Jankowitz*, 523 A.2d 695 (N.J. 1987)]

Potamkin tried to disclaim its responsibility under the warranty, as the back of the retail installment contract disclaimed both the implied and written warranties on the car, even though all of the warranty provisions were contained in the new car warranty offered by GM. The court called the installment sales contract a "masterpiece of ambiguity, inconsistency, and contradiction." It held that under the Magnuson-Moss Act, because Potamkin, as a dealer, is an **agent of the manufacturer**, and the manufacturer gave a new car warranty, Potamkin too "gave" a written warranty, which is inconsistent with its disclaimer of all warranties. Congress invalidated such disclaimers under the Magnuson-Moss Act to prevent suppliers of goods from giving an express warranty while taking away an implied warranty.

The court also stated that to revoke acceptance of goods for nonconformity to the warranty, the buyer must show that: 1) the goods do not conform; 2) the nonconformity substantially impairs the value of the goods to **the buyer**; and 3) the nonconformity was discovered at the time of acceptance of the goods, with the good faith belief that it would be cured, or was realized later only because it was difficult to discover upon acceptance; and 4) the buyer revoked acceptance within a reasonable time.

They also held that because Potamkin, the dealer, was the expert on what was wrong with the car, the work orders showed there was a defect, the defect was not cured at the time of trial, and the consumer allowed the dealer several repair attempts, it was up to Potamkin to prove the defect was in fact corrected. Jankowitz was therefore entitled to return of his purchase price and payments, plus incidental expenses, and damages from breach of warranty, if he could prove the nonconformity existed. It took **six years** from the time Mr. Jankowitz revoked acceptance until the date of his court appeal, which saved him 48 monthly payments on his lemon by use of the Holder-in-Due-Course Rule.

PURSUING A STATE BOND

Some states require automobile dealers to post bonds to make sure they keep the promises made to new car buyers in guarantees and warranties. Check with your state Attorney General's office to determine whether your state does this. A lawyer can assist in securing your rights under the bonding arrangement. Maryland, for instance, requires that manufacturers post a $100,000–300,000 bond to assure they will hold to promises made by sales people and in warranties to new car buyers. The law in Maryland also requires a $15,000 bond for the dealership itself and a $1000 bond for sales people in hopes of giving motorists greater protection.

Because of the bonding requirement in Maryland, many consumers in that state have successfully collected money from dealer's bonding companies. These claims have involved situations where consumers had unknowingly purchased stolen vehicles from dealers, or where consumers purchased vehicles from dealers but could not obtain a good title from the dealer. Lemon owners in states with bonding laws should try to collect money from the dealer's bonding company or the manufacturer's bonding company, if one exits.

CLASS ACTIONS

In some situations a class action suit may be the best approach to solving a consumer complaint. In essence, a class action is nothing more than a group of individuals sharing a common injury from a product or practice who bring a lawsuit against a manufacturer, thus reducing each individual's fee by sharing the costs of hiring an attorney. For instance, a class action may be filed on behalf of all purchasers of the manufacturer's product who suffered in the same way because of a defect in the product.

Thus, the manufacturer is faced not with a couple of individual claims, in small amounts, from the few persons concerned enough to see a lawyer and bring an action, but is faced instead with one gigantic claim representing the total amount lost by each and every victim. The class suit or class action is potentially one of the most far-reaching devices, legal or nonlegal, available to consumers.

The advantages of the suit are:

a. Lawyers in class suits receive a percentage of the total recovery, and with the stakes so high, the most able and aggressive attorneys will be attracted to the consumer side.

b. Public notice accorded the suit will very likely bring to light injured parties who might not otherwise have ever known of the opportunity for recovery.

c. Manufacturers will be made to assume full financial responsibility for their mistakes, rather than meeting the demands of occasional single consumers pressing only their individual claims.

d. Increased manufacturer responsibility will place them under much needed pressure to build more safety and reliability into their products before marketing them.

When consumers win a class suit, the defendant may pay the total verdict (often a large amount) into court; individual members of the class then file claims for their share of the recovery. Class suits are becoming a rallying point of the consumer movement. New York City, for instance, passed a law enabling the city to file class suits for defrauded groups of consumers. Its potential is indicated by the ferocity with which it is opposed by business interests.

The Magnuson-Moss Warranty Act provides for a class action where 100 or more named plaintiffs have claims totaling at least $50,000 (exclusive of interests and costs). The Act also provides for awards of attorneys' fees from the losing manufacturer.

The class action provision makes it paramount for consumers with similar defects to band together in order to get the 100 named plaintiffs. Consumers can report their cars' defects to the Department of Transportation and the Center for Auto Safety so that common defects can be found. Consumers can ask the Department to search its computerized file of defects to find potential plaintiffs.

SECRET WARRANTIES AND CLASS ACTIONS

Discovery of a secret warranty can lead to a class action suit. When the Center for Auto Safety discovered that Toyota was repairing the brake pulsating experienced in 1983–86 Camrys for only those consumers who complained persistently—1000 of whom had complained to CAS alone—they joined the Center for Law in the Public Interest in a suit against the manufacturer. A precedent-setting settlement resulted against Toyota that cost the company $100 million. Under the terms of the settlement, Toyota 1) notified all 400,000 past and present original owners and leasees covered by the suit; 2) reimbursed consumers who already fixed their Camrys for out-of-pocket repair and incidental expenses, such as towing and taxis; 3) repaired any cars in which the defect had not been corrected; 4) arbitrated any disputes through the American Automobile Association; 5) paid $850,000 into a Consumer Support and Education Fund; and 6) paid $250,000 in attorneys' fees.

The brake pulsation defect threatened drivers with a loss of control and caused excessive deterioration of the car's tires and lower control arms. A whistle-blower exposed Toyota's secret warranty that authorized free repairs without notifying owners of this defect, meaning that thousands of Camry owners were paying $790-$1,380 for brake pulsation repairs, excluding the cost of further damage this defect caused the vehicle. The suit charged Toyota with breach of express and implied warranties, false and misleading advertising, fraud, deceit, breach of obligation of good faith and fair dealing, and unlawful competition.

JOINT SUITS

Where there are not enough consumers for a class action, individuals with similarly defective cars can hire an attorney together. Where one or two people cannot afford a lawyer, four or more might be able to afford one. See Chapter 11 for examples of consumers placing ads in newspapers to find other unhappy owners of the same make and model lemon. Under the Magnuson-Moss Act, such groups of individuals may still get into federal court if the total damages incurred by the group due to a common injury is $50,000 or greater. This joint Magnuson-Moss action is more attractive to private attorneys because the Act specifically provides that attorney fees and court costs may be awarded to successful plaintiffs. Chapter 11 contains an example of a successful joinder suit.

ACTIONS INVOLVING FRAUD

Apart from suits against the dealer or manufacturer for violations of your warranty rights, you might be a victim of a fraudulent business practice that would entitle you to cancel your contract with the dealership. You should also watch out for advertising claims which falsely lead you to believe you got a great deal on a car such as buying at one dollar over dealer cost. In these instances, your state consumer affairs department or the Attorney General's office might intercede to file a complaint. See Chapter 4 for examples of state agencies interceding on behalf of consumers in such cases.

Consumer fraud can often be found in the financing agreement. When Roosevelt Davis of Mobile, Alabama entered into an agreement to buy a $30,000 1987 Dodge B-250 van from the dealer, it was on the condition that he could get a loan approved from the credit union. He had offered for trade-in a vehicle valued at $1,000. When the credit union refused his application, he went back to the dealership to cancel the sale, but they refused to tear up the retail contract. He sued the dealer for fraud and conversion of his trade-in, as the dealer still held him to the contract and so would not return his vehicle. A jury awarded Mr. Davis $224,000 in punitive damages against the dealer, a judgment 224 times the amount given in compensatory damages for the value of the trade-in, a record for Alabama. Actions for fraud are intended to punish—and hopefully deter—the dealer from shady operations.

LAWSUITS: WHOM TO SUE

Although new car purchasers come into contact with only the dealer, most lemon problems involve the manufacturers, and there is no reason not to sue them. In fact, there are strong reasons to make sure the manufacturer is included in any suit; in some cases, they will be the only proper defendant. In any case, the manufacturer, obviously, would be able to pay larger damage awards than most dealers could pay. Historically, manufacturers placed dealers between themselves and their retail customers to insulate themselves from liability. Now, statutes and court decisions in many states have destroyed the vestiges of this device, and manufacturers can and should shoulder their full liability.

Moreover, it is important that owners bringing lawsuits avoid being blinded by the smoke screen often thrown up by the manufacturers that the dealer is an independent business rather than an agent of the manufacturer. Despite the passage by Congress in 1956 of the Dealers Day in Court Act, which helped eliminate the most flagrant practices by which manufacturers maintained an iron grip on dealers, the manufacturers still manage to exert a subtle but pervasive control over most dealership policies. This control is achieved by means of requirements for detailed financial reporting, loans and subsidies to dealers in financial difficulties, rewards (for achieving sales goals and so forth), or by reductions in the dealer's quota of hot-selling car models, forcing him to achieve his agreed upon overall sales quota by pushing the slower moving models. If a dealer fails to meet his prescribed annual sales volume, he may face the ultimate form of control—a threatened or actual cancellation of his franchise.

In an ironic twist, two Connecticut dealerships were sued by the state Attorney General's office when it was discovered that they allegedly told Subaru of America they sold cars to Sidney Chatpuma and Maxwell Puma. Sidney and Maxwell are cats, and therefore not likely to be new car buyers. It seems the dealerships listed these felines as customers to falsely claim a high sales volume which allowed them to advertise themselves as a "number one" dealer of Subarus. Not only did this scheme defraud Subaru, it also cheated actual Subaru buyers out of warranty protection. Because the time period on warranties began with the fictitious sales, the vehicles bought later by actual people had their warranty periods shortened up to eight months, as their delivery records were altered to the time when the cats "bought" the cars. Though this seems to be a unique scheme, it's best to keep both eyes open when reviewing any sales documents to make sure your rights are being protected.

CHANGE THE LAW

Unfortunately, the Magnuson-Moss Act and state lemon laws or other warranty acts may not cover some of the problems you may have. Even though car problems are consistently the number one complaint for consumers across the country, the present laws do not thoroughly address this crisis. The Magnuson-Moss Act does not have any special provisions for automobile problems, and does not clearly ensure relief in certain situations, such as cars bought for business purposes, leased, or used. The provision for attorney's fees does not specifically state in what circumstances you may recover this expense; certain awards under the Act must be appealed to provide for full reimbursement.

Lemon laws offer their own set of imperfections. Even though most states now have these laws which cover vehicle owners exclusively, not all of these laws are written to provide you with effective relief. Some require you to submit to binding arbitration, which means you cannot go to court if you lose at this stage. Some arbitration programs offered as prerequisites to relief are run by the manufacturer and are biased. Some allow the manufacturer to appeal an arbitration award, and assess the costs of litigation against you if they succeed in reversing your recovery. Others have unfair offsets for use of lemons.

If you feel federal laws can do a better job of protecting your rights, you should write Congress with your concerns and your suggestions. The committees listed below are responsible for passing and improving consumer protection legislation. You can find out the name of the current chairperson (to whom the letter should be directed) by consulting a Congressional Directory. The committees are as follows:

Senate Committee on Commerce, Science,
    and Transportation
Consumer Subcommittee
U.S. Senate
Washington, DC 20510

House Energy and Commerce Committee
Subcommittee on Telecommunications and Finance

Your Legal Rights

U.S. House of Representatives
Washington, DC 20515

House Energy and Commerce Committee
Subcommittee on Commerce, Consumer
Protection and Competitiveness
U.S. House of Representatives
Washington, DC 20515

You should also write to the chairperson of the full committee as well, because he or she will have authority to propose or advance consumer protection legislation, even if the subcommittee is inactive. Send copies of your letters to your own representatives in both the Senate and the House of Representatives and to the Federal Trade Commission, Bureau of Consumer Protection, Washington, D.C., 20580. State level officials, particularly the Attorney General, could also be helpful in rallying support for new federal legislation. In fact, the National Association of Attorneys General is very active in fighting the FTC's proposal to mandate federal procedures that would limit the access of consumers to effective remedies under the law.

To affect state legislation, you should contact your state representatives and the state Attorney General's office, as well as local consumer protection agencies who could join you in supporting consumer legislation. Building a coalition of others who are concerned with the same issues will not only ease the tremendous amount of work involved with passing or amending legislation, but will accentuate the importance of your ideas.

CHAPTER 7

STATE LEMON LAWS

Frustrated by the countless unsuccessful repairs to his new car and ongoing debates about whether or not Connecticut should pass a lemon law, Thomas Ziemba decided drastic action was necessary. Letters to the editor may be fine for some people, but they do not grab the national attention he received by buzzing the state capitol building in Hartford for one hour, while flying a plane with a banner reading, "My 1982 Chevrolet is why we need the lemon law." After delivering this message to state legislators, he flew around the rest of the state to rally the support of other disgruntled consumers. Both the Associated Press and United Press International wire services covered the story, resulting in appearances in nearly every major newspaper across the country. NBC Nightly News hired a plane to follow him as he recreated the event to air on their evening broadcast. Connecticut shortly thereafter became the first state in the nation to pass a lemon law, perhaps the most significant consumer protection legislation for car owners since the federal Magnuson-Moss Act (see Chapter 6). Led by Connecticut's success in breaking the auto industry's strangle grip on state legislatures, California and many other states shortly thereafter passed lemon laws; today almost every state in the country has one.

What makes the lemon law a major tool for consumers is that it defines what a lemon is. Under the Uniform Commercial Code, a consumer is entitled to a refund or replacement of a lemon that a manufacturer cannot fix. But it is up to the courts to define what a lemon is, prompting the auto companies to say "sue us because we have never seen a lemon we couldn't fix given a reasonable number of attempts." Yet that was the rub; what was reasonable to the car companies was clearly unreasonable to consumers. During a hearing before the California Assembly on its proposed lemon law, **a Ford executive had the audacity to testify that sometimes 30 repair attempts were required to cure a lemon.**

The conceptual beauty of lemon laws is that they define a lemon in English so plain that even a car company can understand it—i.e., a car is a lemon if it cannot be fixed within a precise number of repair attempts or if it's out of service a set number of days within the warranty. Once the law is triggered, the manufacturer cannot require additional repairs before replacing the vehicle or refunding the consumer's money.

In practice, lemon laws vary from state to state, with some states having great lemon laws and others having lemon laws that are almost lemons themselves. This chapter will help explain lemon laws so you can maximize the benefits of your state's lemon law and avoid any pitfalls. Additional information on your state's law may be obtained from your state Attorney General. For general information about lemon laws, see the April, 1985 issue of *Consumer Reports*. Appendix F is a handy summary of each state's lemon law.

LEMON LAW PREREQUISITES

Most states define a lemon as a car that requires three or four repair attempts for the same problem, or that has been out of service for thirty days within the first year or 12,000 miles of the warranty period. The defect or condition must substantially impair the value, use, or safety of your car; e.g. repair of cigarette lighters would not qualify, but power windows could. In some states, if you have made *one* unsuccessful repair attempt for a safety-related problem, you qualify for relief under the lemon law.

To prove you have met the threshold requirements of the lemon law, keep close track of the number of repair attempts and the time the car is out of service. Submit a written, dated list of problems to the dealer each time the car is in for repairs, keeping a copy for yourself. List the symptoms the car has; for example, "stalling" instead of "check carburetor." This establishes a record of what problem was addressed, even though the dealer may work on different parts in attempting to fix the problem. The number of repair attempts applies to **problems** so that a stalling car qualifies even though the dealer makes four different repair attempts to the fuel injectors, fuel pump, ignition, and electronic control module. The days out of service can apply to different problems and repairs. To show you have met these requirements, get a copy of the repair order that lists the symptoms described, repairs done, any parts replaced, and the days the car was in the shop.

LEASED CARS AND LEMON LAWS

Some states have not caught up with modern car marketing techniques and do not apply their lemon laws to leased cars. Leading states such as California and Connecticut recognize that a lemon is a lemon, whether you buy it or lease it. If your state's lemon law does not apply to leased cars, work to get it applied. Meanwhile, check with a local lawyer about rights you have under laws other than the lemon law.

Mark Davis of Cambridge, Vermont successfully defended an appeal of his $6000 arbitration award for his leased lemon, a 1986 Pontiac Grand Am that stalled repeatedly. Vermont's Motor Vehicle Arbitration Board ordered GM to refund the bulk of the monthly leasing payments Mr. Davis had already made, in addition to the $500 down payment he made on the car. The Assistant Attorney General of Vermont, Susan Sussman, joined the case at the appeal level; the state interpreted the lemon law to cover people who lease vehicles for long-term use and who should be given the same protection against lemons as those that buy them.

NOTIFICATION—FIRST STEP TOWARD RELIEF

Before seeking a replacement or refund for your lemon, most state lemon laws require that you give the manufacturer (and the dealer in some states) written notification that the dealer has been unable to fix the car, and allow the manufacturer a reasonable opportunity for one last chance to fix it. Send a copy of this notice to the zone/regional office listed in your owner's manual or warranty booklet. Make sure you send this letter by the time you take the car in for the repair attempt which qualifies it as a lemon. Give the dealer a copy of the letter when you deliver the car for the repair. If the problem has not been corrected after this attempt, you should inform the manufacturer in writing, and request a refund or replacement—whichever you want. Any correspondence should be sent by certified mail. Be sure you keep copies of your letters, as well as all receipts and correspondence from the repair shop, dealer and manufacturer. At this point, a letter from a lawyer could put the dealer and manufacturer on so much notice that they decide to settle your complaint, as the letter below illustrates:

Jim Satcher, Inc.
Dodge-Chrysler-Plymouth
Johnson, SC

RE: Mrs. Jackie C. Eubanks
       1981Chrysler VIN 2C3BJ62EOBR135011

Gentlemen:

I represent Mrs. Jackie Eubanks with reference to the above referenced vehicle. I believe you are familiar with the automobile; it has been in your repair department numerous times.

Before commencing any legal proceedings on behalf of Mrs. Eubanks, I have advised her to bring her automobile to you for one last repair, replace, or whatever may be necessary to put her automobile in good condition. You have a record of multiplicity of defects and shortcomings both of the automobile itself and your woefully inadequate attempts to make good of its defects.

In the event her complaints are not fully satisfied on this occasion, please take notice I am prepared to advise her to commence suit against you and Chrysler Corporation for damages under applicable provisions of the Magnuson-Moss Act and the Uniform Commercial Code (15 USC 2301 et seq. and Title 36, Chapter 2, Part 3, South Carolina Code of Laws, 1976).

I shall be interested in your response.

Julian M. Sellers
Attorney at Law

Within ten days of receiving this letter, the dealer and manufacturer offered the consumer a replacement of her car **and** $800, even though all her repairs were performed under warranty without charge. Mr.

Sellers was so pleased with the outcome that he did not charge the consumer for his services. (This was an extraordinary act of generosity, however, and you should expect to compensate your lawyer for her or his services. Make sure they get the manufacturer to pay attorney fees as part of the settlement.)

ARBITRATION PREREQUISITES

Unfortunately, most manufacturers and dealers will view your notice letter as just that—notice that if the last repair is unsatisfactory, you will invoke the lemon law. After giving notice, many lemon laws require you to go through a manufacturer-run arbitration program before you file suit. The decision of this board is not binding in the vast majority of states, but the manufacturer must obey the decision if you choose to accept it. However, you don't have to arbitrate if the manufacturer's process does not comply with Federal Trade Commission (FTC) rules known as the Section 703 guidelines. Make sure to find out if these rules are being followed **before** you arbitrate. Very few arbitration boards comply with the 703 requirements, but you may want to use this process anyway; you could be given a refund or replacement without the expense and delays of a trial. Avoid an arbitration panel, however, that issues a decision that is binding on the consumer. You do not want to be stuck with a bad decision with no recourse in a court of law.

You may be in a jurisdiction that has a state-run program. This will be preferable to one run by the manufacturer, since it will be more objective and generally more concerned with your rights. The District of Columbia runs its own arbitration program, which is very favorable to consumer interests. Mr. and Mrs. Shurter decided to go before the Board for the hesitation problems in their 1988 Ford Taurus when the manufacturer and the dealer said nothing was wrong with the car (after seven repair attempts). According to the Shurter's lawyer, Robert Lotstein, the engineer representing Ford admitted the company would lose but it was not their policy to settle cases. Not surprisingly, the Shurters were awarded a buyback, attorney's fees, and incidental and consequential damages in the amount of $17,000.

New York's state-run program awarded buybacks or refunds to

1,120 New Yorkers in 1988, which represents two-thirds of all consumers using that program. New York's lemon law was amended in 1986 to provide for an impartial arbitration panel run by the state, after consumers complained panels run by the manufacturers did not give them a fair hearing. Consumers must pay $200 to use the program, which uses panelists from the American Arbitration Association, but they get this money back if they win their cases; the manufacturer then pays for the hearing. The average refund under New York's program is $14,126. Though a handful have been challenged by the manufacturer, consumers have prevailed in over 90% of these appeals.

WHAT TO DO WITH YOUR BAD CAR WHILE YOUR CASE IS PENDING

If you go through arbitration under a state lemon law, you may drive the vehicle to the extent it's driveable. If you have to sue after arbitration or you sue at the outset, what you can do with your car becomes more complicated and varies from state to state. Unfortunately, lemon lawsuits commonly take one to two years to resolve. A growing number of states recognize that a car is an essential means of transportation so that it can continue to be used during litigation. However, in many states, you cannot continue to use the car while a lawsuit is pending without jeopardizing your position that it's a lemon. Consult with your attorney about what to do. (See Chapter 6 for a more detailed discussion of this issue.)

HIRING A LAWYER DURING ARBITRATION

Consumers do not need lawyers to go through arbitration hearings, although you are allowed to use one if you want. Some lemons laws, like the District of Columbia's, provide for the award of attorney fees in arbitration. In such states, it is a good idea to hire a lawyer. If you do not use an attorney, prepare yourself for arbitration by getting manuals and materials from your state Attorney General's office, or consulting with someone familiar with the arbitration process. If the mechanism permits, attend an arbitration hearing before yours to learn more about the process.

WINNING AFTER LOSING: LITIGATING AFTER ARBITRATING

In most states, the arbitration decision is binding on the manufacturer but not the consumer. You can refuse it, and still sue the dealer/manufacturer in court under the lemon law. However, if the arbitration program meets the FTC guidelines, the decision rendered by the arbitrator may be admissible in your court case. It is not unusual for consumers to get nothing in arbitration and then to get more than the purchase price in litigation to compensate them for their aggravation and expenses. For example, Rosalyn McDonald of Detroit got nothing from the BBB but got $17,163 for her $13,000 1981 Buick in court. GM had to pay her attorney an **additional** $8,000 bringing the total to $25,000.

Joel Borden of North Woodmere, New York wrote to the Center about his experience of winning in court after losing arbitration:

> The BBB Arbitrator asked the GM Representative what he wanted to do about the problem and then so ruled. You recommended me to a lawyer after the adverse BBB decision. Prior to picking a jury, the car had about 60,000 miles, was 4 years old and the case was settled for $21,000 (the car then valued at $7,500 plus $14,500 in cash).

DAMAGE CLAIMS AVAILABLE UNDER THE LEMON LAW

Most lemon laws provide for not only a refund of the purchase price of your car, but also for reimbursement for expenses incurred in buying the car, such as sales tax, registration fees, delivery charges, and finance charges. If you ask for a replacement vehicle, it should be one that is fully acceptable to you, and is of comparable value to the car you originally bought had it not been a lemon.

If you elect to receive a refund, you may have to pay a small offset for use of the car. However, the offset should only be for the trouble-free use of your vehicle, which is the mileage at which the defects first showed on your car. If they began at mile one on day one, then there should be no offset even if you drive the car for 15,000 miles until you win under the lemon law. You should not accept any depreciation calculation that includes operating expenses, such as gas or maintenance, since these are costs that you, the consumer, have already expended. A simple depreciation deduction for use is the formula you should advocate.

Frank and Pauline Donofrio of Clearwater, Florida were awarded $39,000 in damages under Flordia's lemon law for a 1984 Chrysler Fifth Avenue that was plagued by continuous stalling problems, where the engine would suddenly die even at high speeds. The car was so unreliable—and dangerous—that it remained parked in the Donofrio's driveway for two years, becoming "a high-priced storage place for golf clubs."

After trying to get relief from mechanics, dealers, and Chrysler officials, the Donofrios arbitrated their case before the Chrysler Consumer Arbitration Board, but found the Board offered satisfaction in name only. At trial both parties agreed to a stipulated amount of damages; the issue for the jury was one of liability only. They decided Chrysler was liable to the Donofrios, entitling them to collect $24,000 to cover the price of the car and another $15,000 for the expense of leasing a car for the interim.

Some lemon laws allow you to sue for incidental damages, i.e., those expenses you incurred because your car kept breaking down. The law is supposed to put you in the position **you should have been in** had you bought a reasonably trouble-free car. A refund of the purchase price or replacement of the car may not account for all the added costs you unnecessarily suffered.

If the lemon law does not specifically provide for incidental damages, other laws like the Magnuson-Moss Warranty Act and the Uniform Commercial Code often enable consumers to recover other damages. In some states, you may be able to recover expenses such as towing charges, rental car costs or lodging if the car broke down while away from home (See Chapter 6). Often, you can recover these additional damages in small claims court after winning a refund through arbitration (See Chapter 9).

THE SWEET SMELL OF LEMON LAW SUCCESS

Lemon law suits have a very high success rate. "Winning" is a subjective term, however; you may not always get a full purchase price reimbursement or a refund of expenses such as finance charges, but still may be awarded substantially all you asked for. It is difficult to quantify how many consumers actually "win" their cases, since the majority never proceed to trial (although they may not settle until the eve of your court date). Usually, the pleadings filed before going to trial will flush out the merits of your case, and the manufacturer or dealer won't want the adverse publicity or expense of losing a lemon law case.

Manufacturers respond to lawyers, even though they will attempt to stall their efforts, and consequently will take the consumer's complaint more seriously. Once a lawyer is involved, "the meter is running," so it is less likely that the manufacturer will rely upon the consumer giving up out of frustration. And the threat of legal action with its attendant expense and bad publicity usually encourages a settlement attempt.

Dale Irwin, an attorney in Kansas City, Missouri, brought suit on behalf of a client after his car's transmission failed twice almost immediately after he purchased it. The car, an Oldsmobile Firenza, was a demonstrator and had 6,000 miles on it when the consumer bought it. After filing suit, Mr. Irwin discovered from dealer records that the car's transmission had failed several times while in service as a demonstrator. GM decided to settle the case, and reimbursed the consumer for all payments made on the car, plus incidental and consequential damages totaling $13,000. He was also awarded $3,400 in attorney's fees, and was given a brand new Oldsmobile Firenza with a list price of $8,400.

Peter Alan Mittenthal, a lawyer in Van Nuys, California, sued on behalf of his client after his Volkswagen suffered through five engine replacements. Only one month after Mr. Mittenthal sent a letter to the manufacturer demanding a refund of the purchase price, Volkswagen settled the case for $13,500 plus $500 in attorney's fees. No lawsuit was ever filed; the case was resolved on the basis of one letter from the consumer's lawyer.

Sometimes, your compensation may require some compromise. Edward Westbrook of Charleston, South Carolina was retained by a consumer whose 1981 Lincoln Continental started vibrating, belching smoke and losing pick up immediately after delivery, along with several other minor problems. The car was not fixed by the dealer, even after 13 repair attempts. This time, Ford did have a better idea. After receiving a letter demanding action for Mr. Westbrook, they offered to give the consumer a 1983 Lincoln in exchange for his 1981 model, if he would agree to extend payments for one year. The consumer agreed, and the case was settled without having to go to court.

It sometimes takes a lot more persistence, however, to be relieved of your lemon. Alfred Ilves wasn't about to abandon his complaint over his 1986 Oldsmobile Cutlass Ciera, even after 40 trips to Oldsmobile dealers to service excessive vibration and another six visits to independent service stations. Oldsmobile insisted the car functioned normally, but the independent stations believed the vibration was caused by a manufacturer's defect.

After ten months trying to get his new car serviced, Mr. Ilves hired "lemon lawyer" Patrick Tillman of Santa Clara, California to seek a buyback under the state lemon law. Mr. Tillman successfully argued for a full refund of the purchase price, and Oldsmobile also had to pay attorney's fees of $3,050.

PITFALLS AND BENEFITS OF SPECIFIC STATE LEMON LAWS

Even though all lemon laws generally provide the same relief—a repurchase or replacement after a fixed number of repair attempts or days out of service—there are certain differences within each state's law that can provide you with added benefits and pitfalls to watch out for. For instance, some laws allow you to recover double damages if the manufacturer brings a frivolous appeal. Others allow you to recover money spent to arrange financing. Some **limit** the incidental damages you can claim. The lemon law outlines below illustrate some of the differences found in these laws across the country. (A complete listing of lemon law summaries is contained in Appendix F.)

1. CALIFORNIA

The California lemon law applies only to new cars, vans, or trucks sold in California on or after January 1, 1983, and to new vehicles leased after January 1, 1985, for terms exceeding four months. To qualify as a lemon, a vehicle within the first year or 12,000 miles must be subjected to four unsuccessful repairs on the same problem or be out of service for thirty-one or more days. If the vehicle is dangerously defective the above requirements may be lessened. In fact, if the problem is safety-related, the number of repairs needed may be as little as one or two.

Additionally, the lemon law requires that (1) the problems are covered by the warranty and substantially reduce the use, value or safety of the car; (2) you notify the manufacturer directly about the problems you are having with your car if required to do so—check your warranty; and (3) you submit a complaint about your car to a "qualified" third party dispute resolution program, free of charge, if one exists before you proceed in court. The manufacturer will notify you in writing if a program is available.

If you do not agree with the decision you may reject it and proceed in court. If you are legally entitled to a refund or replacement under the lemon law and the manufacturer or dealer refuses to honor your request, you may be awarded up to **three** times your actual losses, reasonable attorney's fees, and court costs, due to the manufacturer's willful violation of the Song-Beverly Warranty Act.

The California Department of Consumer Affairs provides a free booklet titled "Lemon-Aid for New Car Buyers" to assist you in preparing for lemon law cases.

2. INDIANA

The Indiana lemon law applies to cars and trucks purchased after February 29, 1988. If a car has been returned to the dealer for repair four times within the first eighteen months or 18,000 miles, or has been out of service thirty-one or more business days, the car qualifies as a lemon.

To invoke the Indiana lemon law, you must submit written notification to the dealer and manufacturer listing when and where you bought the vehicle, the problem, the number of times it was serviced, and where the service was performed, as well as whether you seek a refund or replacement vehicle. You must also include photocopies of the written repair summaries and service records. As in California, if a qualified arbitration program exists, you must use the program before proceeding to court. You are not bound by the findings of the arbitration program if you do go to court.

If the vehicle is declared a lemon, the manufacturer has thirty days to provide you with a refund or replacement vehicle. If you go to court, you may recover your attorney fees and reasonable costs of litigation.

The Indiana Attorney General's office provides a guide entitled "The Lemon Law: Your Rights and Responsibilities."

3. NEW YORK

The New York lemon law applies to vehicles purchased or leased in New York, registered in New York, and normally used for personal, family, or household purposes. The lemon law also extends to subsequent purchasers during the duration of the warranty. To qualify as a lemon, a vehicle within the first two years or 18,000 miles must have four unsuccessful repair attempts on the same problem or remain out of service because of repair for thirty or more calendar days.

A consumer in New York has the choice of either participating in an arbitration program or suing the manufacturer directly in court. Either action must be commenced within four years of the date of delivery to the consumer. If you use the New York State Lemon Law Arbitration Program and win, the manufacturer must comply with the decision within thirty days or pay an additional $25 for each business day of noncompliance up to $500. If you proceed in court and win, you may be awarded reasonable attorney's fees. In either case, a successful consumer recovers state and local sales tax in addition to any other awards.

The Attorney General's office provides a guide titled "New Consumer's Guide to the New York State New Car Lemon Law."

4. NORTH DAKOTA

The North Dakota lemon law applies to cars and trucks under 10,000 pounds. A vehicle which has four unsuccessful repair attempts or is out of service for thirty or more business days within one year of the warranty qualifies as a lemon.

North Dakota does not have state-sponsored arbitration programs. Consumers are referred to arbitration boards sponsored by automobile manufacturers. Furthermore, a consumer who proceeds under the North Dakota lemon law is foreclosed from pursuing any other remedy arising out the facts and circumstances giving rise to the claim. This is an example of a bad lemon law.

5. TEXAS

The Texas lemon law applies to all vehicles. To qualify, the vehicle must be subjected to four unsuccessful repair attempts or remain out of service for thirty days or more within the first year of express warranty.

To be eligible for relief under the lemon law a consumer must (1) report the defect to the dealer within the first year or express warranty; (2) be able to show that the defect still exists and it substantially impairs both the use and market value of the vehicle; and (3) notify the manufacturer in writing and give the company one more opportunity to cure the defect. A complaint must be received by the Texas Motor Vehicle Commission within eighteen months of ownership or six months following the expiration of the warranty along with a $35 fee.

The Commission reviews all the complaints and if possible first tries to mediate and settle the issue. As a last resort a hearing will be held. Either party may appeal the decision from the hearing within thirty days.

The Texas Motor Vehicle Commission provides a one page summary of the lemon law as well as "Texas Motor Vehicle Commission Lemon Law Rules."

CHAPTER 8

ARBITRATION

When William Winslow of San Mateo, California bought his diesel Cadillac in 1981, he expected the kind of transportation usually provided by a luxury car. He paid a premium for the diesel engine because he was promised this would increase both the mileage and the lifespan of the vehicle. Instead, he got 7 years of constant breakdowns and repair bills, including engine and transmission replacements. In December of 1988, he took his case through arbitration, seeking both a buyback and reimbursement for his repairs. The arbitrator found that the vehicle had never operated satisfactorily, the problems occurred repeatedly, the consumer proved through evidence submitted that his damages were caused by the vehicle's mechanical problems, and GM failed to show any evidence of abuse or failure to follow recommended maintenance procedures. Consequently, he awarded Mr. Winslow a buyback of his Cadillac in the amount of $13,601.32, with depreciation taken for only the first 27,000 miles of use, and an additional $2750 for reimbursement of repair expenses. Total award: $16,351.32. Mileage at the time of arbitration: 107,000.

Lemon Times, Summer, 1989

When it works, arbitration offers a relatively quick and inexpensive way to seek relief for your lemon, whether you are trying to get a replacement vehicle under your state's lemon law, or reimbursement for repairs made on your diesel engine. Instances in which you should consider arbitration include:

1. As a means for reimbursement for excessive repairs or breakdowns of your vehicle where you meet the time and mileage limits of the program.

2. As a prerequisite for relief under the lemon law. Some laws require you to submit to arbitration before going to court, if certain guidelines are followed by the manufacturer, and this requirement is specifically stated in your car's written warranty.
3. As a means for obtaining a buyback of a lemon when you meet the time and mileage limit of the arbitration program or when time and mileage limits are suspended under a Federal Trade Commission (FTC) order.
4. As an alternative to filing a complaint in small claims court, if such an opportunity is provided in your jurisdiction.

Arbitration is an informal proceeding, in which you and the manufacturer's representative present your case before an arbitrator or a panel of arbitrators. In some instances, presentations are made only in writing. In others there is an oral hearing. In all instances, the arbitrators are supposed to be independent of the manufacturer.

Some manufacturer-run arbitration panels, such as that of Chrysler, allow written submissions only, making the need to document and support your case even more crucial, as you are not given an opportunity to explain any discrepancies between your submission and that of the manufacturer. When Robert and Joan Farmer of San Diego, California experienced severe surging problems with their new Chrysler that kept it in the shop for more than 30 days in its first six months of ownership, they decided to seek a buyback under California's lemon law. First, they took their case to the Chrysler Customer Satisfaction Board, who told them they did not have to be present because the dealer involved was not going to appear. Since Chrysler was running the proceeding, however, they insisted on appearing as was their right under the lemon law. At the hearing, the Board reported that a Chrysler representative had submitted a statement saying the Farmers had not picked up their car when it was ready for repair, a fact crucial to their case because of the 30 day trigger under the lemon law. This allegation was untrue, but had the Farmers not been at the hearing, they would never have known of it, and not been able to prove it was false. They reported this violation of their rights to the FTC, as should you if your arbitration procedure is not following FTC regulations for informal dispute programs. You should also report such infractions to your state Attorney General, state and federal legislators, and any consumer group in your jurisdiction that could intercede on your behalf.

Most arbitration proceedings routinely involve an oral hearing, where you can question—and be questioned about—the facts surrounding your case. No one else is usually present except for witnesses either side chooses to bring with them. No formal rules of evidence or procedure are followed; instead, the arbitrator generally accepts all of the documentation and testimony of each side (within reason) and gives each submission weight based on its apparent credibility. The arbitrator then makes his or her decision shortly after the hearing or submission of evidence. Sometimes, a panel of arbitrators is used in these types of proceedings, depending on who is running them and what is being arbitrated.

Preparation for arbitration is essentially the same as that for enforcement of your rights under the state lemon law, the Magnuson-Moss Act, small claims court, or any other complaint procedure—thorough documentation of defects and repairs. If you know your case well, have organized your evidence so that it can be clearly and logically presented, and have a good understanding of how and what you must prove to gain relief, you should have an excellent chance of prevailing through arbitration. Unfortunately, the programs are not always run in compliance with their own rules, the arbitrators are not always well-trained, and some procedures have a built-in bias against the consumer. For example, when Dennis King of North Tanawanda, New York decided to go through arbitration over his 1988 Corsica, he was convinced he would prevail. He had numerous repair orders, service bulletins, and the opinion of the arbitrator himself during a test drive of the vehicle that the car was performing ineffectively. The decision of the American Arbitration Association, however, was "no award." In spite of these pitfalls, however, thousands of consumers every year receive complete relief for their lemons through a buyback award, reimbursement for repairs, or both. What will give you the best chance for success is thorough preparation, knowledge of the rules, an awareness of the types of programs available to you, and a full understanding of what to look for and avoid in the arbitration process.

PREPARATION FOR ARBITRATION

KNOW THE RULES

Your first step once you decide to arbitrate should be to contact the program running the arbitration. Whether it is the Better Business Bureau, Ford Appeals Board, or a state-run board, find out what the rules are. (A description of the various arbitration programs is contained in Chapter 4.) Explain exactly what you are seeking, and that you would like a complaint form to initiate the process. Request a copy of any pamphlet or brochure that explains the program. Familiarize yourself immediately with all steps in the process so you do not miss a deadline for submission of materials or response to information sent to you. Ask questions about anything you do not fully understand or agree with; after all, the manufacturer has had a lot more experience than you have with this process, and will send a representative to the hearing who has probably been there many times and has his rhetoric well-rehearsed. It's only fair that you be fully informed of the process you are about to initiate to enforce your rights.

It is particularly important to know the rules if your car is eligible for arbitration pursuant to an FTC consent order. For example, as a settlement of its complaint against GM for its lemon diesels and certain specified components, the FTC ordered the company to arbitrate claims involving the powertrain through the Better Business Bureau, regardless of the age or mileage of the vehicle, through 1991. In spite of this clear directive, some local BBB offices have erroneously rejected claims to arbitrate, and many arbitrators have denied relief because the car was "too old" to qualify for reimbursement or replacement. When Paul and Ethel Lubarsky contacted the BBB in Farmingdale, New York, the office told them they were ineligible for arbitration because the car was five years old and had over 50,000 miles on it. But the Lubarskys had read several articles on the consent order, had secured letters from both the FTC and GM stating they met the arbitration requirements, and contacted the Council of Better Business Bureaus in Arlington, Virginia with their complaint. They were finally granted a hearing, but not until more than a year after their original application.

FIND OUT IF THE PROGRAM IS BINDING

Before you begin mediation or negotiation to initiate the process, you should find out if the arbitration decision will be binding on you. This means you cannot seek future relief. If so, you will likely want to find out if there are any other arbitration programs you can use, or may forego this step and go right to court. Even though a lawsuit is more time consuming and costly, it does provide you with greater protection in how and what you present during your case, and the right to an appeal if a bad decision is reached.

BE SPECIFIC ABOUT WHAT YOU WANT AS A REMEDY

To initiate the process, you will have to indicate to the arbitration program exactly what kind of relief you are seeking. For example, the BBB will send you a form called "Agreement to Arbitrate," which states exactly what is subject to arbitration. Read this form carefully: if you want a buyback but you are only authorized to arbitrate for a repair reimbursement, you will not want to sign this form until this discrepancy is straightened out. You cannot be awarded anything beyond that which is stated on this agreement, so make sure everything you seek is clearly laid out. This should not be difficult, because you probably decided what you wanted when you filed a complaint. It is very important to include a complete list of all expenses or repairs for which you seek reimbursement in the agreement. The arbitrator is bound by the terms of this agreement and it determines what he or she is authorized to award you. La Vonne Slama of Gresham, Oregon found out about this limit the hard way when she was awarded a buyback of her 1984 Oldsmobile Cutlass for $10,700 but denied several thousand dollars in additional expenses not listed on the agreement to arbitrate. She complained to the Center for Auto Safety that:

> The Oregon BBB office is one of the most poorly informed programs that I have ever seen. They do not tell you that if you do not put all your costs in your complaint that you can't add to them. Thus we did get a buyback but no reimbursement for down payment nor out-of-pocket expenses.

In general, you may arbitrate any vehicle problem for up to the purchase price of the car **plus** repair bills. You don't have to ask for money; you may ask for a needed repair which the manufacturer and/or the dealer has not performed. Normally arbitration will not cover such expenses as substitute transportation, lodging, lost wages or other incidental or consequential damages. Nevertheless, you should ask for compensation for these damages; it is up to the program to explain if they are not eligible, and the arbitrator may be influenced by these other damages in deciding the award for covered damages. In at least eight states—Connecticut, District of Columbia, Kansas, Maine, Maryland, Massachusetts, Vermont and West Virginia—you are clearly entitled to incidental and consequential damages under state law, but the manufacturer may not agree to arbitrate them. If arbitration does not cover these expenses, you may later file in small claims court to get them.

A buyback of a car at its original purchase price may be awarded. This is an appropriate request when your car has had major and/or repeated breakdowns or if the manufacturer and its dealers have not repaired a major problem. (Some manufacturers, however, do impose age or mileage restrictions on vehicles eligible for a buyback if the car would not be eligible for these remedies under the lemon law.) Requesting a buyback does not make your arbitration an all or nothing proposition; an arbitrator is free to award something less than a buyback if you are unable to convince him or her you should receive the buyback. Buyback requests are inappropriate for minor repairs where monetary damages are adequate.

MEDIATION BEFORE ARBITRATION

After you've initiated the arbitration process, some programs will attempt to mediate your case by forwarding your complaint to the manufacturer, which may attempt to work out a settlement with you. The majority of complaints have ended at this point. It is not known whether consumers were satisfied with the settlement offer or simply quit out of frustration. Do not feel pressured to settle if you are not satisfied with what the company offers. As long as you meet the eligibility requirements, you have the right to present your case to an arbitrator. Even if you lose the arbitration, you still have the right to go to court. William Crawford of Phoenix, Arizona was one consumer who benefited greatly by not ending his case during mediation. The BBB originally mediated a settlement of $325 with GM for his 1983 Oldsmobile Cutlass, and advised him to accept it, since depreciation losses were not subject to arbitration. He decided to take his case to arbitration, and was awarded $8,256 for a buyback of the car, which had 41,123 miles on it at the time of the hearing.

PREPARE YOUR CASE THOROUGHLY

The key to success in arbitration is documentation and organization. To clarify the case for your own sake, for your oral presentation and to make it easy for the arbitrator to award you a buyback, have a summary of all repairs and breakdowns listed in chronological order, with the relevant date and mileage indicated next to each entry. Have copies of corresponding receipts, correspondence and repair orders labeled and ready to present to both the arbitrator and the manufacturer's representative.

Evidence that your vehicle's defects are common in that model can be particularly helpful. Besides conducting research of newspaper and magazine articles, obtain a computer printout of complaints the National Highway Traffic Safety Administration (NHTSA) has received on a particular problem in a model through its Technical Reference Division, Room 5108, 400 Seventh St. SW, Washington, D.C. 20590, (202) 366-2768. This office also has the service bulletins that manufacturers send their dealers about problems in their vehicles. A service bulletin on a defect is good evidence of a widespread pattern, and if your vehicle has continued to exhibit a problem despite a supposed "fix" described in a bulletin, you bolster a claim that the manufacturer and its dealers cannot repair your vehicle's defects. (You can obtain a printout of bulletins on a particular model and component problem and the bulletins themselves from the Technical Reference Division.) Ask the dealer and manufacturer to provide you with copies of service bulletins relevant to your vehicle.

To check if your car is under investigation for a safety problem or has been recalled, call NHTSA's Auto Safety Hotline at 800-424-9393. You can order the public documents related to any investigation from NHTSA.

GM and Volkswagen must make available both indexes to and copies of all service bulletins or Product Service Publications. There may be some restrictions on availability of earlier model years. To order GM bulletins, call 800-551-4123 and get an index for your make and model. For Volkswagen and Audi, call 800-822-8987. For Ford, call 800-241-8450. Even if you find such documentation for a model year before or after your own, you can argue that the problem was not yet detected or not yet fixed, whichever is applicable. (See Chapters 3 and 4 on how to gather this type of information.)

You should also have either a notarized statement or an affidavit from a mechanic or other automotive expert, if possible, which states what problems exist with your car. This will help negate the argument made by the manufacturer that the problem is your fault, caused by lack of maintenance or poor driving habits. (Both of these tactics are commonly used by auto makers.)

Gather all relevant evidence and make arrangements with potential witnesses well in advance of the arbitration hearing. If the manufacturer or its dealer have evidence or witnesses (such as a dealer's mechanic) that you need to make your case in arbitration, you should write them well before the hearing to request that they send you the evidence promptly or agree that the witnesses you need will be at the hearing. If the evidence or agreement to testify is not provided voluntarily, it may be possible to write the program to request that the arbitrator issue a "subpoena." Even if the arbitrator does not issue a subpoena, give the arbitrator a copy of your request to the manufacturer or dealer. Ask the arbitrator to rule in your favor on the facts that would have been revealed by the evidence or witnesses that they refused to provide.

It is also extremely helpful to use an arbitration guide or manual to assist you in preparing for all phases of the proceeding. Several State Attorney General offices have such guides available, as well as local consumer affairs agencies. The Center for Auto Safety publishes *A Consumer's Guide to BBB Arbitration*, available both for all car owners and for diesel owners specifically, the latter of which includes articles, orders and service bulletins on the diesel lemon. Such manuals can provide invaluable information to assist you in the proceeding, as many consumers have no idea what to anticipate from the arbitrator, manufacturer's representative, or the process as a whole. The following is one of many letters from consumers who put the Center's Arbitration Manual to good use:

May, 1987

Dear Center for Auto Safety:

We received a buyback of $13,175 for our 1982 Chevrolet Caprice Classic station wagon with 92,000 miles. We feel our case was successful because of the information we gained through "A Consumer's Guide to BBB Arbitration" put out by you. I quoted from you in my written presentation which blew holes in the GM representative's comments.

Sincerely,
N. & L. Adams
Ukiah, CA

ARBITRATION AT LAST

If you and the manufacturer do not reach a settlement through mediation, the program with which you have filed your complaint will arrange an arbitration hearing. Recontact them to ensure they do. These hearings should be held within a specified number of days of when you made your complaint; look to the program rules for this information. You may have the choice of a personal hearing, a telephone conference call or submission of your case in writing. A personal hearing is the best way to make your claim. It may be necessary for you to travel a short distance to accommodate the proceeding, but every effort should be made to make the hearing location convenient for you, especially if your car is not operable.

SELECTING AN ARBITRATOR

You may have the option of choosing an arbitrator from a list of potential candidates, with brief biographical sketches included. Eliminate any from the list with whom you have a conflict and rank the rest according to your preference. The only proper reason for eliminating an arbitrator from the list is if you have a business or personal relationship with him or her, not because of where or for whom they work. The arbitration program will select a single arbitrator or a panel of three arbitrators based on the highest common preference between you and the company. Most of the manufacturer-run panels are comprised of representatives from both the auto industry and consumer community. Others are run by manufacturer representatives only. In these kinds of programs, you will not have a choice of arbitrator.

INSPECTION OF YOUR CAR

If you want the arbitrator to inspect your car, make your request well before your hearing. It is best to anticipate at least some delay with this request, and therefore try to be sure that the inspection is conducted in time to be discussed at the hearing. You may also request the arbitrator to provide a neutral expert to inspect your vehicle and to submit findings at the hearing. The arbitrator decides whether an inspection or expert will be provided. In some cases, if the vehicle is inoperable, the manufacturer must arrange to tow it to the hearing at their cost. You can always hire your own expert and present his or her findings at the hearing, or have the expert appear at the hearing to present testimony.

MAKING YOUR CASE IN ARBITRATION

The key to success in arbitration is thorough, advance preparation. You should collect, learn and bring to the arbitration all evidence relating to your claim. The testimony and the evidence you submit will not be restricted to legal rules of evidence, except that neither you nor the manufacturer may contact the arbitrator outside of the hearing unless the other side is present or has given written permission. Insist on receiving copies of any documents that the manufacturer's representative presents to the arbitrator in support of its case. The manufacturer's representative may likewise request copies of your documents. Both you and the manufacturer's representative may question the other's witnesses.

At the hearing, explain to the arbitrator in your own words what happened to your car, what the mileage was at the time, and what the manufacturer and its dealer did or did not do about it. Be as specific as possible about your car's breakdowns and how much it cost for repairs and other expenses. Support your story with repair bills, mechanic's testimony, any letters written to the dealer or manufacturer, and any other evidence of the problem.

List your money losses or damages for the arbitrator. Have a copy of a bill for every expense, if possible. For items which should last the life of the car (such as an engine or transmission), ask for full reimbursement. The owner's manual may be helpful in establishing how long a component should last. For example, if the manual does not call for servicing of the automatic transmission until 100,000 miles, that indicates it should last at least that long. Even if your arbitration does not cover incidental or consequential damages such as towing charges, lodging or transportation, list them anyway. The arbitrator may decide to increase the award to implicitly cover such damages.

BASE YOUR CASE ON COMMON SENSE, FAIRNESS AND APPLICABLE LAW

The guiding principle of arbitration is supposed to be to do what is fair or reasonable. Technically, the arbitration is not governed by law as is a court case, so certainly you should not assume that an arbitrator is familiar with the law applicable to your case. Nevertheless, you should become familiar with the most important aspects of the applicable law and not hesitate to make arguments based on the law. These arguments should bolster your arguments that are based on common sense and fairness. You should suggest to the arbitrator that a just decision should give you at least what the law entitles you.

Warranty law is most relevant to your complaint. The first step is to examine the written warranty itself. Its plain terms may aid your case (see Chapter 6).

A "lemon law" may also be relevant to your case. These laws, now in effect in almost every state, make clear that you are entitled to a refund or replacement if a new car develops problems that are not repaired within a reasonable number of attempts. They set a cap on the number of repair attempts and days out of service that are considered "reasonable" under the law. (See Chapter 7.)

ARBITRATING POST-WARRANTY CLAIMS

If failures and expenses occurred after expiration of your written warranty, emphasize to the arbitrator that the length of the written warranty does not govern the arbitration, nor does any decision rendered obviate any terms of the warranty. Rather, as noted above, the basic principles of arbitration are common sense, fairness and justice. Thus, your task is to convince the arbitrator that it is fair to hold the manufacturer—not you—responsible for your car's post-warranty problems. One way to do that is to show that you have suffered abnormal and/or excessive post-warranty failures. Your case is particularly strong if you have evidence suggesting that the failures are due to defects or poor dealer repairs of your car.

Holding the manufacturer responsible for your post-warranty problems is not only what is fair, often it is also the law. For example, a fundamental principle of warranty law is that if you complained about a problem during the written warranty period, the manufacturer is responsible for a proper fix regardless of whether the warranty has expired before the repair was made. In addition to the written warranty, there is an implied warranty of merchantability that the car is fit for its ordinary purposes and free of defects.

Normally, manufacturers attempt to limit implied warranties to the same length as their written warranties, but in at least nine states— Connecticut, District of Columbia, Kansas, Maine, Maryland, Massachusetts, Mississippi, Vermont and West Virginia—they are prohibited from limiting implied warranties. In those states it is especially clear that the manufacturer is responsible for hidden defects that pop up after the written warranty. (See Chapter 6 for more information on warranty rights.)

Emphasize that the written warranty period does not govern the arbitration result even if the manufacturer does not raise the warranty limitation in arbitration, because many consumers have reported to the Center for Auto Safety that their arbitrator erroneously believed that the written warranty is controlling. You should indicate that if the manufacturer has agreed to arbitrate post-warranty complaints, the written warranty cannot be controlling. In the case of GM engines and transmissions and VWoA engines, the FTC issued specific instructions that the terms of the written warranty do not define the scope of a manufacturer's liability and a consumer may recover for failure regardless of mileage.

HOW TO GET THE MOST FOR A BUYBACK

If your arbitration is for a buyback, you not only need to be prepared to show that the manufacturer should repurchase the car, but also the price that they should pay. Stress that you are entitled to a full refund of the purchase price. Your argument for a full refund is stronger if your vehicle is still relatively new. If your vehicle is older, emphasize the early mileage at which your vehicle's problems occurred, and that you have received very little trouble-free subsequent mileage. Argue that at the very most, a deduction should only be made up to the mileage when your vehicle began to experience problems: i.e., for its trouble-free use. Elizabeth Knight of Washington, D.C. was awarded a full purchase price buyback and a reimbursement for repair award totaling $11,610.05 for her 1985 Buick, which was three years old at the time of arbitration. The arbitrator stated that "due to the nature of the problems encountered by the consumer, mileage deduction was not warranted."

Whenever a buyback is requested, the issue of deducting for use will be raised. The manufacturer will submit unduly low estimated repurchase prices. You need to be prepared to discuss a truly fair repurchase price. If a deduction is under consideration, remind the arbitrator of your expenses, loss of work time and other inconveniences.

It is clearly improper for the arbitrator to focus on the market value of your car because a buyback at market value leaves you no better off than if you sold your car. Nevertheless, go to the arbitration knowing the approximate market value of your car so you can object if the manufacturer's estimate is too low. The Kelley Blue Book and the *NADA Used Car Guide*, available at your bank, are two sources in addition to newspaper advertisements.

Barbara Rose of Wichita, Kansas won a $16,605 buyback for her 1985 Chevrolet van and a reimbursement award of $492.23 for a transmission repair. It seems the garage put the transmission in backwards, causing the car to die on a single lane entrance to a highway. Ms. Rose said that tractor trailers were passing her by inches, cursing her, while she prayed she would not be hit or stranded there for hours. The arbitrator in her case ruled that because numerous problems that appeared early in Ms. Rose's ownership of the van were not repaired by the dealer, and because the repair that was made caused even greater problems, she was entitled to both a buyback and reimbursement.

Remember that a buyback represents a cancellation of your deal, because you were sold a defective car. The focus should be on the original purchase price. If anything is to be deducted, it should only be some small amount to reflect the benefit you received from use of the vehicle. Manufacturers like to suggest 20-25 cents a mile as a deduction because that's what the IRS allows as a tax deduction when a personal vehicle is used in business.

The IRS figure is much too high because it includes expenses such as gas, oil and maintenance, which **you** have already paid. A more appropriate measure is the average depreciation per mile of similar cars on the road which is roughly one-third of the IRS value. This reflects the maximum loss of value that consumers should absorb in using their cars. When Bruce Jones was awarded $16,690 for the buyback for his 1987 Oldsmobile Delta 88, the arbitrator explained that the repurchase price was calculated by deducting 5 cents/mile from the original purchase price. The car had been in the repair shop 67 days for a leaking rear window and a defective arm rest. The arbitrator said the primary problem was the total breakdown in communication between the zone representative and the dealer. Because of the "very lackadaisical attitude" of the zone representative toward adequate repair, he found a buyback was warranted.

RESPONSES TO THE MANUFACTURER'S DEFENSES

The manufacturer may claim that many breakdowns are due to inadequate maintenance, or even your abuse of the car. In this way, the manufacturer suggests to the arbitrator that you are to blame for your car's problems. While it is the manufacturer's burden to prove that you were at fault, you will present the strongest case by showing you took good care of your car and maintained it properly. Bring service records if you have them, or testimony from your mechanic. Even letters from friends who know your driving habits or care of your car can help. Articles or other materials showing your problem is part of a widespread defect in your model are also helpful. If you have driven cars in the past without any problem, state this fact. Even if you do not have thorough records, point out to the arbitrator that the FTC

Arbitration

says this is not controlling. Most consumers do not save maintenance records and the manufacturer must prove improper maintenance. Have your owner's manual handy. Don't let the manufacturer charge you with more maintenance obligations than are listed in your manual.

When the fuel injector, transmission, and engine in his 1981 diesel Buick Park Avenue all essentially self-destructed, DeVaughn Bird filed for arbitration with the Orlando, Florida BBB. At the hearing, the GM representative accused him of using contaminated fuel and said he was supposed to treat the diesel fuel with an additive to prevent sludge build-up in the diesel tank. When Mr. Bird showed GM had never made this recommendation, the representative changed his story and said all the problems were caused by poor maintenance, since no one else had experienced the problems Mr. Bird had with his car. In fact, hundreds of consumers had the exact repair history as Mr. Bird with their diesel engines. The arbitrator awarded him $230.02 for his fuel injector repair, $467.20 for his transmission repair, and a buyback of $10,400.36 for his car with 40,000 miles on it at the time of the hearing.

The manufacturer may also blame the dealers for not repairing your car, saying that dealers are independent businesses and the manufacturers should not be held responsible for their mistakes. (Normally, the dealers are not a party in the arbitration.) There are several responses to this claim:

1. Argue that the cause of the need for arbitration was a problem in the vehicle itself, which is the manufacturer's responsibility. Therefore it should also be responsible for the ensuing difficulties that would not have happened except for the initial problem.
2. Point out that dealers are the manufacturers' official authorized repair agents. Indeed, to get your repairs covered under warranty, you have to have them done at a dealer.

If your vehicle was involved in a class action suit, the manufacturer may try to use this against you by saying that you should get no more than was offered in the class action, which often covers repairs only up to 50,000 miles. Argue against this by saying class settlements are compromises in which individual members of the class trade getting full reimbursement for all members of the class getting some recovery. Consumers who want full recovery file individual lawsuits or go through arbitration exactly like you. Turn the manufacturer's citing of the class action into an advantage by saying it proves the existence of a defect, and that the arbitration issue is the amount of compensation for you.

AFTER THE HEARING, BEFORE THE DECISION

With some programs, **before the decision**, you may request that the hearing be reopened to consider additional evidence by writing to the arbitration board. The board should forward the request to the other party and the arbitrator, who decides whether to reopen the hearing. You can only get a hearing reopened if you can present "new evidence" that was unavailable at the time of the hearing, e.g., if you locate a missing witness or your car broke down after a hearing.

RECONSIDERATION OF YOUR CASE

If you believe the final decision is impossible to perform by its terms, contains a misstatement of the facts of your case, or contains an error in calculation (such as a mistake in the subtraction of deductions taken), immediately contact the program in writing. Other grounds for a reconsideration could be that the decision is too unspecific or unclear to be executed. The program should forward your notice to the other parties in the case for review, but it is strictly up to the arbitrator whether the decision will be modified.

If a consumer can show a hearing was tainted by impropriety, contact the national program and ask for a new hearing. Richard Howell of Irvine, California asked the BBB for another hearing after the arbitrator in his first hearing refused to accept evidence he presented including published defect data and a tape of Mr. Howell's car showing its hard start condition. The national Council of BBB's in Virginia told the local BBB, "In an effort to provide fairness in our arbitration programs, the Council is requesting your office to rehear the entire case with a new arbitrator." Three months later on May 21, 1986, the second arbitrator awarded Mr. Howell a full purchase price buyback of $17,809 for his 1980 Cadillac with 40,000 miles.

AFTER THE FINAL DECISION

Once the decision is final you have to decide whether to accept or reject it. If you want to accept it, make sure you notify the program of your acceptance within the time specified in its letter to you, or the decision will be considered rejected and the manufacturer can refuse to comply with the decision. If you reject it, you retain your rights to pursue other recourse against the manufacturer, including a lawsuit. If you accept what is offered, it is a legally binding resolution of all issues that were arbitrated. Thus, make sure you can live with what you are accepting. This is especially important if you were awarded a repair decision. Make sure the decision specifies that the problem with your car is to be fixed, instead of prescribing a certain repair which may not be the proper solution. The decision should also state where the repairs are to be performed, and when they are to be completed, so you are not stuck for months while the shop "is working on it." The time allowed should be no more than 30 days from your acceptance of the decision. The decision should also state that if you have any problems within a specified "interim period" after the repairs have been completed (generally 30-45 days), you have the right to reconvene the hearing to seek a more satisfactory resolution.

Whether you reject the decision entirely or were unable to arbitrate for all claims you are entitled to (such as incidental expenses) you can proceed to small claims court to be made whole on your complaint. Bruce Knight of St. Paul, Minnesota was awarded $3,200 for the buyback of his 1982 Oldsmobile Cutlass after he submitted records of the car's crankshaft problems, transmission malfunctions, and fuel injector pump defects, which made his car a moving fire hazard. After the arbitrator's award, he won $1,000 in small claims court for ancillary costs not subject to arbitration, such as insurance, rental car expenses, and towing charges. (Chapters 6, 9 and 10 explain how to use the court system to file your claim.)

If new problems arise after the decision is final or if the repaired problem reappears after the interim period has passed, you can file for a new arbitration hearing. Thus Jim Nauert of New Berlin, Wisconsin was reimbursed for a third transmission at 110,000 miles and for a third engine at 127,000 by going back for new BBB arbitration hearings each time.

HOW TO ENFORCE AN ARBITRATION AWARD

If the manufacturer fails to carry out an arbitration award, first contact the program board. Even if they cannot compel the manufacturer to voluntarily comply with the decision, they are authorized to arrange for an attorney for you to enforce the decision in court, and charge the manufacturer for your litigation costs. You must first contact the program before bringing suit, however, to see if you qualify for this arrangement. If they can't help, you can bring a suit on your own to enforce the decision.

Sometimes, it takes a lot of persistence to collect your award. After nine repair attempts, eighteen letters to the Ford Motor Company, and an arbitration award of $13,000 under the New York State lemon law in August of 1987, Angelo Fabrizio thought his endless headache with his 1986 Ford Taurus was finally over. It had just begun. Even though the car experienced engine problems, stalling, transmission problems, low mileage, and failed to pass New York State's emissions testing program (among other problems), Ford has now lodged four appeals of the original arbitration award.

Ford appealed the arbitration decision to the New York State Supreme Court and lost. Six months later, it appealed this decision to the Appellate Division Court; all five judges unanimously upheld the earlier two decisions. But Ford was just getting warmed up. After the Appellate Division Court's decision, Mr. Fabrizio tried to collect his award which had been posted by Ford as bond money for over a year. No deal. Ford took the case to the Court of Appeals in Albany, now challenging the constitutionality of New York's lemon law, abandoning its earlier argument that the car is not really a lemon, a tactic virtually meritless in law. The Court of Appeals dismissed this attempt by Ford to deny relief once again, and Mr. Fabrizio thought his case was finally won. Not yet. Ford has now filed for "leave to appeal" the Court of Appeals decision once again.

As of November, 1989, Mr. Fabrizio was still waiting for the $30,000 Ford owes him for his car, interest, and legal expenses. Though manufacturers rarely compensate consumers without some resistance,this case is exceptional. Some lemon laws, however, allow you to apply for double or triple damages for meritless appeals filed by the manufacturer. In this case, Ford would still be getting off easy.

Arbitration

Hopefully, your experience will be closer to that of Rebecca Mize's, who arbitrated her case before the BBB in Houston. She was awarded a buyback of $10,583.70 (representing a 10 cents per mile deduction for depreciation) and a repair reimbursement of $3,373.79 for her **used** Cadillac. In giving the reasons for her decision, the arbitrator stated:

> There is no evidence that Ms. Mize abused the automobile or failed to maintain it. In fact, she had the oil changed every 3,000-5,000 miles, as recommended, and the dealer's service history on her car shows that it was also maintained prior to her purchase of it. Additionally, the repairs to the car seem to involve rather premature failure of parts. The transmission and engine were replaced prior to 50,000 miles and the dealer's warranty record shows that the fuel pump was repaired or replaced three times; on the first of those occasions, the car had 0 mileage.
>
> I think that Ms. Mize has been subjected to a lot of expenses and hassle for such an expensive automobile, which should have given her years of carefree service.

You can't be guaranteed of an arbitrator who is this sympathetic to your complaint, but even if you do not prevail at the arbitration stage of your complaint, it will prepare you well for future action.

CHAPTER 9

SMALL CLAIMS COURT

An Auto Giant Takes a Fall
By Jim Brewer

An extremely disenchanted customer took the world's largest automobile manufacturer to court and won. It happened in Marin County small claims court where attorneys are forbidden to participate.

Judge Robert A. Smallman ordered the Chevrolet division of General Motors to reimburse a 37-year-old geologist for the cost of replacing the engine in his 1972 Vega. The car broke down last year with just over 25,000 miles on it.

It was a victory for John T. O'Rourke of San Anselmo who said he decided "to fight it out" in small claims court because "it was me against them—no high powered lawyers."

Under court rules, he will only collect $500 of the $678.83 it cost him to repair the engine, but O'Rourke said it was worth it. Five hundred dollars is the maximum claim allowed in small claims court.

"The consumer has been shafted too often," he said. "The people who buy this kind of car just can't afford to put a new engine in."

O'Rourke made his case upon a three-month old consumer report which urged the Federal Trade Commission to require that auto makers notify car owners of any warranty extensions.

The report, by the Center for Auto Safety in Washington, D.C., said "General Motors and other automobile manufacturers" sometimes double the life of a warranty (to two years or 24,000 miles) for selected owners . . . without disclosing such extensions to the public or the affected owner."

Small Claims Court

It specifically cited "under the table extensions by General Motors on 1971 and 72 Vegas because the cooling systems in these models often break down."

The report did not say who the "selected owners" were, but O'Rourke wasn't one of them.

GM officials said the damage to the car was due to "excessive hard carbon buildup on the pistons" and not "product failure." William Perry, a Chevrolet Motors representative, told Judge Smallman that warranties were not selectively extended to some Vega owners but said his company, in some instances, "made policy adjustments to keep our customers happy."

"The way I see it, policy adjustments and warranty extensions are the same thing," Judge Smallman said. And he ordered Chevrolet to pay O'Rourke $500 plus $27 in court costs.

San Francisco Chronicle, April 23, 1974
Copyright Chronicle Publishing Co., 1974

Small claims courts, designed to provide a fast, efficient and inexpensive way to resolve claims of individuals against merchants or large corporations, are potentially a great resource to consumers. They are one of the best ways for consumers to settle disputes with a dealer, service station, repair shop, garage, or auto manufacturer.

Small claims court is just what it sounds like—a forum for claims not large enough to warrant a full-scale trial, yet worthy of argument before a judge. Virtually every state has small claims courts, each generally having county-wide jurisdiction. Claims limits range from $300–$5000, which means that this is not the appropriate court to seek a buyback or replacement of a lemon, or if you are seeking considerable damages and expenses. If you win a buyback through arbitration, however, you are free to file for reimbursement of incidental expenses such as towing, lodging or rental cars through small claims court, since these claims are not subject to arbitration and will usually be under the claims limit.

Thus James Adams of Oceanside, California used small claims court to recover incidental expenses after he was awarded a refund on his 1980 Pontiac Catalina station wagon through the Better Business Bureau. Because the program does not consider out-of-pocket expenses, such as towing and loss of use of the vehicle, he would not sign a complete release against GM, and sued them in small claims court. He won a judgment of $1000, but GM appealed, forcing him to defend their suit in Superior Court. Even though he represented himself and GM hired a high-powered law firm, his judgment was upheld.

A major advantage to small claims court is that they are so simple you don't have to hire a lawyer to represent you; in fact, some courts do not permit lawyers. Even if the auto maker brings in high-priced lawyers to fight your claim, as GM did with James Adams, do not be intimidated or discouraged. Small claims court is meant to provide an informal, simple method of justice where consumers can easily explain their problem and the remedy they seek. The judge may help present the case by asking appropriate questions. Formal courtroom procedures and the use of legal rules are usually ignored, providing an informal atmosphere in which consumers making claims can more easily talk out their problems before the judge.

Information and other resources are available for the consumer to use in preparing to go to small claims court. A few courts and many consumer groups and agencies publish guides or consumer manuals on using small claims courts, with emphasis on the local procedures involved. (See Appendix J for list of titles and where they can be obtained.) Even though a lawyer is usually not necessary in a small claims court suit, some legal assistance or advice may be helpful. Free legal help may be obtained from law students who are participating in a legal clinic, such as the Law Students in Court Program in Washington, D.C. Call the nearest law school to find out whether there is such a program in your area. Often, legal assistance is available from neighborhood legal service organizations or legal aid societies which are set up to help low-income or minority groups. Where legal assistance is necessary, some courts will provide indigent consumers with a lawyer at the consumer's request.

PROCEDURES

FILING A COMPLAINT

Small claims courts are located in county or other local courthouses in your state. The plaintiff (person who is suing) usually must file suit in the area or district where the defendant (person being sued) lives, works or has his or her place of business, for example, where the dealership or repair shop is located.

The small claims court in your area will be listed in the telephone book under Courts for either your city or county government, or there may be a general information number for Courts. (See Appendix H for a state small claims court table indicating for each state the type of court, availability of appeals, maximum amount of suit, use of lawyers, and whether the procedure is informal.)

After finding the court in your area, ask to speak to the clerk of the small claims court. Tell the clerk that you wish to file a complaint. Ask the clerk whether the court can handle your kind of case and whether it has jurisdiction over the party (or parties) you wish to sue. As a general rule, the defendant must live, work or do business in the court's territory. Since automobile manufacturers do business in all areas of the country, they can be sued in just about every small claims court. Thus, choose the court in an area where the dealership is located when suing the dealer and manufacturer.

The clerk can assist in filling out the necessary form. The basic and perhaps only form you need to fill out is the complaint. Many small claims courts will have a sample, completed, complaint available. The complaint includes your name and address, the names and addresses of the persons whom you are suing, the amount of your claim and the reason for your suit. (See Appendix G for a sample complaint.)

The amount of your claim should include the cost or repair in the case of a defect or accident and the overcharge in the case of a fraudulent or incomplete repair, as well as any consequential damages arising out of the problem. For example, if a repair shop charged you $30 for a tune-up—and in the meantime you had to hire a taxi costing $20—and consequently you hired another mechanic to perform the tune-up for $25, then you should sue for $50 ($30 to get back what you paid for no tune-up and $20 for the cab; do not ask for the $25 because that is what you are paying the honest mechanic for the tune-up actually performed). If fraud is involved, you may be entitled to triple damages.

Be certain the business name of the organization you are suing (which you write on the complaint) is the official *legal* title. John's GM Shop may not be enough: it may be legally registered as John Brown's General Motors Showroom, Inc. Some courts will dismiss the suit unless the company is identified in the complaint exactly as it is registered for legal purposes. Ask the court clerk whether the exact legal name is required, and, if so, how to find the correct name. This information can usually be checked with the city or county clerk, or the secretary of state. See if the dealership or repair shop has an operating license posted on an office wall with the legal name on it. Auto companies are required to have an agent for service of process which may be the Secretary of State in which you live if they do not name an agent.

When you fill out the complaint, be precise. State exactly what part of the engine, for example, was defective or malfunctioned. The clerk will give you a summons to be completed with the complaint. A summons is the official notification of the case delivered to the party you are suing, which will be sent to the defendant after you have filed your complaint.

After you fill out the forms, you will pay a small filing fee which usually will be returned if you win since the losing party pays it. The clerk will then give you a copy of the forms and usually a "docket number" (identifying the case) and a date for the hearing of your case. The hearing date is usually scheduled for 2-8 weeks from the date of filing. Some courts notify plaintiffs by mail telling them whether the defendant was served with the summons. If the defendant cannot be located, you are responsible for finding the address where they can be served.

PREPARING YOUR CASE

Try to attend a session of the court to learn the procedure so you will know what to expect and how to prepare for your own hearing. At least come to court early on the hearing date and observe the cases that come up before yours, in order to become more at ease with the procedure.

In small claims court, a consumer can do a good job by going before the judge and telling the story of his or her complaint from the beginning. To do this easily, write down the history of your complaint. Arrange the events in the order they occurred, checking the dates. Pull together all the documents related to your claim, such as written estimates, repair orders and canceled checks. If the record keeping system in Chapter 3 is followed, the important papers needed to show your side of the story will be readily available. Also bring physical evidence (broken or defective parts) if possible.

Where possible, get written statements or affidavits that support your complaint. One example is a statement in writing from a car mechanic describing what is wrong with the car and why it would be considered a defect as opposed to normal wear and tear. If the mechanic is willing, have it notarized by a notary public. This evidence lends credibility to your case. Another piece of helpful evidence would be a report from a diagnostic inspection center in the form of a computer printout or checklist, listing what is wrong with the vehicle. If your case involves a manufacturing or design defect, obtain a printout of service bulletins and other complaints similar to yours from the National Highway Traffic Safety Administration to help build your case, as suggested in Chapter 4.

The vast majority of small claims suits are decided without witnesses. If you do bring witnesses, make arrangements with them prior to the hearing. It is best to get a witness to testify at the hearing on a voluntary basis rather than by court order. If the witness is not willing to come to the hearing, ask the witness to make a written statement or affidavit indicating his or her knowledge of the case.

In the rare case where success depends upon a witness actually appearing in court, and the witness will not come voluntarily, check with the court clerk to see if the small claims court has subpoena power (ability to order a witness to appear in court). For example, a mechanic at the dealership who repaired the car admitted that the failure of a part was due to a manufacturing defect. Since the dealer will not let the mechanic appear at the hearing, a subpoena is the only way to get the mechanic in court to tell the story. There is a beneficial side-effect of a subpoena issued in such a case; not only will you win if the mechanic testifies, but the dealer loses a mechanic for the day. Confronted with such a situation, the dealer may very well offer to settle out of court after the subpoena arrives.

SETTLEMENT

Many small claims suits are settled out of court before they can come to trial. Once a dealer, garage or manufacturer sees that a consumer means business by going to small claims court or beyond, he or she frequently agrees to meet the consumer's demands. You can even settle in the courtroom on the day of the hearing before court actually begins. Some courts have clerks, other assistants or even judges available to expedite this settlement process before trial.

If you want to settle, be prepared to bargain. Make sure you understand all the terms before you settle and get the terms of the settlement in writing. Do not settle for anything you feel is unfair. Upon settlement, file a copy signed by both parties with the court so that the settlement can be enforced by law. If the court allows, arrange to appear in court to clarify with the judge the settlement terms. Try to negotiate reimbursement of court costs as part of the settlement.

THE HEARING

If there is no settlement, you will have your day in court. Most small claims courts call the roll of cases and parties at the beginning before taking each case in order. If a party is late or does not appear, the case can be decided immediately in favor of the party who is present, so be on time.

When the clerk calls your case, the judge will ask each party to tell his or her side of the story. In the course of presenting your case, give the court copies of any written evidence you have. If you have any witnesses, call them before the judge and ask them to tell what they know. The judge will not expect you to have any legal knowledge; he or she will merely ask you to state the facts as clearly and concisely as you can. The judge will ask questions to clarify anything that was not clearly presented. The other party will then be given an opportunity to present his or her side. Many small claims courts have cross examination of witnesses only, not the parties. The following suggestions will help you present your case at the hearing:

1. Rehearse your presentation before going to court. If you know your case well, you should be able to present the facts easily and with confidence.
2. Provide the court and the auto manufacturer's representative with a copy of each repair order (with canceled check attached) as you describe each repair attempt to the judge. Label each submission with corresponding exhibit letters (A,B,C, etc.) so they can be easily referenced.

3. Bring copies of supporting documentation of defects or problems with your car, including recalls, service bulletins, studies, articles, fact sheets, and similar consumer complaints to present to the judge and the opposing party. Label each with exhibit letters as well.

4. Be as organized as possible. Have a summary listing of each breakdown or repair, together with the relevant date and mileage indicated in each entry. Repair information should include the garage's diagnosis, the repair work actually done, the repair order number, and the amount you paid for each repair.

5. When asked questions during the hearing, take a moment to think about how to respond, especially if the other party is questioning you. They may try to phrase their questions so that the only reply you can give will sound damaging. Rephrase the question to expose this tactic and respond accordingly.

The judge may give a decision at the hearing, or notify the parties of the decision by mail. If you lose, you may have the right to appeal; if you win, the defendant may be able to appeal. Check with the clerk about the appeal procedure (see Appendix H).

ARBITRATION

Some court systems provide for arbitration instead of or in addition to small claims courts. (See Appendix H for a list of jurisdictions where this is an option.) Both are very similar, with the main difference being that in arbitration, one goes before an arbitrator rather than a judge. This method enabled a Buffalo, New York couple to get $780 from General Motors for the repairs and other expenses incurred when their Oldsmobile Cutlass broke down. The DiDomenico family was on a motor trip when the engine in their Cutlass failed and had to be completely rebuilt at a cost of $540. They had to cancel their vacation plans, rent a car and return home. Although the car had just over 13,000 miles on it, the manufacturer's district representative refused to make any adjustment. The DiDomenicos threatened legal action and would have settled for a much smaller amount than that which they actually ended up winning in small claims court. But General Motors remained unresponsive. A local legal aid office suggested suing General Motors in small claims court.

In Mrs. DiDomenico's own words:

> This entire experience was frightening, inasmuch as we had never been involved in a lawsuit; consequently we had no lawyer to ask for advice, and we felt completely helpless dealing with this giant corporation.
>
> Throughout, a pattern emerged whereby my husband would first try to reach an agreeable settlement by telephone or in person, and he would be given sympathetic understanding and be temporarily pacified, first by the dealer/repairman, then by the Olds Division representative, then by the Olds Division in Lansing, Michigan, and by the local dealer from whom we had purchased the car. But in each instance a point was reached where they turned off, became unavailable, unresponsive.
>
> After we had threatened legal action and they didn't offer to settle (we would have accepted just about any reasonable amount: $200 or $300) we seemed to have no alternative but to go ahead. It was as if they were calling our bluff, daring us to take General Motors to court.

Armed with receipts to show proper maintenance, motel accommodations when they were stranded, rental car fees, long distance phone calls and the repair bill itself, they submitted their claim to an arbitrator provided by the court. General Motors had a lawyer present its case and even brought an expert witness to testify on its behalf. The DiDomenicos had no lawyer, but they did have good records and concrete evidence (the engine parts which had to be replaced) to give credibility to their case. They were awarded full recovery: $780 from General Motors.

Mrs. DiDomenico sent her advice to other consumers in a letter to the Center for Auto Safety:

> In retrospect I would say that it is most important to keep complete, accurate records of all work done on the car. In case of a problem, speak directly to the proper person and be persistent and don't back off.
>
> Small claims court is the best possible place for the average consumer to take his legal matter. Every conceivable type person was among those filling the courtroom: individuals suing individuals (some still arguing), individuals having complaints against businesses, many businesses represented by lawyers.

A clerk called the docket to first determine whether anyone had failed to show up, and when General Motors was called, there was such a gasp of reaction in the room that we couldn't hear the response. But of course they were present and we both agreed to an arbitrator. We did have a completely fair and thorough opportunity to have it all out.

Finally, small claims court is the place for the consumer to have his faith in equal justice restored. Every person should make it a point just to visit his local Small Claims Court one day and realize it is not necessary to have legal knowledge or a lawyer to have his chance to get a fair hearing.

Auto manufacturers should be held responsible for defective products, and should compensate you accordingly. Your persistence can ensure that both of these goals are met. And small claims court could provide you with the most effective forum in which to achieve them.

Ann and Paul Murphy of Wellesley, Massachusetts got relief for the chronic brake problem in their 1984 Buick Skylark by taking the dealer to small claims court. They complained several times to the dealer who refused to fix the car, instead suggesting they put sand in their trunk. Several letters to GM and calls to the Buick Hotline went unanswered, or referred them back to the dealer. It was not until the car was in an accident that the dealer looked at the brakes carefully, finding a hairline crack. Instead of acknowledging a defect, the dealer attributed the fracture to excessive braking required when driving down a steep hill, a diagnosis Mr. Murphy found to be outrageous. Refusing to accept this treatment, he hired a metallurgist to examine the brake drums, who in his written analysis reported the problem to be a manufacturing defect. Armed with this evidence, Mr. Murphy went back to the dealer, who simply laughed at him. Unable to gain relief any other way, the Murphys filed a complaint in small claims court, and won a judgment for $461.39 for repair of the brakes.

ARBITRATION PANELS

The concept of resolving consumer complaints outside of the courtroom is becoming more and more popular across the country. The superior court of Santa Clara County in California has court-ordered arbitration. Three hundred and fifty lawyers arbitrate cases in their respective areas of expertise. The program, run according to the rules of the California Arbitration Practice Guide, has been operating since 1982 at no cost to the consumer. Many other counties in California have adopted programs similar to this one.

The American Arbitration Association has similar programs in cities all across the country. In Philadelphia, the program was so well received that local courts adopted it into their systems. You should be warned, however, that the filing fee is $300, even though the lawyers who run it are all volunteers.

In Orlando, Florida, the local bar association has operated a Citizen Dispute Settlement Program since 1975. About 70 lawyers volunteer to hear the cases, which are initiated when consumers call the program to arrange a hearing. The Program then sends notice to the other party, whose attendance is voluntary. The decision rendered is not binding on either party. The program operates at no cost to the consumer. Appendix H lists those jurisdictions which offer dispute resolution mechanisms as an alternative or prior resort to small claims court.

As stated before, if you are denied relief through arbitration, you still have the right to go to small claims court unless you submitted to arbitration that is binding on the consumer, which is rare, fortunately for these kinds of programs. That's the route James Larkin of Garden City, Michigan took when the transmission on his 1984 Oldsmobile Delta 88 malfunctioned. He tried to get a repair reimbursement through the Better Business Bureau program, but lost his case because the word "transmission" did not appear on the work orders for repairs made under warranty, which would show that the problems began early on. Armed with a letter from a transmission shop which stated the transmission was defective and showed no sign of customer abuse, he sued his dealer in small claims court, and was awarded the full $1281.82 for the repairs on his transmission.

COLLECTING THE JUDGMENT

Unfortunately, some consumers who win in small claims court do not always collect the full amount of the award. Some defendants refuse to pay or simply do not have sufficient funds to pay. The court is not responsible for the actual collection of judgments but it can help enforce the judgment. In most auto cases, the winning consumer has little difficulty in collecting since the losing party is frequently a multi-billion dollar auto company or well-to-do auto dealer that can scarcely plead lack of funds to pay the judgment. However there are horror stories about consumers trying in vain to collect a judgment as the following letter shows.

October 28, 1988

Center for Auto Safety
Washington, DC

Dear Sirs:

Last April we purchased a 1981 Plymouth Sapparo from Affordable Autos . . . The car was to be inspected and was to have a tune-up. After realizing a week later that the car was not tuned up, we returned to the car lot many times only to find that the owner was never there. We finally decided to have the car checked by a reputable garage. After receiving the report that the "unibody frame on the right side is rotted real bad" we tried to contact the owner again. Once during the two week period we were successful and he stated that he would not take the auto back even though the warranty was still in effect.

After calling office after office in the state department, we were directed to the Department of Motor Vehicles, Division of Vehicle Safety. We received the forms for a formal complaint and submitted them. A few weeks after submitting the complaint . . . Mr. William Hawkins telephoned and stopped by to check the car. In his opinion, the car should have never passed inspection and, therefore, should have never been sold under the law. He suggested, because of the fact that the property on which the car lot was located was in the process of being sold or rented, that we submit a claim to small claims court for the amount of $2000. We did this and had a court date set for August 16, 1988. Neither of the owners in the car lot showed up in court that day. We, therefore, received a judgment in the amount of $2064.25. We believed that we were on the road to receiving restitution. We contacted a lawyer who sent a letter with the judgment decision, but, of course, no response was received. So to date, this judgment was only a piece of paper.

In the meantime a hearing was set with the Department of Motor Vehicles from the state of New York on September 19, 1988. Once again, neither owner was present. So once again, this was

159

only a formality for us—it meant nothing to either man since they knew nothing was going to be done. Since they didn't show up a fine was imposed but our feeling at this time is that it will never be collected.

We then proceeded to file a small claims judgment with the Sheriff's office. We were naïve enough to believe that this was the end of the "work" for us. The lady in the office said "I have six other claims against this person—I believe you're wasting your time and money with this claim." I believe at this point we felt that we were only wasting our time and money too. . . .

We've been through many channels, come to many dead ends, and still have a car that cost over $2,500 and is not safe to drive on the road and will never pass an inspection. Is this fair?

> Sincerely,
> Mr. & Mrs. M. Dockal
> Schenectady, NY

At the hearing, ask the judge to order the entire amount to be paid at one time in a single payment. If notification is by mail, contact the defendant and ask for the money. If the defendant does not pay within a reasonable time (2-3 weeks), go back to the small claims court clerk. Fill out the necessary forms, and the clerk will tell you how to get a sheriff or marshall to collect the money owed by the defendant. The cost of a sheriff or marshall can be added to your judgment. File with the clerk a list of all the costs accumulated in trying to collect the judgment.

If the sheriff or marshall cannot collect the money owed to you, ask the court clerk for information about what to do next. If an oral examination of the defendant is possible, request a hearing before a judge to decide what action can be taken to make the defendant pay the judgment. At the hearing, you can find out whether or not the defendant actually has the money to pay you. If he or she does have the money, request an attachment on the defendant's wages, money in a bank account, or other property until you have collected your money. The clerk can again help you fill out the necessary forms.

However, persistence does pay off, as one consumer proved when he sued the Ford Motor Company. Bob Repas of East Lansing, Michigan had a serious rusting problem with the tailgate of his Ford Torino station wagon. The difficulty began when the car was new and continued to get worse despite frequent trips to the shop for repairs. By the time the car was only three years old, the entire tailgate was rusted and required replacement at a cost of $291.90. Mr. Repas won his case and was awarded a total of $305.30, with the extra $13.40 for court costs. However, Ford stalled for several months before paying. After additional hearings he received the original judgment plus 74 days interest on the sum.

Mr. Repas wrote in a letter to the Center for Auto Safety:

> I am most irked about the way this company stalled on paying the judgment. . . . it is determined to give anyone a hard time who doesn't accept their verdict as final and infallible.

Mr. Repas's persistence made him a winner.

SUING WITHOUT A LAWYER

Even where nearby small claims courts do exist, some consumers have chosen to file suit in a higher court because the jurisdictional amount (limit on the amount you can recover in a given court) is too low in small claims court. In order to avoid legal fees, some consumers have pursued the case on their own, without hiring a lawyer. Others did so because they couldn't find a lawyer willing to take on an auto manufacturer.

One example is Toby Cagan who took Chrysler Corporation to court and won—without a lawyer—over her defective Dodge Aspen. She had complained over and over again about her "lemon" to Chrysler dealers and to the manufacturer, but Chrysler treated her complaints callously—responding with form letters and rude, reluctant service.

Before Cagan signed for her Aspen, she took a test-drive and found many problems with the car, including difficult steering, sticky windows and doors, stalling and dents. When she complained to the salesperson, he told her that, "It's a new car and these problems have to work themselves out." Trusting the salesperson at his word, Cagan drove away in her new Dodge. When the car developed more problems within a week, she took the car back to the dealer. For the next several months, Cagan tried to get six different Chrysler dealerships to repair her car, but still without satisfaction. She sent letters and made telephone calls to Chrysler. All she received was the run-around. By this time, the consumer was quite angry. "The car had been defective since the date of its purchase. After three government recalls, numerous problems and defects, I was afraid to drive the car," she said.

So Toby Cagan filed a lawsuit against Chrysler Corporation in Civil Court, in the city of Queens, New York. Planning ahead, she saved all the repair orders to document her "lemon" story, showing how she had brought the car into numerous Chrysler service departments again and again with no success. Chrysler simply could not fix her car. As her story unfolded in the courtroom, the shabby treatment Chrysler gave the consumer was exposed. She brought in a mechanic to verify the defects in the engine and drivetrain. A body shop owner testified that her car had formed rust.

Cagan also brought in reports from the Center for Auto Safety, describing how the Center had written to Chrysler Chairman Riccardo about the large number of complaints on the Aspens and the identical Volares. Most of the complaints, which were similar to those Cagan had experienced, concerned carburetor, brake, driveline and steering problems. (Chrysler had earlier denied the Center's charges, calling the group's claims "irresponsible." But within the next six months, Chrysler had initiated four large recalls for the very same defects experienced by consumers writing to the Center and Ralph Nader. About 80% of all Aspen and Volare owners had their cars subject to all four recalls.)

Although Chrysler brought in an expensive New York City lawyer, its only witness was a zone official who admitted, incredibly, that the car was defective, as Cagan claimed, but that given enough opportunities Chrysler could fix all the defects. After hearing Cagan's witnesses at the trial, Chrysler gave in and offered to refund the consumer's purchase price minus $500 for the 18 months she had owned the car.

Cagan and other consumers who do not give up easily prove that you don't always need a lawyer to take a giant corporation to court and win. But you do need persistence and planning. Toby Cagan had plenty of both, much to Chrysler's dismay.

CHAPTER 10

WORKING WITH A LAWYER

Mrs. Warren Marx had chronic problems with the diesel engine in her 1982 Oldsmobile Cutlass wagon, which finally failed completely when the car was five years old. Even though she tried to repair the engine while it was under warranty, GM refused to acknowledge that anything was wrong with the car. Unwilling to suffer the financial loss for a car that was obviously a lemon, Mrs. Marx consulted Michael J. Jannuzzi of Huntington, New York, a lawyer with a specialty in GM diesel cases. He negotiated a buyback of $13,000 for the wagon, which had 60,000 miles at the time of settlement. Mrs. Marx wrote the Center for Auto Safety, "It was a matter of principle and money. GM was made to take responsibility for their product and we did not suffer a total financial loss." She credited her success to the "excellent" assistance of Mr. Jannuzzi.

Lemon Times
Summer, 1989

Hiring a lawyer to win a buyback or reimbursement of repair expenses may seem like a daunting proposition, given the cost of legal fees. Yet it could be the most effective way to succeed against an auto manufacturer, even if you never enter a courtroom. Manufacturers respond to lawyers, even if they attempt to stonewall them, and consequently will take the consumer's complaint more seriously. Once a lawyer is involved, it is harder to believe that the consumer will eventually give up out of frustration, a strategy many manufacturers rely upon. And the threat of legal action with its attendant expense and bad publicity usually encourages at least a settlement attempt.

The frustrated lemon owner has a number of legal options for getting the lemon replaced or repaired. These options include many tactics less expensive than a lawsuit, but which are often just as effective.

An attorney can be helpful in finding a successful and inexpensive tactic short of actually filing suit. For instance, a simple, direct letter from an attorney is often enough to startle a stubborn dealer or manufacturer into fixing your car or revoking acceptance. Beyond this, a lawyer could call the dealer, guide you to a regulatory agency, to small claims court, or actually file a lawsuit.

Before hiring a lawyer, consult with one. Many attorneys will give free consultations for up to half an hour or so to evaluate your case. He or she can point out deficiencies in the case, indicate the likelihood of success, the amount of damages, and the cost of bringing a suit. At the same time you can appraise the lawyer—whether she or he seems competent and interested in your case. At such an initial consultation, there is no requirement on either the lawyer's or the consumer's part to hire or be hired.

WITHOUT A LAWSUIT

A letter or telephone call alone from an attorney to the dealer or manufacturer shows them that you mean business. Sometimes they will offer to fix the car, settle for money damages, or otherwise resolve your complaint. Another inexpensive use of a lawyer is a letter to the manufacturer or dealer. When Mark Steinbach, a lawyer with a practice in Washington, D.C. and Maryland, was contacted by a client to help him rescind a car purchase, Mr. Steinbach sent the dealer the following letter:

Herson's Honda   May 1, 1989
Rockville, MD

Re: Leonard Kopp
    1989 Honda Prelude
    Vin: JHMBA414OKCO36057

Gentlemen:

I represent Leonard Kopp, who came to your store with an interest in purchasing a car over the weekend.

By this letter, Mr. Kopp cancels any purported purchase of the above-referenced automobile. He has the unconditional right to do so pursuant to Section 11.12.01.15 of the Maryland Motor Vehicle Regulations, which provides in pertinent part:

> Until the buyer signs the instrument and **receives a copy of it signed by the seller**, the buyer or **prospective buyer has an unconditional right to cancel the instrument** or order and to receive immediate refund of all down payments of deposits made on account of, or in contemplation of, the agreement or order. [Emphasis supplied.]

Mr. Kopp has never received a copy of any instrument signed by you. He therefore has the right to, and hereby does exercise, his right to cancel any purported transaction. He will hand you his keys to the car, along with a facsimile copy of this letter.

Mr. Kopp also demands that you return to him the trade-in which he left with your personnel. Should you fail to do so immediately, Mr. Kopp will rent a car and hold you responsible for these and other damages. No further notice will be afforded.

Alternatively, Mr. Kopp rejects the tender of delivery. The driver's seat is completely unsatisfactory, and there may be other problems with the car as well.

If you have any questions, please feel free to call.

Sincerely,
Mark H. Steinbach

The dealer agreed to cancel the sale on the spot. This shows the importance of acting quickly, especially before financing arrangements are made.

FILING A LAWSUIT

If the dealer and manufacturer do not respond to the attorney's first few contacts, a lawsuit may be necessary. But this does not necessarily mean a lengthy and expensive trial will result. Sometimes by filing a lawsuit, an attorney can resolve your case without going to trial. Dale Irwin, a lawyer from Kansas City, Missouri was able to settle his client's case against Nissan after the court ordered the auto maker to produce the names and addresses of all owners of cars that accompanied the client's car on the trip from Japan. He wanted this information to rebut Nissan's charge that the defects in the client's car—including body cracks, premature tire wear, alignment problems, and a transmission replacement at 10,000 miles—were caused by customer abuse, because the car was used to deliver bagels! Mr. Irwin's tactic was to show that the defects were caused in transit. Rather than produce the names and addresses of all owners of the cars, Nissan and the dealer settled for a combined recovery of $13,500. In addition, the consumer recovered $4000 from the sale of the car.

The act of initiating litigation against the dealer or manufacturer often brings about a settlement. Joel Borden tried arbitration before taking GM and his dealer to court for the stalling problem in his 1985 Buick Park Avenue. During the hearing, the arbitrator asked the GM representative what he wanted to do, and then ruled accordingly. After this experience Mr. Borden turned to the Center for Auto Safety for lawyer referrals, finding Richard Clifford of New York City. Although GM dragged out the lawsuit for two years in the New York courts, the case was settled just prior to trial for $21,000; the car was four years old with 60,000 miles and was valued at $7500. According to Mr. Borden, "Apparently, their lawyers know how to stall litigation as well as their engineers know how to stall engines. . . . I want to commend Mr. Clifford and would heartily recommend him for any litigation."

A letter from your lawyer can also establish the basis for your suit, the grounds upon which you are claiming relief, and a notice of intended revocation. This creates a framework from which your case can build.

GOING TO TRIAL

If the parties to a lawsuit do not settle before trial, the case usually will be heard in court, where many consumers have been successful. James and Kay Orrell weren't about to give up on their 1976 Ford F-350 pickup that appeared to be a bumper to bumper lemon after four years of complaining to Ford and the dealer. The final straw came when Ford offered only to rebuild the engine at 23,000 miles rather than replace it or the vehicle. So after four years of frustration, the Orrell's hired "lemon lawyer" Phil Clarkson of San Louis Obispo, California to file suit under the state lemon law on April 28, 1980. Nearly five years later, the Orrells got their day in court on June 18, 1985, and won a jury verdict of $82,941. This included the full purchase price and interest, plus attorney fees of $30,720 and civil penalties of $32,569 against Ford and the dealer for their refusal to remedy the lemon as required under the lemon law.

GETTING OUT OF LEGAL HOT WATER

When a lemon owner has taken certain types of direct action, such as withholding car payments or stopping payment on a check, an attorney is usually necessary to untangle the legal tape. For example, if you have paid for a new car by check, and immediately discover it has defects so serious that the car is unfit for use, you can stop payment on the check, return the car to the dealer, and inform him by letter of your refusal to accept the car. (See Chapter 6 for an example of this in the *Zabriskie* case.) An attorney's help is essential here; the dealer may file suit to force you to pay for the car, or may in some places be able to obtain a warrant for your arrest.

A special need for an attorney may arise when you stop payment on a new car because the dealer is unable to repair a defect. For instance, a dispute as to whether a needed repair will be covered under the warranty may leave you without a car for weeks or months, and make continuing payments a serious problem. In this situation, a lawyer may be able to solve the problem and at the same time avoid respossession or damage to your credit rating. **Do not stop payment without consulting an attorney**.

Forest and Barbara Snyder found themselves in legal hot water when they refused to pay the $1,500 balance owed on their Cadillac lemon. The dealer, Cal Connel Cadillac, took them to court. The $1,500 judgment was granted for the dealer, and the Snyders had to pay. But the Snyders consulted with their attorneys in time to file a third-party complaint against General Motors. One of their attorneys, Warren Tipton of Louisville, Kentucky, took the case to trial.

The Snyders's major problem in going to trial was finding an expert who would testify that the car was defective when purchased. The lawyers finally convinced a Louisville service station owner, who had serviced Cadillacs for years, to testify on the Snyders's behalf. During the trial, the Snyders described the broken water hoses, unpredictable windshield wipers, collapsing front wheel and other problems with the lemon. Mrs. Snyder told of repairs costing over $1,000 and of more than $500 in car rentals while her car was being "fixed." She explained how the car broke down on expressways and all the problems associated with the unreliable and unpredictable car. The service station owner testified that the car was not worth the money the Snyders had paid for it. The Snyders persisted against the world's largest auto manufacturer. They beat General Motors in court, winning a $2,500 judgment plus court costs.

FINDING A LAWYER

In finding a lawyer, look for two things: competence and low cost. Surprisingly, some of the best lawyers are free, because they work for programs designed to help the needy, or for nonprofit organizations that look for test cases that can set legal precedents.

Similar aid may be obtained from law students who are participating in a legal clinic, such as the Law Student in Court Program in Washington, D.C. Call the nearest law school to find out whether there is such a program in your area. In many cases, a bright enthusiastic third year law student at a good law school may be more than a match for an overworked and unenthusiastic lawyer retained by a dealer. Legal assistance is available from neighborhood legal service organizations or legal aid societies that are set up to help certain minority and low-income groups. Government-supported legal services programs often provide legal services free of charge. These services are potentially very helpful, but only for those who meet rather strict eligibility standards.

Under the federal Magnuson-Moss Warranty Act and many state lemon laws, you can recover your attorney's fees from the manufacturer for certain kinds of cases. Traditionally, lawyers have been reluctant to handle lawsuits against giant corporations such as the auto companies, because the legal fees can easily be greater than the judgments awarded to the consumers. The Magnuson-Moss Act improves the economic feasibility for consumers to pursue remedies against the auto manufacturer in court.

When Asif Daqiq bought his new 1984 Corvette, he was not expecting the bugs that came with it. It was equipped with a racing suspension which produced a horribly stiff ride, especially over rough pavement. The original engine also required replacement after one month when water got into one of the cylinders, which kept it out of service for 28 days. In addition to these problems, the transmission shifted roughly and the air conditioning ran noisily. Fed up, Mr. Daqiq sold the car for $10,000 three years later and sued GM for his losses. The court awarded him $30,127 in damages ($10,000 of which was punitive) and $27,797 in attorney fees. Without the fee award, his recovery would have been diminished to just over $3,000.

If you do not have a Magnuson-Moss warranty case or a suit under the lemon law, and do not qualify for or cannot find good, free legal assistance, look for a lawyer who is willing to take the case on a contingency or percentage basis, where payment depends on winning.

To find a competent attorney, do some research. Contact consumer groups or faculty members of a law school in your area for guidance to finding a good lawyer. Call a local judge's law clerk for assistance in finding a competent lawyer. Ask friends or business associates to recommend an attorney. Contact the local lawyer's referral service if one exists in your area. The state bar association can also provide you with such information.

A national multi-volumed directory, Martindale-Hubbell, contains short biographical listings of most attorneys and law firms in the country. Available at most public libraries or county law libraries, this and other directories provide valuable information about attorneys. In evaluating attorneys that you do not know, ask them if they have ever sued an auto company or dealer and what happened. Look for interest as well as experience. Too many uninterested lawyers agree to represent consumers in auto cases only to drop the client later. One sign of interest is willingness to take the case on a contingency basis.

WHAT TO EXPECT FROM A LAWYER

In order to best handle your case, the attorney needs to know the facts; exaggerations or distortions will not help you. When you visit the attorney's office, bring all the receipts and records you have collected documenting your case. Be sure not to mark up or alter any documents. Having a summary of the repair history and breakdowns of your car, including any accidents or near accidents you have had, will also help a lawyer evaluate your case. Be sure to bring any service bulletins, articles, recall notices, engineering analyses, and related documentation with you for her or his review.

LEGAL FEES

Ask the attorney to describe the methods of payment so you have a clear understanding of how you will be paying attorney fees and other expenses. Attorneys base their fees on many considerations, including the time required, the difficulty of the case, chances of winning, the amount involved, the method of payment and the attorney's experience, reputation and expertise. The most common fee arrangements include:

1. **Contingent fee:** This fee is a percentage of the damages collected where payment depends on winning. If the case is lost, there is no fee, other than out-of-pocket court costs. The "contingent fee" basis of paying is often used when the client seems to have a good claim but cannot afford to pay a flat fee or hourly rate. Consumers can negotiate with attorneys over the percentage of the recovery the lawyer gets. In negotiating the percentage, be sure you and the attorney understand which of you will pay the investigation and court costs. These expenses are independent of attorneys' fees. Most lawyers' fees require 40% of any reward obtained if the case goes to trial and up to 25% if the case is settled before trial. Such an arrangement should be entered into only where filing a lawsuit is inevitable; settlements arising out of a simple attorney letter should be billed on an hourly basis.
2. **Flat fee:** This fee is based on the attorney's experience with similar cases. Usually applied in routine matters such as drafting a will, the flat fee is not generally used in cases concerning auto problems.
3. **Hourly rate:** This method of payment varies a great deal from one lawyer to another, from city to city and from case to case. Rates generally range between $50 and $175 per hour, with $100 the average rate. For example, settlements arising out of a letter written to the dealership about the client's auto problems should be billed on an hourly basis. If you think the lawyer's hourly rate is too high, shop around. Ask the lawyer for a memo stating the nature of the fee arrangement.

ATTORNEY-CLIENT PRIVILEGE

A good attorney-client relationship is based upon trust. If you do not like or do not trust an attorney, find someone else. You must feel free to discuss everything with the lawyer. A lawyer should be fully informed of all the facts of the case in order for his or her client to obtain the full advantage of our legal system.

The conversations between a lawyer and his or her client are protected by the "attorney-client privilege"—a technical term used in keeping the client's confidence and secrets out of the "evidence" in court. The conversations are also protected by the ethical obligation of a lawyer to guard the confidences and secrets of his or her client. These restrictions on the lawyer's use of a client's private matters help maintain a balance between the nature of the legal system and respect for an individual's privacy.

KEEPING INFORMED

Be sure the attorney understands that you expect to be informed of the progress on your case including deadlines that must be met. A mistake made by many lawyers is the failure to keep the client fully informed. That does not mean daily reports, but it does mean advising the client of what is being done. Ask that copies of the following be sent to you routinely as they are produced:

1. All correspondence
2. Memoranda of fact and law
3. Pleadings and briefs
4. Filing and court deadlines
5. Offers of settlement or negotiation
6. Responsive papers from the other parties involved, including the court.

COMPLAINTS AGAINST ATTORNEYS

Before they are admitted to practice in every state, lawyers must take an oath to uphold the law and comply with the rules of ethics approved by the courts and bar associations. Unfortunately, they do not always live up to this oath. If you have been unfairly treated by an attorney, first try to work out disagreements with your attorney in case they are due to misunderstandings. If you are not satisfied, report him or her to the state bar association. Attorneys are subject to disciplinary proceedings by the state bar upon charges of unethical conduct. If an attorney made a major error, such as failing to file suit before the statute of limitations expired, you can file a malpractice suit against the attorney.

While litigation is often a "last resort" option, with all the added concerns it can bring, it could provide the best resolution of your car complaints. Bringing a successful lawsuit will also establish good case precedent, which makes it easier for future lemon owners to win their cases. This creates excellent incentive for dealers and auto manufacturers to be more responsible for the vehicles they market and produce.

CHAPTER 11

WHEN ALL ELSE FAILS: TELLING THE WORLD ABOUT YOUR LEMON

Man Changes Car Into "Portable Backyard"
Protests GM's Refusal

by James Carbone

A Delmar man yesterday cooked hot dogs and marshmallows where the engine of his 1984 Pontiac Fiero used to be while his dog sat in the driver's seat. Robert Stein Jr. said he turned his car into a "portable backyard" to protest the fact that General Motors refuses to recall the model although 300 of the 126,455 cars sold have burst into flames because of a faulty engine design.

Stein said his car caught fire Oct. 2 while his 16-year-old son, Dan, was driving to school with his girlfriend. "I looked in the rear-view mirror and there were flames shooting out of the engine," said Dan Stein. "At that point, we pulled off the road and got a fire extinguisher and put the fire out."

The Center for Auto Safety said it has received numerous complaints about the cars. Engine rods in the model break and are sent through the engine block releasing oil into the engine, resulting in fires. Some of the fires are caused by engine coolants and oil leaking and splashing on engine components.

Robert Stein said there have been six injuries caused by burning engines of the 1984 Fieros. "The reason there haven't been any fatalities is that there is generally at least a five-minute lapse between the time the car stops running and you notice the flames and the time the gas tank is actually reached by the flames."

Stein says he hopes the government will order a recall of the cars. NHSTA has asked GM to recall the cars, but GM has refused.

"I don't think people should be subjected to driving along and having their cars burst into flames," said Stein. "I think they're [GM] waiting to see what the body count will be. If they can start piling up bodies like charcoal then they'll be much more impressed with the fact that there really is a problem."

The government has the legal authority to order a recall, but has not done so. Stein said GM should pay a flat fee of $6000 to buy the cars back or $7000 allowance toward trade-ins. The auto giant knew of the defective engine rods before the cars were built and changed the design for the 1985 model, he said.

GM spokesman David Hudgens said the auto maker has been unable to determine the exact cause of the fires.

From United Press International
Albany Times-Union, Oct. 1987

In addition to the publicity Mr. Stein received by appearing in newspapers as far away as Japan, GM bought back his converted Fiero for a figure well above the sticker price. He said they quickly crushed the car, which had, among editorial comments painted on its exterior, a choice of "rare, medium, or well-done" on the back fender. After they flattened the car, he asked if he could have it back to use as a coffee table, but "GM didn't think that was very funny."

When writing letters does not help and lawyers want too much money, take your case to the public. Dealers fearing the financial repercussions of adverse publicity are often willing to reconsider complaints to clear the air.

The right of consumers to tell the world about their lemons is rooted in the First Amendment of the U.S. Constitution and in most state constitutions. The First Amendment protects the individual's or group's freedom of expression or "free speech." By making their lemon problems known to the public, consumers occasionally receive replacement cars or refunds from embarrassed dealers.

But, like other tactics that have proven effective against business interests, picketing and the use of lemon signs are controversial. Businesses claim a competing right—the right not to be injured in the conduct of their business. Thus, dealers have occasionally involved the authority of the courts and the police in attempts to halt its use. The courts are divided in upholding the right of consumers to use lemon signs and picket dealerships. The cases frequently turn on a minor point such as whether the picketers were on dealer property or interfering with consumers trying to enter the dealership.

Lemon owners have used many techniques to inform the public about their lemons. The most frequently used tactics include picketing and lemon signs, classified advertisements in newspapers, and flyers handed out to prospective customers at the dealership. A few local consumer groups specialize in picketing dealers. Many successful consumers and groups who have used this tactic have encouraged others with similar complaints to organize "lemoncade" lines of cars covered with lemon signs, driving slowly around the block where the uncooperative dealer is located.

PICKETING

Group picketing and demonstrations are most effective because they dramatize the fact that many consumers share a dissatisfaction with the dealer's unresponsive attitude toward the lemon owner's plight. Some consumer groups have organized on a local basis to provide their members with participants whenever picketing is necessary to protect a member's rights.

One group, the Consumers Education and Protective Association International (CEPA), of Philadelphia, Pennsylvania, has frequently picketed uncooperative dealerships with success. Over its 21-year experience with complaint handling, CEPA has developed a three-step grievance procedure for use in lemon or other consumer complaints: (1) investigate, (2) negotiate and (3) demonstrate.

Jack and Emi Sparks of San Diego, California, members of a group called "Lemon-Aids" won double damages for their Honda lemon, plus court costs and attorneys fees—a total of $13,000—from a unanimous jury verdict. They had been picketing San Diego Honda for over a year, along with fellow Lemon-Aid members, in spite of a court order forbidding them to come within 100 yards of the dealership. Not only did they get relief for their lemon, but the American Civil Liberties Union filed a suit challenging the constitutionality of the restriction of their free speech. The Sparks planned to continue picketing until they got an apology from the dealership and the ACLU's lawsuit was resolved.

LEMON SIGNS

Lemon signs alone frequently bring success to consumers. For example, attach large lemon signs to your car reading: "THIS FIRE-EATER IS A $12,500 LEMON, BOUGHT FROM SHADYDEAL MOTORS. MANUFACTURER'S DEALER CAN'T FIX." If your gripe is against the dealer as well as the manufacturer, you might add to the sign: " SEE ME BEFORE YOU BUY." Then locate your car conspicuously near the dealer's showroom (but not on his property). This expresses your plight in a way that cannot fail to bring a fast reaction.

Donald and Sheryl Clemons of Lexington, Kentucky were fed up with the constant problems with Ms. Clemons's 1988 Dodge Daytona, especially after the dealership refused to fix it. To register their displeasure, they plastered the car with lemons and parked it near the dealer, who had them arrested. This did not stop their protest, however, as the next day they drove the car back and forth in front of the dealership. A jury took just twenty minutes to acquit them of the charge of disorderly conduct. They are now suing Chrysler under the Kentucky lemon law.

The lemon sign tactic has the advantage of being a very flexible device. You can drive around town with the lemon signs prominently displayed, or you can park the car in a public place near the dealership's entrance and go off to work. Or you can stand beside your lemon to explain the signs and pass out leaflets or flyers about your lemon experience.

One successful consumer who painted lemon signs all over his defective car had reached a point where he could no longer put up with the cost and inconvenience of owning a lemon. W.L. Lanzone, Jr. of Long Beach, California, said his troubles began the day he took delivery on the new Chevrolet Blazer. In his letter to the Chevrolet Motor Division Owner Relations Manager, Mr. Lanzone complained about his four-wheel drive lemon:

> Since the purchase of the Blazer on March 13, it has been nothing but trouble. At the end of this coming week it will have been in for repair not less than 38 days.
> So far they have removed the transmission three times, trying to locate an oil leak. They have replaced the valve cover gasket, rear

end seal, rear end housing, rear bearings, two relay horn switches, new oil pan and three new oil pan gaskets. In addition, two weeks ago part of a front spring fell off while driving on the freeway and [last week] . . . the left front shock absorber became detached from the frame.

Mr. Lanzone followed the above lemon sign suggestions in the Center for Auto Safety's first edition of this book, *What to do with Your Bad Car: An Action Manual for Lemon Owners*. He painted on the side of his Blazer:

> **This $5000.00 LEMON! Courtesy of C. Cannon Chevrolet. This is tough as . . . JELLO LEMON.**

and on the back of the vehicle:

> **This $5000.00 LEMON! Please RETURN FALLEN PARTS! This CHEV . . . A 4 letter word!**

Lanzone drove around town with this custom-lemon paint job announcing to everyone that his Blazer was a lemon. Not long afterwards, he succeeded in getting a new Blazer from the dealership.

HOW TO PICKET AND PROTEST WITHIN THE LAW

If you decide to picket or use lemon signs, there are certain guidelines which you should follow to remain within the law. This will help you defend your actions if the dealer requests a court order prohibiting the signs, picketing, demonstrations or other activity, or simply calls the police. First, do not picket or otherwise protest until you have tried to negotiate with the dealer or manufacturer. When this fails, picket.

The purpose of your protest is twofold: to announce to the public that you have been treated unfairly and to settle your complaint. If your goal is to interfere with the dealer's business activity or put him or her out of business, your demonstration, picketing or lemon signs can be legally enjoined or stopped by court order. Thus, avoid statements that might be interpreted as attempting to coerce the dealer into a course of action or into paying you money. Direct your disparagement at the vehicle, rather than at the dealer personally.

The key to legal picketing is to be nonviolent, non-obstructive, and honest. It is advisable to notify the local police and news media ahead of time. Do not interfere with the operation of the dealership's day-to-day activities. Be careful not to block traffic in the street or to prevent people from entering the showroom. You may distribute flyers or leaflets to explain and clarify the message on your signs and car. Above all, do not interfere with the free flow of customers. Let them come to you or to your display. The location of the picketing is as important as the purpose. Generally, you have to remain on public property such as city sidewalks. If you picket or park your car with lemon signs on the dealer's property, you can be thrown off for trespassing.

Picketing a dealer's home or corporate executive residence may work, but it can get you in trouble with the law. If you want to try residential picketing and are willing to fight it out in court, be aware that private residences are generally heavily shielded by the courts when confronted with the issue. Courts weigh the competing interest of a consumer exercising his or her rights of free speech against the individual householder claiming his or her right to privacy and domestic tranquility.

The law does not protect acts of blatant coercion, physical intimidation or destruction of another's property. The courts attempt to find a fair balancing point between the First Amendment right of the picketer to speak out and the property rights of the business being picketed. When First Amendment rights are exercised peacefully and all statements are true, they are most often upheld. (Appendix K traces the history of protest law in greater detail.)

Recognizing that court orders against picketing are difficult to obtain, some dealers resort to libel and slander suits alleging large damages in efforts to get consumers to back down on their protest activities and demands. By and large, these are frivolous suits, particularly if consumers observe the above guidelines for picketing legally.

Consumers can turn these harassing law suits to their advantage if they refuse to back down and instead, counter-claim for their damages. For instance, Mr. and Mrs. J. Waterbury of New Rochelle, New York were sued by their dealer, Tappan Motors of Westchester County, New York. They had parked their Volvo station wagon in front of the dealership with a large sign affixed to the car describing the repair history of the automobile. Ultimately, the dealer dropped his suit. The Waterburys settled for a new Volvo, as well as all expenses incurred in the ownership of the original car.

LAST RITES FOR A LEMON

Few people have gone as far to tell the world about their lemon as Janet Greene of Sacramento, California, a very disgruntled—and persistent—consumer who staged mock funerals in California and Nevada for her 1978 GM diesel truck. Enclosed in the flag-draped casket were lemon shaped balloons with the slogan, "GM Mark of Excellence," released during the "last rites." She invited consumer groups, the media, and diesel owners across the country to attend the ceremonies so that "GM will be forced to wake up and stop producing lemons." Ms. Greene was particularly upset about the chronic break-down of their diesel engine, because during one engine failure (two miles from their home, and only four days after the car had been "repaired") her husband was mugged while stranded on the road waiting for a tow truck. Hoisted above the coffin was a sign reading, "Genuine Craps Mobile. Three engines totalling $12,436.22 and a vehicle failure that nearly robbed me of my life at gunpoint. GM makes business decisions to save a few dollars per vehicle that nearly got me shot!"

She decided to stage the funerals after continually being stonewalled in her attempt to arbitrate for reimbursement of the three engines replaced in the truck. Both GM and the Better Business Bureau claimed she was ineligible for the program by which GM was ordered by the Federal Trade Commission to arbitrate diesel claims, regardless of the age or mileage of the vehicle. (See Chapter 8 for more information on this program.) She also wanted other consumers like herself to learn of the danger created by defective diesel vehicles.

When she tried to get background documents from GM on the FTC consent order, they refused to release them. Undaunted, she wrote to Congressman James Florio, then Chairman of the Subcommittee on Transportation and Tourism in the House of Representatives, to help her secure this information. She sent copies of the letter to several television stations, Ralph Nader, the chairman, general counsel, and consumer relations representative of GM, and Guy and Diane Halferty, the founders of Consumers Against GM.

After her claim was refused in a hearing before the BBB, she sought information from the FTC, Attorney General of California, and GM service bulletins to prove her eligibility, which finally paid off when she was granted a new hearing. She also successfully challenged the limits to which GM agreed to arbitrate, arguing she was entitled by her claims to much greater compensation.

After generating a file of documents, articles, reports, and correspondence four inches thick, GM settled Ms. Greene's claim. Although it seems unlikely she will ever want to repeat the tremendous amount of perseverance and hard work it took her to gain relief, it seems equally unlikely GM will ever want to tangle with her again.

NEWSPAPER AND TELEVISION

In addition to picketing there are other effective ways of conveying your lemon story to the public. If your lemon story has an unusual twist to it, or if you have devised a novel way of getting results, it might be considered newsworthy by the media. Certainly any dramatic reactions to lemon signs you get from local dealers or manufacturers could be material for a consumer-oriented feature writer or TV newsperson.

Unfortunately, the news media are reluctant to run lemon feature stories because they do not want to threaten their lucrative automotive advertising business. For example, K. Schoenberg of Great Neck, New York, called the local newspaper before she put lemon signs on her car and picketed the dealership, Jamaica Lincoln Mercury Corp. She described her frustrating experience in a letter to the Center of Auto Safety:

> The newspapers did not seem to want to touch [it]. The N.Y. Post took pictures and a complete statement. It was never printed. The enclosed ad is no doubt the reason. [A large ad was placed by the Jamaica dealership in the New York Post classified ad section. Part of the ad read, "We're furlongs in front when it comes to pleasing the customer."]

If the major newspapers in your area refuse to run what they admitted was a newsworthy story, send a "letter-to-the-editor" challenging this policy. Send copies of the letter to the Center for Auto Safety and the Federal Trade Commission.

NEWSPAPER ADVERTISEMENTS

If the press will not do a feature on your lemon struggle, try placing an advertisement to generate publicity of your own. A.G. Southern ran the following ad in the *Cornell Daily Sun* in Ithaca, New York:

MY RENAULT STINKS

Does yours? Are you disgusted with your Renault and local authorized service? Add your name to the list of dissatisfied owners. Maybe we can rectify the situation. Call 555-1111 (days) or 555-1112 from 5 to 7 p.m.

Besides announcing your lemon story to the public, the classified advertising tactic is valuable in rounding up other owners of the same model lemon. As a group, you can picket the local dealerships, form a lemoncade and drive through the town or file a lawsuit against the manufacturer of the lemons.

Vicki Huff of Wilton, Connecticut used the following advertisement to locate other Chrysler lemon owners who could help protest. Their reluctant "lemoncade" received national news coverage including a major story in the *New York Times*.

ATTENTION! Aspen and Volare owners. Consumer group forming to seek redress for all manufacturing defects in our 1977 cars. Please call 555-3308 for details.

Advertisements can also be used simply to tell others how defective your car is, as opposed to gathering other lemon owners to form a consumer group. Ralph and JoAnn Sigman of Hays, Kansas ran the following ad in the "Automobiles For Sale" section of the Hays Daily News complete with an illustrated lemon:

How much would you be willing to pay for a 1987 Dodge Charger "lemon?" Benefits include rebuilt engine, new carburetor, new left hand strut, new right hand wheel bearing, new battery, alternator, fuel pump, vapor-lock kit, power module and rear main seal. We will include six low mileage salvage tires plus two salvage tires on vehicle as well as two good tires. Other benefits include a noisy speedometer, gasoline smell in car, poor gas mileage and temperamental hatchback cylinders. Package includes hard starting, loss of power and hissing gas cap. Our "lemon" cost us $9,200 and many days in the shop; what is it really worth? Send replies to:

We've Been Soured
1728 Donald Dr.
Hays, KS 67601

This strategy, like lemon signs and picketing, is protected by the First Amendment right to freedom of expression—as long as you stick to the truth.

A highly publicized lemon advertising campaign was run by David Merrick, the well-known Broadway producer of such shows as "Breakfast at Tiffany's," "Irma La Douce," "Oliver," and "Promises, Promises." In 1967 Merrick spent $14,000 on a Chrysler limousine which proved to be defective. After owning the car several years and investing more than $6,000 in repairs, he realized the company simply could not keep it in running order. So he placed an ad on the front page of the *New York Times* reading, "MY CHRYSLER IMPERIAL IS A PILE OF JUNK. [signed] David Merrick." When further negotiations with Chrysler failed, he had a cartoon ad prepared of a horse pulling a Chrysler into a junkyard. The caption read "Good Riddance!" and his signature was across the bottom. Of the eleven papers he submitted it to, the Miami Herald was the only one to run it. He had no success whatsoever in placing a third ad. Then Harper's Bazaar ran a full page photo of a young couple emerging from a car, captioned: "Whatever David Merrick says about Chrysler Imperial, I like it." When asked whether Chrysler placed the full page photo, Harper's said that it was part of an editorial spread on women's attire. After creating a lot of bad publicity for Chrysler, Mr. Merrick sold the lemon Imperial for $3,750 and switched to taxis.

MAKE A GIFT OF YOUR LEMON TO THE MANUFACTURER'S CHIEF EXECUTIVE

J.M. Robertson of Oneonta, New York, devised a last resort which was imaginative, but not exactly suitable for the average new car buyer.

When Mr. Robertson's new $6900 Chrysler Crown Imperial turned out to be a lemon, he decided to make a gift of it to Chrysler Chairman, Lynn Townsend. He dropped it off at his local dealer together with a check for $94 to cover shipping charges, so that the car would be delivered directly to Mr. Townsend in Detroit "with my compliments."

THE SLOW BURN

Eddie Campos of La Habra, California, had saved for five years to buy his 1970 Lincoln Continental. Despite innumerable trips to different Ford dealers, he could not get his lemon fixed. Problems with the car began the day after he bought it when the entire ignition system fell out. Other problems occurred repeatedly with the ignition, air conditioner, electrical system, power windows, carburetor and front end alignment.

On August 31, 1971, after a year of "constant agony" with the car's mechanical problems, Campos drove the car onto the middle of the lawn at the Ford Motor Company assembly plant, poured gasoline inside, and set it ablaze. A sheriff's deputy on the scene said of Campos: "He was perfectly sober, perfectly rational and completely disgusted."

Campos later hauled the remains of the car to his Los Angeles office and put signs on it reading, "Eddie Campos has a BETTER idea," and "We want cars, NOT Lemons." He also cut a hole in the car's roof and stuck a lemon tree through it. After he set fire to his lemon, Campos received over 120 letters and telegrams in support from other irate lemon owners from at least 30 different states. Many consumers even enclosed contributions.

A REAL HATCHET JOB

When Calvin LeBuffe received no satisfaction from his Oldsmobile dealer, even when the brakes on his 1985 Toronado failed, almost killing his wife, he decided to make a point. He took his brand new car back to the dealership, and hacked it into pieces with a sledge hammer. He, too, was arrested when the dealer called the police and accused him of disorderly conduct. Fortunately, Mr. LeBuffe lives in Connecticut and got John Woodcock to represent him. He is the state legislator who was the chief architect of Connecticut's lemon law, the very first one passed in the nation, and an expert in consumer protection law. When Mr. Woodcock argued to the judge that Mr. LeBuffe's reaction was a totally normal response to the complete lack of satisfaction he received from the dealer for an extremely dangerous car, the case was dismissed on the spot. Spectators in the courtroom rose to their feet and cheered the verdict. GM bought back the car (rather, the pieces of the car) from Mr. LeBuffe to settle his complaint. According to Mr. Woodcock, the dealer was very anxious to keep Mr. LeBuffe's demonstration and eventual vindication as quiet as possible.

POST LEMON FLYERS TO RALLY SUPPORT

Shortly after Dan Shaktman purchased his 1986 Dodge Colt E in San Francisco, he noticed an opaque oily residue on the inside of his windows and windshield. After taking hours to scrub it off, it would reappear in three to seven days. Not only did this make driving dangerous because it impaired his visibility, he feared the substance was toxic. The manufacturer told him to use Ivory soap to remove the residue; when this failed, the dealer suggested a mixture of vinegar and water, which also was unsuccessful. In spite of frequent visits with his zone representative and promises that he would hear further from them, he was given no assistance. Instead, some Chrysler representatives stated they never heard of the problem while in the same breath told him they tested the substance for its toxicity. Convinced the manufacturer was not going to provide a solution he enlisted the support of other Dodge Colt owners by posting flyers reading the following:

DODGE COLT OWNER
Can you see through your windshield?
Constant oily build-up on the glass?
Always cleaning the windows?

YOU'RE NOT ALONE if your Colt is experiencing the frequent and continual build-up of OILY RESIDUE on the INSIDE GLASS SURFACES.

HAZARDOUS DRIVING CONDITIONS? Along with others, have you found that this oily residue is difficult to clean away, returns very rapidly, and is a hazard to safe driving?

TOXICITY? What's it doing to your lungs? Skin? Eyes? Chrysler denies toxicity, but has not publicly produced evidence to support this statement.

RESALE VALUE ADVERSELY AFFECTED?

CLEANING DOES NOTHING? Chrysler and affiliated dealerships acknowledge the problem. They suggest the use of "Ivory Liquid" or vinegar for cleaning, and "Armor-All" for sealing the vinyl upholstery. These "solutions" do not have lasting effect!

* * * *

Help us help you . . . if you have this problem, please contact:

Dan Shaktman
123 Main Street
555-1212

He was able to find several Dodge owners who shared this problem, who joined together to demand that Chrysler find a solution for this safety hazard.

THE TRIP TO THE ZONE OFFICE

Another unusual effort to publicize dissatisfaction with cars was undertaken by a group from the Hartford Auto Research Center, an offshoot of the Nader-sponsored Buyer's Action Center. On March 22, 1972, over twenty disgruntled Chevrolet owners decorated a bus with signs about the manufacturer's unresponsive attitude and went to the Chevy Zone office in Tarrytown, New York. The surprised and embarrassed Chevy people promised to devote serious attention to all the problems described.

AUTO SHOWS

Take your lemon, appropriately labeled, to your local armory or amphitheater the next time the annual auto show is presented. Ask for a prominent location to insure that visitors get a balanced view of what it can mean to own a new car. If you are refused entry, park your lemon near the entrance.

S. Israeloff of Forest Hills, New York, took his Dodge Challenger to the International Auto Show at the New York Coliseum and parked in front. He put a sign in the window reading "4-sale. Please buy this car.

It's a lemon and my Chrysler dealer won't fix it." The *New York Times* reported:

> To a rapt consumer audience, Mr. Israeloff . . . detailed the misfortunes that had befallen him since he took delivery. Only seven of the eight cylinders worked, the distributor was defective, the oil pan was cracked, the water pump broke.
>
> As Mr. Israeloff finished listing his car's ailments, a policeman approached. "I think you'll have to move that car out of here," he said gently.
>
> "I don't know if it will start," said Mr. Israeloff.

Before he left, Mr. Israeloff won a promise of an investigation from a Chrysler official attending the show.

LAST RESORT RESULTS

Many car owners outraged in this way have come up with these and other inventive last resort measures. Politic and impolitic, we have presented them all here in the hope that one or more may be appropriate for you when all else has failed.

If you have suggestions to add to this list, please mail them to:

Center for Auto Safety
2001 S Street, N.W.
Washington, DC 20009

for possible inclusion in future editions of this book.

Imaginative last resort measures might succeed for you. However, they fail to bring about any basic change in the situation giving rise to the problem in the first place. To score successes benefiting wider numbers of consumers, and to bring about changes in the system which generates the abuses, it is absolutely essential to broaden your base, join others, and eventually to organize.

CHAPTER 12

BEFORE BUYING A CAR

June 1, 1977

Dear Mr. Nader:

I purchased an Oldsmobile as a new car and paid a new-car price. I still have the written contract and bill of sale. Lately, Miss America decals have been showing through the paint on both car doors of my convertible! I went to the dealer from whom I bought the car and asked what they would do about this. I was told to have my lawyer contact theirs. I feel either the dealer from whom I bought the car, or GMAC, has defrauded me by selling me a new car which has obviously been represented on my written contract and bill of sale as demonstrator, or some other classification other than new.

Yours truly,
/s/
A.L. Draughton
Huntington, WV

Consumers experience auto problems of all types. Some problems show up right away. Others show up many years later, as did the Miss America decals in the above letter. Some auto ownership pitfalls can be avoided through wise and prepared shopping. Other problems simply cannot be anticipated, even by the best prepared consumer.

Before buying a new or used car, you should decide whether you need a car at all. In these days of soaring insurance, gasoline, parking and car prices, a second car or even a first car may cost too much. Individuals living in large urban areas may well find it cheaper and easier to rely on public transportation, taxis and rental cars rather than buying a car.

COSTS OF OWNERSHIP

The escalating costs of buying, owning and operating a car push many consumers to the edge of their resources. The top expense in owning a car is a hidden toll: depreciation, the difference between the price paid for a vehicle and its trade-in value. From January 1988 to January 1989 depreciation costs increased from an average $1,778 to $2,018, according to figures released by the American Automobile Association (AAA). A study by the Hertz rental car company estimated the total depreciation cost for a 1987 compact car, bought new and driven 10,000 miles annually for five years, at 17.7 cents per mile or $1,744 per year. According to AAA, the total cost in 1989 for owning and operating a new car driven 15,000 miles was $4,595. The longer you keep a car and the further you drive it, the lower the cost per mile to own and operate. For example, if the typical intermediate 1987 model is driven 10,000 miles a year then traded after the first year, the cost-per-mile averages 62.5 cents. If the car is kept for five years, this costs falls to 51 cents for the same rate of annual mileage. If you keep the car for the full expected life of 12 years, the annual cost drops to about 30 cents per mile. The lower depreciation rate for an older car offsets higher maintenance expenses.

Other expenses of owning a car include gas and oil, maintenance and repairs, insurance and registration, finance charges on auto loans, parking and tolls. Operating costs for a small car are much less than those for a standard-size car.

For car owners who wish to reduce new car purchase and operating costs, shop wisely for the best price and interest rate on your new car. Select options that increase gas mileage such as five-speed manual transmissions; use radial tires, join a car pool, keep your car well-tuned, obtain insurance tailored to your particular needs and look for insurance discounts given to good drivers and for safety equipment like airbags. Avoid adding power-robbing features to a small car, in order to take advantage of its improved fuel economy.

One way to reduce the costs of car ownership is to buy a used car, since most depreciation on a car occurs during its first three years. Buying a three- to four-year old car and keeping it for three years will save a consumer at least $4,800 over buying a new car and keeping it for the same period.

MATCHING A CAR WITH YOUR NEEDS

Through television, radio and print advertising, and with the additional help of extensive market research and glossy sales brochures, auto manufacturers bombard consumers with images of the perfect car. The dealer reinforces the selling efforts of the manufacturer by convincing you that the car is even more than the answer to your lifelong dreams, for only $159 over invoice. However, all references to safety, quality, and the dealer's responsibility to prepare the car properly and honor the warranty is usually glossed over with glowing generalities. It is up to you to introduce these criteria into your dialogue with the salesperson.

One of the foremost factors in selecting a new car is size—full-size, intermediate, compact or subcompact. Choosing the right size car is at present a compromise between economy and maneuverability (which you can get with small cars) or more comfort, capacity and safety (with the larger cars). For most consumers, an intermediate-sized car is the largest they will need. Fortunately, government-run crash tests indicate many cars are getting safer. For example, the 1988 Ford Taurus and Mercury Sable showed remarkable improvement from previous years in NHTSA's New Car Assessment Program (NCAP). Modifications to the steering column, steering wheel assembly, front sheet metal and seat belt system allowed those cars to easily meet the injury criteria for head and chest. Small cars that weigh less than 2,500 pounds can be made safer than present large cars with currently available safety technology such as advanced airbags. (See Chapter 17 on Auto Safety.)

A good example of a safer compact car is the Ford Escort, rated one of the five best subcompacts in NCAP crash test performance. The NCAP tests, conducted by NHTSA, indicate that driver and passenger would survive a frontal impact at 70 MPH into a similar-size parked car without severe injury or death. The Escort features a motorized shoulder belt system. In fact, consumers will find a well-designed compact car will provide more than adequate internal space while offering very economical operation.

SELECTING THE CAR: SAFETY FEATURES

Despite lip-service which auto designers pay to safety, many features of "modern" cars cause accidents or maim and kill a large proportion of accident victims. Even now, with the results so plainly evident, the auto makers build and advertise family vans with inadequate occupant protection and egg-shell bumpers, recreational vehicles without seat belts for all seats, small utility trucks with high rollover propensity, and many more deadly features. The trivial gimmickry of hidden windshield wipers creates a cavity which clogs up with snow, ice, and debris; the raised sheet metal edge that forms the top of the cavity may slice rearward like a neck-level guillotine in a serious crash. Most of these suicidal options were originated by stylists, and heavy advertising has led an unsuspecting public to pay stiff extra costs for them.

The enormous cost of motor vehicle accidents due to the lack of safety is readily seen in the National Highway Traffic Safety Administration's estimate that in 1986, the cost of motor vehicle accidents exceeded $74 billion. This estimate includes such costs as lost wages, medical expenses, insurance administration costs, property damage, legal fees and court costs. The enormous cost of motor vehicle accidents reflects the outrageous number of people maimed and killed. On our nation's roads and highways, an accident involving injury occurs every 18 seconds, while one involving deaths occurs every 11 minutes. Each year, nearly 50,000 people die in motor vehicle accidents.

Safer cars not only will reduce this appalling total but also will save consumers money. Already some insurance companies such as Allstate offer lower insurance premiums for cars that have less severe accidents. Most insurers offer discounts up to 30 percent for cars with airbags. If consumers do get in an accident with a safer car, the likelihood of severe injuries and costly medical bills is reduced. Safer cars in general mean less diversion of police, ambulance and fire services, fewer children tragically orphaned by accidents, and a decrease in the number of paralyzed adults whose productive lives are cut short. Although all cars must meet minimum federal safety standards, some cars, such as the Buick Electra, are much less safe than others. NHTSA administers crash tests to new models each year under its New Car Assessment Program (NCAP). Each model is scored in three categories—head injury criteria, chest acceleration, and femur load (force) exerted on the upper leg. You can obtain NCAP results from NHTSA's Auto Safety Hotline and in *The New Car Book* each year by Jack Gillis.

To select a car which does more than just meet minimum federal standards, use the following checklist.

1. Visibility for the Driver
a. Adequate Field of Vision
The driver should be able to see a small child standing fairly close to any part of the car. In backing up the car, wide panels between the rear window and the side windows require as much use of the ears as the eyes and make lane changing unnecessarily dangerous.

b. Distortion
Vision through all windows must be clear and undistorted. The rakish angle of many windshields seriously obstructs vision. Fastback rear windows also often distort vision, and easily collect dirt and snow.

c. Reflections and Glare
When sitting in the car in the sunlight you should see no reflections (in front and rear windows) of the dashboard or the rear deck. There should be no glare from the wiper blades or other chrome ornaments. In many cars, when the sun is shining from overhead, reflections become so bad that safe vision is impossible. Even when reflections are minor, they can dangerously increase eyestrain and fatigue.

d. Rear Window Defroster
The rear window should be equipped with an electric defroster (optional on some cars, standard on others) and, if available, a rear wiper and washer. These accessories help insure clear vision in inclement weather.

e. Rearview Mirrors
The driver's outside mirror should be far enough forward to let you use it without turning your head too far to the side. Passenger side mirrors have become standard on most new cars and a worthwhile option. The inside mirror must be high enough not to obstruct forward vision, and low enough to allow you to see through the rear window when the trunk is loaded. (Have two people sit on the rear bumpers to check this.)

f. Non-Obstructing Headrests

Headrests should not block the line of vision through the rearview mirror, nor should they be bulkier than necessary. The Volvo ladder-shape offers good visibility and good protection for the head and neck.

g. Windshields

Fully tinted windshields (as distinguished from those with a band of tint running only along the top edge) are unacceptable because they drastically reduce dusk and night vision, making pedestrians and obstacles hard to see. The combination of a windshield with standard tinting and the usual 60-degree tilt cuts incoming light by 35%, and worse yet, it cuts red light (important to the partially colorblind) by 51%. Cars can usually be ordered with clear-glass windows unless tinted glass is standard in those vehicles.

2. Visibility of the Car

a. Raised Tail Lights

The higher the tail lights are, the better. Stop lights at roof level (as on school buses) and those at rear deck levels can help to prevent rearend chain collisions. High mounted brake lights are required on all new cars starting in 1986 but are still not required on light trucks and vans. According to the NHTSA studies, these brake lights reduce rear collisions in urban areas by up to 40 percent.

b. Turn Signals

Side, front, and rear turn signals must be large enough to be plainly visible and, like tail lights, must be as high as practical.

c. Color

Light-colored, single-tone cars are more easily distinguished from the surroundings by other drivers. Studies made by the New York Port Authority have shown that light-colored cars have significantly fewer collisions. According to one study released by the Minnesota Department of Safety, the safest color for an automobile is a greenish yellow shade. As a general rule red and black are the worst; cream, yellow, and white are best.

3. Operating Equipment

a. Brakes

The brakes must be able to stop the car repeatedly from high speeds without any noticeable deterioration in effectiveness. Brake fade must be low enough that even the weakest driver will still be able to stop the car with ease. Ideally the brakes should bring the car to a controlled stop from high speeds even with the gas pedal pressed to the floor, as if the accelerator were stuck.

The oldest and simplest rule for brake design, which has been used for many years to calculate minimum values of braking strength, states that brake horsepower must be greater than engine horsepower. This means that the brakes should be capable of stopping the engine even when the gas pedal is floored. (We do not advise testing your brakes for this capability—you'll be in trouble if the brakes flunk the test.) Larger engines, of course, require larger brakes; your salesperson can advise you whether heavier-duty or four-wheel disk brakes may be available on the car. The brakes must be stronger than the engine, not only when they are applied, but also until the car comes to a complete stop. If the brakes fade, they must still be able to stop the car, even with a fairly weak driver.

Disc brakes are standard equipment on the front wheels of cars, vans and light trucks sold in the U.S. These tend to resist fading and improve directional stability when compared to all-drum brakes. Power assist is virtually universal, but would be most worthwhile only if brake effort seems excessive without it. Four-wheel disc brakes are standard or available on several vehicles and are worth considering especially if the vehicle will be driven hard or used to tow a trailer.

Some newer models provide an antilock braking system **(ABS)**. On wet pavement or during an emergency stop, a computer senses that wheels are locking before a skid and automatically pumps the brakes, preventing loss of control. First offered on some Chrysler models in 1971, antilock braking systems are only offered in 3% of the cars sold in the U.S., primarily in models costing over $20,000. However, one Chrysler official has predicted that they will be available by 1991 in all but the Omni and Horizon models.

b. **Suspension**

American cars used to be so softly sprung that they needed heavy-duty, police car type suspension to be safe for emergency maneuvers. Now that cars are smaller and lighter due to regulations on fuel economy, fewer models require heavy-duty suspension. The suspensions of downsized vehicles are much tighter, thus improving their emergency handling.

c. **Power Steering**

Most cars of compact size or larger come with standard-equipment power steering, and some subcompacts offer it optionally. To determine whether power would be a good option, try parking the car in a line of cars parallel to the road. If you can easily back in and pull out without power steering, that particular car may not need it, but if you need the muscles and arms of a gorilla to park, you'll probably want power steering. Also, check the vehicle's handling in normal driving maneuvers; if the manual steering requires a seemingly large amount of turning in quick maneuvers, or if emergency handling is sluggish, you may want to invest in power steering. Cars with power steering must be easy to steer if the engine stalls when driving since stalling causes loss of power assist. This is fairly easy to test—while coasting through a large empty parking lot, with plenty of extra room to spare, shut off the engine and attempt to maneuver the car quickly.

d. **Tires**

From the vehicle's load capacity which is usually listed on the side of the driver's door or on the inside of the glove compartment door, determine the passenger and luggage load capacity for the size of tires on the car. Allow at least 150 pounds per passenger and 50 pounds each for heavy suitcases. Some cars, especially station wagons, are delivered with tires of such a low weight-carrying capacity that the car can only be partly loaded before an unsafe tire load is reached.

e. **Gauges and Controls**

All gauges and warning lights must be placed, marked, and lit so that they can be easily read day and night. You should be able to reach all the controls easily with your shoulder belt fastened and to operate them without taking your eyes from the road. Controls should be readily distinguishable from one another, to prevent potentially tragic mistakes.

f. **Seat Adjustments**

If unusually short or tall drivers will be using the car, make sure the seat can adjust to allow good vision and proper pedal reach for all of them.

g. **Engines**

At least for the present, 5000-pound cars with their gas-guzzling 400-plus cubic inch engines have been virtually banished from the U.S. marketplace. Smaller engines, properly tuned, provide enough reserve power for safe passing maneuvers. An overpowered car is uneconomical and can be unstable during wet-weather driving and hard acceleration, or uncontrollable if the accelerator sticks. Since the auto companies began to eliminate hundreds of pounds of unneeded weight in their cars in the late 1970's, a V-6 is adequate for all automobiles—even those equipped with air-conditioning. A 4-cylinder engine is adequate for intermediates, compacts and subcompacts. If you need to pull heavy loads frequently, a small V-8 such as 301 or 305 cubic inch engine should be satisfactory. Multivalve engines with four valves per cylinder improve both fuel economy and performance. A 16-valve 4-cylinder engine can outperform a standard 6-cylinder engine.

4. **Minimum Crash Protection**
a. **Bumpers**

Bumpers should be solid enough to withstand pushing and low-speed collisions. If the bumpers are up against the body of the car, minor collisions will push the bumpers into the sheet metal, causing expensive damage.

Bumpers on 1980-82 model year automobiles were required to meet a federal safety standard that prohibited all damage in 5 MPH front and rear barrier impact tests and 3 MPH corner impact tests to the car and bumper itself. Despite the widely recognized effectiveness of this standard, it was relaxed in 1983 to levels even below the pre-1980 standard. Legislation is pending in the U.S. Congress to restore the 5 MPH bumper standard for 1992 and later cars and to extend it to light trucks and vans.

b. **Seat/Shoulder Belts and Passive Restraints**

The best restraint system now available is the passive restraint system, which includes automatic seat belts and airbags. A passive restraint is a device that protects occupants of a car without requiring them to buckle up or take any other action. The benefits of an airbag system have been known since the early 70's when General Motors first discovered a 50% reduction in death and injury rates when they were deployed. Airbags are designed to protect front seat occupants in the event of a frontal crash and are effective even if a safety belt is unfastened. Once used, the bag must be replaced.

Some manufacturers offered some sort of passive restraint system—either automatic safety belts or airbags—prior to enactment of mandatory legislation. Automatic safety belts, by their nature, curb reluctance on the part of consumers to wear belts at all. The motorized versions move across a track when the car door is open or closed to allow entry or exit. Non-electric belts are attached to the door, also moving in and out of place as the door is opened or closed.

Seat and shoulder belts make driving about five times as safe as driving without the belts. Two types of seat belts have been criticized by a consumer group, however, for causing serious injuries in the event of sudden stopping. These are rear seat lap belts and the type of shoulder harness which operates much like a windowshade. Rear lap-only belts allow "jackknifing" of rear seat occupants in frontal crashes, which considerably aggravates spinal and internal injury. The "windowshade" harness allows a passenger to move but locks tightly when the brakes are suddenly depressed or the car decelerates; these devices can introduce too much slack into the harness, thus aggravating crash injuries.

Following European and Japanese auto manufacturers, U.S. automakers began installing rear shoulder belt harnesses in most 1989 cars. Those who have not done so voluntarily are now required to do so by a rule issued under a new Federal Motor Vehicle Safety Standard. Effective December 1989, the rule requires all passenger cars manufactured after that date to be equipped with rear-seat lap shoulder belts.

5. Other Features
a. Pedestrian Gougers

Five years before Congress passed the National Traffic and Motor Vehicle Safety Act, a nine-year-old girl was riding her bicycle near her suburban home outside Washington, D.C., when she struck the rear bumper of a parked automobile. The collision hurled her flush into the sharp, protruding tail fin on the 1961 Cadillac, and she was fatally impaled. Years later, in April, 1989, the son of Senator Albert Gore, Jr. (Tenn.) was struck and seriously injured by a passing car as he left a Baltimore Orioles baseball game.

Such tragedies are not unusual accidents. Hundreds of thousands of pedestrians, cyclists and motorcyclists are injured every year in collisions with vehicles—stationary or moving—whose sharp exterior ornamentation inflict additional injury. These protruding ornaments— blade-like front fenders, cutting grill patterns, sharp headlight eyebrows and other designs— not only threaten pedestrians, but are also purely stylistic in purpose. While many of the worst protrusions such as Cadillac's lethal tail fins of the late 1950's and early 1960's have disappeared, there are still sharp protrusions which should be barred at a life and cost savings to consumers.

No new car buyer plans on running into any pedestrians, but few can avoid the pedestrian who runs into them. Your chances of striking a pedestrian are much higher than you might expect—in 1978, about 8,000 pedestrians were killed by automobiles and another 100,000 were injured. Recently, the U.S. Senate passed legislation requiring NHTSA to complete a rulemaking within two years which would consider ways to minimize injury caused by vehicle components. Until effective measures are enacted, avoid models with sharp corners or protrusions on the front end. High front ends on cars tend to push pedestrians under the wheels, so cars with lower flattened bumpers should be chosen. Luckily for pedestrians, the rounded contours of more aerodynamically styled current cars may inflict fewer injuries on those unfortunate enough to end up being hit.

b. **Gas Tanks**

Gas tank location is an important safety consideration on any car, new or old. Two gas tank locations are generally acknowledged as safer than others. One of these is behind the rear seat area, above the rear axle, with a firewall to separate the fuel tank from the rear seat lest fuel escape from a ruptured tank into the passenger compartment. The other preferred location is under the rear seat, ahead of the rear axle. Many vehicles with front wheel drive use the latter design, which locates the fuel tank far forward of the rear of the car. Avoid designs that locate the fuel tank close to the rear of the car or near potential puncture sources. The late Ford Pinto is an example of a car with poor gas tank design. Also, stay clear of vehicles that expose fuel lines or fittings within the trunk area, or vulnerable fuel filler location.

UNNECESSARY OPTIONS

Optional equipment on cars all too often adds to the price of the car and causes excessive repair bills. The auto industry pushes options because they boost profits. Even a President of the National Automobile Dealers Association, Hugh R. Gibson, criticized many options as wasteful and unwanted by consumers but forced on them by the auto manufacturers:

> Another way for our manufacturers to cut the price of cars to the consumer is to stop putting unneeded and unwanted accessories and gimcracks on cars, regardless of whether the public needs or wants them.

These are what the manufacturer calls "mandatory options." That's a funny phrase, isn't it? "Option" means you have a choice. "Mandatory" means "you have to." So, "mandatory option" means there is a choice but it is the "manufacturer's choice" and the public **has** to accept it.

A typical car with radial tires, bumper guards, side moldings, day-night mirrors, and fancy interiors can run up the price $400 to $500 higher than it needs to be.

I call on our manufacturers to stop loading their cars with fancy gadgets that add hundreds of dollars to the cost.

Avoid delicate options with a high frequency-of-repair record, such as power seats, automatic speed controls, eyelid head-lamp covers, power windows, power antennas, sun roofs and moon roofs. (See Chapter 11 for further discussion on "delicate options.")

One method of selling options is to offer them in "packages" or "groups." You end up paying for unwanted frills in order to get the equipment you really want. Option packages pad the profits of the dealer and manufacturer, and frustrate consumers who seek to order only the times they want. *Consumer Reports* finds that adding extras can inflate the sticker price by as much as 20%. Often the only new cars available from the dealer's lot are "loaded" with options. If you are willing to wait for delivery and if the options you want don't come only in expensive packages, you can special order a car with only the options you really want instead of settling for the extravagantly equipped cars available for immediate delivery. This simply means planning a month or two ahead on buying a new car. The wait will mean initial savings of hundreds of dollars in the price of the car and (a later savings of) **fewer** costly repair trips to the garage.

SERVICE CONTRACTS

Optional extended warranties or service contracts are available through many dealerships. There are different types, including those offered by auto manufacturers and independent insurance companies. Coverage and costs vary from plan to plan. For example, some auto companies offer extended warranty coverage to 7 years/84,000 miles for a one time payment of about $750, 36 months/36 thousand miles for a one-time payment of about $100 to $300, depending on the make and model. Some insurance companies offer renewable yearly contracts. Basically, these plans are a form of insurance in case the need for a costly repair occurs after the regular warranty expires. If you live in a strong consumer protection state, such as Maryland, with statutes preventing car companies from limiting their implied warranties, you are better off without the service contract. Even in other states you could do better by putting the money in a high-interest money account than in an extended warranty contract from which it may be difficult to collect.

Mr. and Mrs. Lloyd of Garfield Heights, Ohio had an eye opening experience with the five year extended warranty they had purchased for their 1980 Chevy Citation. The starter mounting bolts had been sheared off the engine block with 13,000 miles on the odometer. Upon checking the terms of the warranty, the Lloyds found the engine and the starter in the list of covered items and also noticed that the bolts were not listed among those items **not** covered. However, when they filed their claim with the warranty company, Servicegard denied that the bolts necessary to mount the starter to the engine were covered, although the engine and starter were. The Lloyds eventually recovered the cost for these bolts after the Center for Auto Safety contacted the warranty company on their behalf.

When considering service contracts, be sure to ask the following questions:

1. What repairs does the policy cover? What is excluded from coverage?
2. What is the procedure for filing a claim?
3. Is the policy transferable to a subsequent buyer of the car during the coverage period?
4. What are the requirements in vehicle maintenance and repair parts before a claim is honored?
5. Where can you get repairs under the contract?
6. Does the policy begin with the purchase of the car or after the manufacturer's written warranty expires? Remember that the car comes with a written warranty for at least 12,000 miles or 12 months, whichever comes first.
7. Does the company have the option to drop the service contract when your car gets older and in need of more repair?
8. Does the policy require prior authorization in order to perform

the repairs? What is the normal lag time between a request for authorization and the company's response? What happens if the car breaks down on a long trip?

9. Is the customer expected to pay for completed service and then file for reimbursement?

WHAT VALUE TO GIVE TO EPA FUEL ECONOMY RATINGS

All new cars should have an EPA/DOE fuel economy label on the window which shows expected gas mileage for city and highway driving. When the EPA ratings first came out in 1975, they were good estimates of real world fuel economy even though they were based on laboratory tests. But by 1979, the auto companies had learned how to beat the ratings system so well that EPA dropped publication of the **highway** ratings and used only the city rating until 1985 when both city and highway ratings were reinstated. Ironically EPA permits the car companies to continue to use the inflated ratings to determine compliance with gas mileage standards but deflates the city rating by 10% and the highway rating by 22% for the ratings released to the public.

HOW TO CHOOSE A DEALERSHIP

The best possible dealership is one convenient to your home or place of work and one that has a solid reputation in sales and service. The number of trained or licensed mechanics can be a good indicator of efficient service. A good dealership performs warranty work when needed without giving consumers unnecessary delay. If you still cannot judge, ask the dealer a few questions, such as:

Do you give customers copies of warranty repair work orders?

Is warranty work as high a priority here as non-warranty work?

Do you fully prepare every new car before delivery? Do you give customers copies of that work when it is completed? How much does it cost the customer?

When a car is clearly a lemon, how do you handle it?

Before Buying a Car

What do you do if the car is delivered with many differences from the one the consumer ordered?

When a car is recalled, do you have any trouble obtaining parts?

See if you can get any answers in writing. Such questioning provides the consumer with more information to consider before ordering the car from that dealer.

If you choose a dealership which is 30 miles away just to save $100 on the purchase price, you may regret having done this when you must drive out there every time the car needs warranty work. Many local consumer groups keep listings of recommended dealers, so check with such groups before you buy. Other sources of information on dealers include state and local consumer protection offices as well as the experiences of your friends and business associates. Check with the local Better Business Bureau if no other source of reliable information is available. An excellent example of how a local consumer group can help is the Washington Center for the Study of Services which publishes a report, *Washington Consumer's Checkbook on Cars*, on the quality and cost of repair at local dealers and independent garages in the Washington, D.C. area.

CHAPTER 13

HOW TO AVOID
BUYING A LEMON

Chrysler's Woes

Publicity on Recalls,
Stiffer Competition
Hurt No. 3 Car Maker

Sales of Volare, Aspen Sag
  As Auto Market Softens,
  Others Offer Compacts

Anger at "Lemons" Awards

By Leonard M. Apcar

Last summer Vicki Huff of Wilton, Conn., embarked on a six-week vacation that she won't forget. She loaded her two young children and camping gear into her sparkling yellow, four-day-old Dodge Aspen station wagon and headed west.

But within 100 miles of starting out, she says, the Aspen engine's rocker arms began to rattle, and eventually had to be replaced. As she drove along a Kentucky highway at about 50 miles an hour, the hood flew up, blocking the windshield.

In Colorado, the horn, lights and turn signals all conked out at once. In Iowa the transmission gears jammed, and twice along the way the battery went dead. Mrs. Huff says she spent a major part of the vacation hopscotching around the country-side from one dealership to another—10 in all—of Chrysler Corp., maker of the Aspen.

"My kids saw more of Chrysler showrooms than the sights of the United States," she says.

The Wall Street Journal.
January 18, 1978, First Page

When Vicki Huff returned home, she took out a local newspaper ad soliciting complaints from other Aspen and Volare owners. She received a huge response. The owners banded together, holding a "lemoncade" protest, then a "lemonstration" and even began to prepare a class action lawsuit. Chrysler engaged in four massive recalls of these cars which the Center for Auto Safety named the "Lemon of the Year."

Even the most knowledgeable and prepared shopper can end up with a lemon, but careful preparation and planning can improve your chances of avoiding one. Learn all the important facts about the car you are considering before entering the dealer's showroom. (Appendix Q contains a list of basic references in new and used car buying.)

Try to find a dealership that is conveniently located and has a solid reputation for service. (See Chapter 10 for tips on finding a good dealership.) Do not rush into a deal—the salesperson knows how to exert pressure on you to close the sale, but don't feel the need to rush. Take time to shop around and test drive the models you are considering. Do not hesitate to ask the salesperson for a full breakdown of the cost. You have the right to ask as many questions as you want, so prepare yourself in advance. Remember, you're investing a lot of money in a new car. If the salesperson does not cooperate, go somewhere else, or ask the sales manager for a different salesperson.

ORDERING A NEW CAR

Because of an imbalance in bargaining positions between car makers and car buyers, many of the usual remedies that a consumer would follow when a new product turns out to be defective are not available. It is almost impossible to return or exchange a new car without trouble. Almost any other product you purchase can be easily returned if it doesn't work, but not defective cars. One reason is that the contract you sign for a new car deprives you of **most** of the rights and powers that you would otherwise have (see Chapter 6 for those rights you **do** have).

Though it is unlikely you will succeed (let us know if you do), you can protect your rights by substituting the Consumer's New Car Order Form proposed in Appendix L for the dealer's form. Unfortunately, the dealer's freedom to vary the terms of the contract with you is limited by the franchise imposed by the manufacturer. This proposal to substitute forms tells the dealer that you are not happy with the contract offered and will suggest ways in which the contract can be made more acceptable to consumers. After all, why should dealers write the contract all in their own favor? Exert some old-fashioned bargaining power as a customer.

There are other less ambitious precautions you can take when you order which may help you avoid a lemon.

1. Avoid New Models

Any new model vehicle in its very first year of production usually turns out to have a lot of defects, particularly U.S.-built models. Often the manufacturer is not able to remedy the defective design problems until the second, third or even fourth year of production, if then. When General Motors came out with its heralded 1980 X-car led by the Chevrolet Citation, GM proclaimed it to be the front-runner of a whole new generation of front-wheel-drive cars that would recapture sales from the Japanese with its advanced engineering and quality. Instead, the X-car proved to be nothing more than an advanced lemon that suffered 13 recalls within the first year including failure of steering gear mounting plate on 161,225 vehicles and possible fire from leaking transmission fluid hoses on 224,892 vehicles. While GM apparently handled the teething problems, it never seemed to get a handle on the X-car's most chronic defect, rear brake lockup which could throw the car into an uncontrollable spin. During its protracted litigation with the National Highway Traffic Safety Administration (NHTSA) on the rear brake lockup defect, GM discontinued the X-car at the end of the 1985 model year. The lesson here is that if the manufacturer has not been able to work out a new car's problems by the third year of production, the car will likely be a lemon forever.

2. Delicate Options

Avoid delicate options with a poor frequency-of-repair record, such as power seats, air conditioners, cruise control, turbo-charged engines, power windows, power antennas, elaborate sound systems, sun roofs and moon roofs. Several years ago, Ralph Nader obtained an internal Ford list of warranty repairs that ranked moon roofs, manual sun roofs, electric sun roofs, and power windows as first, third, fifth and sixth, respectively, in repair frequency.

Not only do options like these break down continually and require expensive repairs, they also needlessly run up the sticker price and operating costs of a car. For example, air conditioning costs $750 or more and can detract 2-4 MPG from a car's fuel economy. Cruise control can cost up to $245 and has been linked to instances of sudden acceleration. For a good discussion on desirable versus undesirable options, see *Consumer Reports*, April 1989, "Which Options to Choose."

3. Dealer's Checklist

Request a copy of the dealer's predelivery service and adjustment check sheet (or make-ready list) at the time your new car is delivered. Write the request directly on your new car order. This request informs the dealer that you are aware of the dealer's responsibility to check your car for defects. This may result in the performance of a more careful predelivery inspection when your car arrives. If the salesperson professes ignorance of the check list, show him or her a copy of the exemplary list reproduced in Appendix N.

4. Warranty

As explained more fully in Chapter 6, "Your Legal Rights," the Magnuson-Moss Warranty Act requires all written warranties to be easy to read and understand, but does not require them to be fair to consumers. As a result, auto warranties still protect the manufacturer much more than the consumer.

Since the warranty, like the new car order form, deprives consumers of many of their rights, ask the dealer to use a fairer warranty, such as the one proposed in Appendix M. Although the dealer may say the manufacturer won't allow it, press anyway, and tell us if you succeed. Some dealers, as a sales pitch, will give a longer-lasting warranty, valid only at those dealerships.

5. Tire Warranty

Most major auto makers do not give warranties on tires; they leave that to the tire manufacturer. Specific warranty information and tire adjustments must be obtained from the tire manufacturer's distributors, dealers or retail stores. Ask the auto dealer for a copy of the tire warranty.

PICKING UP YOUR NEW CAR

1. Is It Ready to Drive? The Make-Ready Procedure

The dealer is the final step in the auto manufacturer's inspection procedure. The condition in which cars are delivered to a dealership depends on the manufacturer. For various reasons, a car may sit on a manufacturer's lot for a long time only to be sent to the dealer with signs of exposure to the weather or stolen parts. One dealer contacted the Center about a Jeep which arrived with the dashboard virtually destroyed; before it could be sold the truck was in the dealer's body shop for days. Other times, demand for particular vehicles rushes delivery. The same dealer tells the story about one vehicle delivered to his lot with a different model name on each side. Many cars used to develop paint flaws after exposure to the sun. Fading and paint spotting were eventually attributed to battery acid which had dripped from one car to another during transport. A new paint problem affecting dealers, particularly in the Northeast, is damage from acid rain when cars are left unprotected on lots for long periods.

Manufacturers provide the dealer with an inspection list for each vehicle delivered to the showroom, and reimburse the dealer for any necessary repairs or adjustments, including filling fluid levels and tightening loose parts. Have the salesperson or another authorized representative of the dealer get and initial the predelivery service and adjustment check sheet (make-ready list) as an assurance that the make-ready was actually completed. But don't just go by the make-ready list—inspect the car yourself carefully, before you sign anything saying that you accept it for delivery. See below for detailed steps on inspecting your car.

The important thing for a consumer to realize is that a new (or used) car may be so defective—an actual lemon—that the consumer should "reject" it as soon as possible. You can inform the dealer of your rejection, either before or after taking physical possession of the car, as long as "rejection" occurs within a reasonable time for inspection. Or you can "revoke acceptance" of the car after the reasonable time for inspection has expired. (The legal right of "rejection" is discussed later in this chapter, while "revocation of acceptance" is discussed in

Chapter 6.) Once you take delivery (physical possession) of a lemon, in most cases you will not be able to return it or get a refund of the purchase price without a legal struggle. At the point the consumer takes possession of the car, he or she loses the best leverage over the dealer—the threat of buying an acceptable new car elsewhere.

There are three ways to determine the condition of a car—(1) a diagnostic inspection, (2) a test drive and (3) a thorough self-inspection in broad daylight at the dealer's lot. Unfortunately, many new car dealers will not allow you to take a new car for a test drive, let alone a diagnostic inspection. But every consumer has the right to an inspection of a new car at the dealer's lot and the right to refuse to take a new car that is not in excellent condition.

Dealers give many excuses for not letting the consumer test drive his or her new car. For instance, one dealer incorrectly told a consumer:

> We can't let you take it out on the road until there are plates on the car. We can't put your plates on until the title passes to you, which of course doesn't happen until you've either paid or signed the financing agreement.

If your dealer objects, point out that the law allows the buyer a "reasonable opportunity to inspect" a prospective purchase before he or she is bound to accept it. The Uniform Commercial Code, which is the law in all states except Louisiana, states: "Acceptance of goods occurs when the buyer, after a reasonable opportunity to inspect the goods, signifies to the seller that the goods are conforming or that he will take or retain them in spite of their non-conformity." See the *Zabriskie* case discussed in Chapter 6 where the Court held: "It is clear that a buyer does not accept goods [a car in this case] until he has had a 'reasonable opportunity to inspect.'"

2. Inspection at the Dealer's Lot

The following checklists cover the most common defects which you can recognize in parts or make-ready adjustments in an inspection at the dealer's lot. The specific problems listed are discussed in detail in Chapter 15, "What Usually Goes Wrong."

a. Brakes

Push hard on the brake pedal for at least a minute. If it sinks toward the floor, there is probably a leak in the brake system which could lead to sudden brake failure.

b. **Tires**

Check for cuts, bulges, or other signs of injury. Some assembly plants subject tires to extreme abuse before the car leaves the factory. Check particularly the tread and sidewalls of the tires.

c. **Steering**

On a car with power steering, start the engine. Turn the steering wheel back and forth to see how much free play there is before the front wheels start to turn. If the rim of the steering wheel can be moved two inches (one inch to either side) or more before the wheels move, the steering gear is too loose for safe operation.

d. **Latches, Doors, Lids and Windows**

Check to see that the outside doors, the glove compartment door, the hood, the trunk lid and all windows close securely. The hood has a double latch which should keep the hood down even if it is not quite closed all the way. To test this, open the hood a crack and let go of the hood release lever. Then try to pull the hood open; it should only open about an inch. Misaligned windows not only let in the wind and rain but also cause excessive noise in the interior. Run each window from the fully opened to the fully closed position. If the window sticks or is difficult to move, have the dealer correct the problem. If there is a gap at the top, ask the dealer to fix that.

e. **Body Damage**

Many cars are damaged in transit and, when possible, repaired and sold as new. Look for telltale signs like spray painting in out-of-the-way places such as on the front of the side view mirror or on the underside of the car, slightly discolored portions of the exterior surface (imperfect color match), and hard-to-close doors, trunk lids, or hoods. Sighting along the length of the car can help detect paint problems and variations in the sheet metal indicating damage that was repaired. It is absolutely essential to do this inspection in full daylight since many paint problems or repair signs cannot otherwise be detected.

f. **Options**

Make sure that the car has all the options you requested, especially any safety options. Certain options, such as air-conditioning, that are supposed to be installed by the manufacturer can be disastrous if installed by the dealer. Cars with factory-installed air-conditioning units are designed to accept the extra loads: tires, cooling system and front springs may be beefed up, and the air-conditioner will be integrated into the car's fresh-air system. Many options, such as engines or transmissions, can be substituted or switched without the consumer noticing. For example, manufacturers will sometimes substitute a smaller or larger engine than that ordered if the proper engine is not immediately available on the assembly line. General Motors put Chevrolet engines in 1977 Oldsmobiles, Buicks and Pontiacs without telling the purchasers before being caught.

g. **Engine, Transmission and Brake Leaks**

Even a new car can have an oil, transmission or other system-fluid leak. First, check for visible leaks in the engine compartment—oil on the engine, signs of fluid on hoses and connections for brakes, radiator, power steering. After doing this, drive the car to a clean spot on the lot and leave it running for a few minutes at a fast idle. Then move it and look for any fresh marks that indicate leaks.

h. **Body Water Leaks**

Ask to have the car washed just before you take delivery. Then look and feel for water leaks around all the windows and doors, in the trunk, and under the dash. There is no better test than this to determine whether a new car has water leaks that frequently will cause an unsuspecting new car purchaser unending trouble.

i. **Miscellaneous**

Operate all controls and accessories to ensure that they work (heater, radio, brake and turn signals, windshield wipers, lights, etc.).

Check to see that a new car delivery label is attached to the car (usually on the side window), as required under the federal Automobile Information Disclosure Act. Each label must list certain information, such as: the make, model and identification number, the manufacturer's suggested retail price of the vehicle and each item of optional equipment on the car, destination charges and the final assembly point.

3. Test Drive

It would make a major difference in the car-selling business if buyers as a routine matter were to test drive their cars before making a final commitment. But, such pretesting is only permitted by some dealers. Small dealers more frequently permit such a test, since they tend to rely more on personalized service in order to compete with big dealerships. If a dealer lets you take a test drive, do not limit yourself to a spin around the block. Take it out on a highway to see that it performs correctly at all speeds.

Most people would never think of asking to test drive a brand-new car, on the assumption that if it is a new car, it must be close to perfect. Though most new cars appear roadworthy, many nevertheless have serious defects that become apparent during thorough testing. Raymond and Brenda Bue of Selma, California learned this the hard way. Two hours after purchasing a brand new Eagle Medallion they were back at the dealership as they related in their letter to Chrysler on August 18, 1988:

> I bought the above referenced vehicle from Rodway Buick in Fresno, California on April 15, 1988. I made the mistake of not driving this particular car as it was in the showroom and the salesperson did not offer to bring it out so I drove a Medallion that was on the outer lot.
>
> The same day I purchased the car and drove it off the lot I noticed it did not run properly. I took the car home at 2:00 p.m. but had to return it to the dealership at 4:00 p.m. . . . If I had test driven this vehicle I would not have purchased it.

Many car buyers pass up a test drive or ignore its results, believing that, even if defects reveal themselves, the warranty will cover them or the dealer will assume responsibility for repairs. Don't delude yourself. Letter after letter received by the Center for Auto Safety and Ralph Nader indicate that such repairs are simply not that easy to obtain. For example, the following consumer went through the paper signing process without having seen the actual car he was getting:

December 9, 1988

Dear Mr. Nader:

> I recently purchased a "new" car. The car in the dealer showroom was not to be the car that I was to take delivery of due to a defect on the interior. The sales-person assured me that it was no problem because the dealership had several cars of the same description in stock.
>
> On November 30, at approximately 6:45 p.m. I picked up my "new" car. While in the office processing the necessary forms, a manager of the dealership stated that he was going to take my car outside for me to pickup due to the fact that they were in the process of closing for the day.

The following day, during daylight hours, I noticed that the door on the passenger side was of a different shade than the rest of the car. Within 24 hours of delivery, I called the dealership to inform them that I was not happy and I felt that I had been defrauded since I had purchased a new car and had never been informed that this car had been damaged. The dealership only wants to repaint the door, stating that this is their only responsibility under the Pennsylvania Lemon Law.

Sincerely,
/s/
Ronald L. Gross
Weirton, WV

Dealers, even if their intentions are the best, find it difficult to remedy new car defects because of overloaded repair shops, inadequate compensation from manufacturers for warranty work, unskilled mechanics, defects which simply elude diagnosis or are unrepairable, and poor design.

4. Professional Diagnosis

Have a mechanic or diagnostic center examine your car before you accept it; your test drive may not catch all the inadequacies of dealer preparation, and the frequently neglected make-ready operations are not covered by the warranty. (You have the legal right to such an inspection as explained above.) The investment can prove to be a wise one. Many large cities have diagnostic "clinics" or "lanes" equipped with elaborate machinery to analyze every phase of the car's performance and condition. The quality and honesty of diagnostic centers vary widely, so it is necessary to pick a center with a good reputation. If the diagnostic center has ties to a repair facility, inform the mechanic or service writer that the repairs will be performed elsewhere, in order to eliminate the incentive to add unnecessary repairs to the diagnosis. (For more on diagnostic clinics, see Chapter 4.)

BUYING A USED CAR

If new car "sticker shock" has left you for a loop, you can save money by buying a used car. First, a three-year-old used car costs approximately 40% less than one bought new. Secondly, operating expenses drop after a car's first year. Hertz, the car rental company, reported 20% savings in operating expenditures for a new car kept five years, compared with buying a new car every year. The greatest savings is depreciation, since the original owner already absorbed that loss, which is heaviest during a car's first year.

A key factor in buying a used car is finding a safe and reliable vehicle, since a defective one endangers your safety and pocketbook. Good preparation and patience cut the risk of ending up with someone else's lemon. To help consumers in purchasing a used car, the Federal Trade Commission (FTC) issued a rule, discussed later in this chapter, requiring a disclosure statement to accompany all used cars sold by dealers. A few states such as Wisconsin went even further, requiring any dealer selling a used car to inspect the vehicle and report on the condition of the car's major systems. Consider buying a used car through the classified advertising section of a local newspaper. You can usually get a better price when buying from a private owner, since there are no commission charges, overhead costs or other expenses that a dealership would have. The private owner should be able to give details, including repair records, of the maintenance history of the car. But one pitfall is that most private owners do not offer warranties. You can write out a contract of sale, though, with provisions specifying who will pay for repairs if the car breaks down within a set time period. Be prepared to handle the paper work in transferring the title and getting new license plates.

SELECTING A USED CAR

Many of the same rules in selecting a new car apply to the choice of a used car as well. Unless you're prepared to pay extra, stay away from sport and luxury models. Not only do you have to pay extra for many needless frills, but also these cars are the ones most likely to have problems with power-operated windows and seats and similar convenience features. Such features are trouble-prone: they're expensive to repair, and they raise the price of the car. Steer clear of "orphans" (makes and models no longer in production), very old models, and uncommon imports. Parts and service for such cars may be costly or difficult to find.

In selecting a used car, a consumer must frequently question the dealer or owner in depth to get enough information to make a purchasing decision. Even when consumers ask questions, they often receive insufficient and inaccurate answers. For example, consumers can expect to receive little information from dealers about the safety or other mechanical conditions of a used vehicle which they are considering for purchase. What's worse, many used car dealers intentionally cover up mechanical faults in order to sell cars.

According to the FTC:

> [T]he consumer shopping for a used vehicle is confronted with immaculate vehicles and smooth-talking salespeople who strive to assure the customer that the gleaming beauties are in "mint condition" or "dependable transportation" while maintaining a wall of silence about defects which may lie beneath the surface.

Used car dealers often "misrepresent that used vehicles are defect-free or that substantial repairs have been performed." Such dealers promise to fix any defect that develops, but when confronted with a problem at a later date, they deny having made any promises. These oral assurances have all too often proven empty rhetoric to the buyer of a lemon. Make sure that the dealer puts in writing any promises made on repairs.

MECHANICAL INSPECTION

The lack of reliable information on a car's operating and safety condition makes a thorough mechanical inspection of the car before purchase very important. Always take a used car to a diagnostic center or a good mechanic for an over-all inspection before you buy it. If the used car dealer refuses to let your mechanic inspect the car, go to another dealer. Furthermore, don't buy the car if the dealer refuses to let you personally test-drive it. Offer to take the dealer's mechanic along with you to the diagnostic inspection. Ask to see copies of all repair orders and other maintenance records, particularly when buying from a private owner. Not only does this tell how well the car has been kept up but also indicates whether it has needed such frequent repairs that it is a lemon.

Before taking a used car to a diagnostic center or mechanic for inspection, some simple on-the-lot and on-the-road tests can eliminate many bad used cars. Perform these tests in good weather and during daylight, since some of the worst lemons have been sold at night, in the rain, or under other conditions that discourage consumers from thoroughly examining the car inside and out. For your convenience, we have included the checklist derived from *Consumer Reports* to use in inspecting a used car (see p. 215).

This check list indicates the most important tests that should be done before deciding on a used car. If possible, bring someone along to help with those tests. On the lot, check for appearance items such as rust spots, blisters in the paint, flaking paint and ripples in the metal or different shades of paint on the car's body. Such tests performed by close visual inspection can reveal anything from major corrosion to evidence of a prior accident.

While on the lot, check to make sure that the car's lights, indicators, and accessories are all in working order. Start the engine and listen for unusual noises. Inside the car, make sure that the instrument-panel lights and gauges work, and test the windshield wipers and washers, turn signals, horn and radio (if there is one). Then with the help of someone standing outside the car, make sure that each of the car's exterior lights work.

Get out of the car and push up and down on a fender to check the car's shock absorbers. When pushed in such a manner, the car should go up and down once and stop—in a middle position. If the car tends to keep on bouncing, it may need new shock absorbers or struts. Shake the top of each front wheel—in and out—to check for looseness and noise that may indicate bad wheel bearings or worn suspension joints.

As with the on-the-lot tests, certain defects will be readily apparent by driving the car for about a half-hour on the road. Again, if the seller refuses a road test, look elsewhere for a car. The automatic transmission should engage smoothly when put into drive and then shift itself smoothly into higher gears as the car speeds up. The gears of a manual transmission should also engage smoothly without the clutch slipping or grabbing. With either type of transmission, make sure that reverse operates without clunking or excessive noise. When accelerating from low speed in the forward gears, check for smooth pick-up from the engine, without pinging or knocking. The brakes should stop the car three times from 45 MPH without any swerving or the pedal feeling soft. Accelerate hard from low speed, then check for clouds of blue smoke that indicate oil burning. Finally check for handling and stability, particularly over rough roads. If any item seems question-able, check it with your mechanic during the shop test described below.

If the car passes the on-the-lot and road tests, arrange for a good auto mechanic to do some shop tests including checking the engine compression, brake and exhaust system, battery and any suspected defects. The mechanic should be a person who will be working for you and not for any dealer. Expect to pay the mechanic at least $40 for the shop tests; it's money well spent if it saves you from buying a lemon or a car with low compression that needs a $1,200 engine overhaul within the first 5,000 miles.

USED CAR CHECKLIST

You can use the following list to check out a vehicle and to estimate costs of repairs. The total figure for repair costs can give you a better idea of the real price of a particular car.

	Estimated cost of repair		Estimated cost of repair

On-the-Lot Tests
_____ 1. Interior wear and tear $_____
_____ 2. Worn tires (including spare) $_____
_____ 3. Bad rust spots, flaking paint $_____
_____ 4. Malfunctioning windows and doors $_____
_____ 5. Worn front-wheel bearings or worn suspension joints $_____
_____ 6. Brake-fluiud leaks $_____
_____ 7. Defective lights, indicators, accessories $_____
_____ 8. Worn shock absorbers/struts $_____
_____ 9. Damage to body and frame $_____

On-the-Road Tests
_____ 10. Wheels out of line or out of balance $_____
_____ 11. Smoothness of engine pickup $_____
_____ 12. Problems with transmission $_____
_____ 13. Problems with brakes $_____
_____ 14. Problems with steering $_____

_____ 15. Worn piston rings $_____
_____ 16. Need for repairing shock absorbers, front end, or suspension $_____
_____ 17. Overheating of engine $_____

In-the-Shop Tests
_____ 18. Problems with engine compression (valves, piston rings) $_____
_____ 19. Problems with brake drums, discs, linings, wheel cylinders, master cylinder, front-wheel bearings, or parking brake $_____
_____ 20. Worn or broken seals, rusted or broken muffler or exhaust pipe $_____
_____ 21. Defective battery; other problems $_____

These precautions should enable you to avoid even such lemons as flood-damaged cars which look like good buys superficially. One dealer in Minnesota was hit by a flood which inundated 23 new 1987 Lincolns, Cougars and Sables. The cars were repaired under Ford policy and sold with complete new-car warranties. In response to a lawsuit by the Minnesota Attorney General's office, the dealership agreed to guarantee a refund of the full trade-in value of a similar undamaged model at any future date. The following tactics are suggested to avoid buying a flood-damaged car:

1. Check for sand, silt or salt deposits under the carpeting in the passenger compartment. A stagnant odor may also be present.
2. Ask to remove a seat cushion, then drop it bottom side down on pavement. If salt or dirt falls out, beware.
3. Check recesses in the intake and exhaust manifold and other crevices for indications of sand or silt deposits.
4. Check for sand in chrome headlight rims.
5. Check wiring for signs of corrosion. Note copper connections: they turn green when exposed to saltwater.
6. Ask to see the title to determine if it has been stamped "submerged" or "flood car."

Generally, your best bet in a used car is one that is two or three years old. If cars only a few years old were properly cared for by their previous owners, they still have a lot of life left. If you find several cars within your price range that fit your particular needs, consider the one with the least mileage on the odometer and best general overall condition.

USED CAR WARRANTIES

Although every new car comes with a written warranty, many used cars come without any warranties at all. These cars may be sold "as is" or "with all faults." Often cars without warranties are sold by private parties such as banks and finance companies, that have no service facilities.

Where warranties are given, they often differ, depending on the seller. One warranty may cover parts and labor for 30 days, while another may cover only parts for a certain period of time, such as 60 days. Since some of these are clearly better than others, it is important to shop around for a good warranty.

The reputation of the dealer can be more important than the terms of warranty to a used car buyer. Even with a complete warranty on parts and labor for 60 days, a dishonest dealer can give a consumer the "run-around" for two months without actually fixing the car. If the warranty or the deal itself sounds too good to be true, or if the dealer looks like a fly-by-night, check on the dealer's reputation with local consumer protection agencies and the Better Business Bureau (BBB).

Whatever the warranty, make sure it is understandable and in writing before buying the car. The warranty should spell out the parts and labor guaranteed and the length of coverage (in miles and/or days). The words "60-day warranty" by themselves do not mean anything. Specific components or systems such as the engine must be listed to give the warranty meaning, otherwise, you could get a warranty that covers only the most extreme failures.

If the used car is a recent model, the original manufacturer's warranty may still be in effect. Check to see if coverage is transferred to you before you sign a deal on the car. This transfer should include a warranty book with the name of the new car dealer who originally sold the car.

FEDERAL HELP FOR USED-CAR BUYERS

A few federal laws, regulations and services make used car buying a little easier. Additional help may come from state laws and regulations.

AUTO SAFETY HOTLINE

After selecting a used car, call the Auto Safety Hotline of the National Highway Traffic Safety Administration (NHTSA) to verify the safety-defect and recall history of the vehicle. This hotline is toll-free, serving the citizens of every state except Hawaii and Alaska. The number is (800) 424-9393. In the Washington, D.C. area, the number is (202) 366-0123. When calling, be prepared to give the make, model, year and vehicle identification number of the car.

If you find the car was recalled, check with a mechanic to see if the

ter law makes it illegal for anyone to tamper with a vehicle's
odometer to show the wrong mileage. Neither the vehicle owner nor
anyone else may turn back or disconnect the odometer, except to
perform necessary repairs.

This law protects car buyers from a seller concealing a car's true
mileage by turning back or disconnecting the odometer. The law
recognizes that true mileage is an indicator of a vehicle's condition and
value. Odometer fraud is a widespread practice used against unsuspecting buyers by dishonest sellers of used motor vehicles. Rolling
back odometers to disguise the true vehicle mileage has cost consumers over a $1 billion a year, according to the U.S. Department of
Transportation.

The federal law requires the seller to give the buyer a written
statement of the mileage before the sale for all vehicles, except antique
vehicles and heavy trucks. Under the law, a person who has been
victimized by odometer fraud has a private right of action against the
violator. If you sue the seller in state or federal court and win, the court
will award you $1,500 or three times the amount of damages, which-
ever is greater, plus court costs and reasonable attorney's fees. Consult
an attorney if you suspect the odometer has been changed. Report
violations to the state Attorney General's Office which can bring civil
actions on behalf of consumers. The federal government can bring civil
and criminal actions against violators of the law. In order to report a
violation to the federal government, contact the National Highway
Traffic Safety Administration, Office of the Chief Counsel, 400 Seventh
Street SW, Washington, D.C. 20590.

For a free copy of a pamphlet on odometers, "Consumer Protection
Under the Federal Odometer Law," write the National Highway
Traffic Safety Administration, Office of Public Affairs, Washington,
D.C. 20590.

218

THE USED CAR RULE

To inquire about the used car sales regulation, write the Federal Trade Commission, Bureau of Consumer Protection, 6th and Pennsylvania Avenue NW, Washington, D.C. 20580.

In 1984, the Federal Trade Commission issued its long-awaited, but ultimately for consumers, disappointing, Used Car Rule. In its original form, the Rule would have required used car dealers to disclose all known defects on a window sticker. Although the National Association of Automobile Dealers first encouraged such disclosure because, they claimed, it was less burdensome than mandatory inspection of each car, eventually used car dealers succeeded in lobbying to eliminate this weak disclosure requirement from the law.

Presently, dealers must post a Buyer's Guide in each vehicle describing the type and length of the warranty that comes with the vehicle (not to be confused with a service contract which must be bought separately), and any potential problems. The standard used car warranty covers problems arising within the first 30 days or 1,000 miles of ownership. Some dealers pay 100% of necessary repairs, while others state that they will pay 50%. Any given warranty should be carefully read. If a salesperson makes any verbal guarantees about the car's performance or mechanical condition which are a significant contribution to your decision-making, get the statement in writing and review the final contract to make sure it has been included.

Some states permit dealers to sell cars "AS IS." This is a way for dealers to escape any and all liability for future problems, no matter how extreme. Although some states may interpret these words loosely, be careful: they may serve to extinguish your rights. Don't buy a car sold "AS IS."

If, after carefully choosing your car, it turns out to be significantly damaged, you may be able to pursue legal action under used car lemon laws. See Chapter 7 for more information.

YOUR FIRST DAYS DRIVING THE CAR

The period permitted to complete a "reasonable inspection" of the car includes the first days of possession. After this period, the consumer is said to have "accepted" the car and further efforts to return the car must be based on "revocation of acceptance." If for some reason you were unable to test drive the car or subject it to a mechanical check before taking delivery, put the car through its paces and get it to a diagnostic lane or a mechanic as soon as you can.

If a new or used car turns out to have serious defects within the reasonable inspection period, you have the legal right to "reject" it—unless it is a used car that was sold "as is" (without any warranty at all). "Rejection," which is similar to "revocation of acceptance" discussed in Chapter 6, works best in cases where something major goes wrong during the first few miles, as in the *Zabriskie* case (Chapter 6), or within the first week or so of ownership. Revocation of acceptance, on the other hand, is a legal strategy that can be used months after accepting a new or used car if it takes that long for major defects to appear.

In the *Zabriskie* case, the car broke down only a few minutes after leaving the dealership, and the consumer immediately notified the dealer of his rejection. He stopped payment on the check and notified the dealer that the sale was canceled. The dealer, nonetheless, sent a wrecker to the consumer's home, brought the vehicle in and made the necessary repairs, but the consumer continued to refuse acceptance of the new car. When the dealer sued the consumer for the purchase price, the court upheld the consumer's right to reject the car.

If you paid other than by check or if the check has already cleared before the lemon showed its true colors, you can reject the car, in the same way and demand your money back from the dealer. If the dealer refuses, you may have to file a lawsuit to receive a refund. Many cases have upheld the consumer's right to reject the car and courts have ordered the dealer to return the owner's money.

If you decide to reject the car, follow these general guidelines:

1. Begin rejection as soon as the defect appears. This should be within the first week after delivery of the car. (If you have had the car for more than a week, many courts would conclude that you have "accepted" the car—thus, in that case, follow the similar strategy of "revocation of acceptance" discussed in Chapter 6.)
2. Notify the dealer **in writing** that you are rejecting the car and explain why. Demand your money back, or inform the dealer that

you have stopped payment on the check, whichever applies. Send this information and demand by certified mail with return receipt requested. Keep a copy of this letter with all other records relating to the car purchase.

3. Return the car to the dealer's lot, noting the mileage. Offer the certificate of title and car keys to the dealer. If he or she does not accept them, just hold on to them and mention in the letter that the dealer can have the title and keys at any time. If the dealer does take them back, this helps prove that the dealer has agreed to the rejection.

4. Remove the license plates if they are in your name. If they are the dealer's plates, just leave them on. Return your plates and registration to the Department of Motor Vehicles.

5. Notify your insurance company in writing that you have rejected the car, but do not cancel the insurance until the dispute is resolved. Ask the company to reduce the premium to the minimum needed to protect you while the car is on the dealer's lot.

6. If the dealer has financed the car or has arranged the financing for you, stop making payments on the car. Notify the finance company or bank in writing that you have rejected the car, explaining why. If the dealer or finance company sues you for the balance of the payments, you will need an attorney to represent you. Show your lawyer the section on the Federal Trade Commission's Holder-in-Due-Course Rule, discussed in Chapter 6, which allows the consumer to withhold payments in many cases where the new car is a lemon.

Within a week after purchasing his new Cadillac, Stanley Jankowitz noticed that a warning light on the dash flashed "Stop Engine" and the car would repeatedly cut off. This continued following six repair attempts in as many weeks. Finally, Jankowitz stopped making payments to the finance company, General Motors Acceptance Corp. (GMAC), and informed the dealer that he no longer wanted the car and that they should take it back. When GMAC did not receive Jankowitz's third payment, it brought suit against him. Not only did the court rule in favor of Jankowitz, it also held that he was entitled to a refund of the payments which he had already made.

Without some basic changes in the way the automobiles are sold, it will be difficult to detect certain types of lemons before consumers become stuck with them. But you can take precautions which will reduce the chances of your new or used car being defect-ridden. Perhaps the most important precaution is to avoid, if possible, putting yourself in the position of having no choice but to take the car you ordered even if it is not just right. This may be difficult to do if you have traded in your only car on the new one. But if at all possible, arrange to have some form of back-up transportation available, so that if your car is a lemon, you will be able to return it to the dealer.

CHAPTER 14

MAINTAINING AND REPAIRING YOUR CAR

The average car during its useful life will require some $7,480 worth of repairs and maintenance (excluding gasoline and oil purchases). Proper care and maintenance of a car help insure safe performance, reliability and efficiency. A poorly maintained car wastes money, fuel and the owner's time, and can even endanger the owner's life. A properly maintained car should provide trouble-free driving of 120,000 miles or more unless it's a lemon. While warranty service must be performed by an authorized dealer, regular maintenance and repairs not covered by the warranty can be serviced anywhere.

Even during the car's first few years of operation, the manufacturer's warranty obligations do not cover regular maintenance items such as tune-ups, oil changes and replacement of worn out brake linings. It is up to the vehicle owner to properly care for and maintain the car; any car problems resulting from neglect of maintenance will not be covered by the manufacturer because they are considered to be "owner abuse." Taking care of your car is necessary to protect your warranty rights because if a car owner can prove that the car had been properly maintained, the manufacturer cannot claim "owner abuse."

DIAGNOSTIC AND SAFETY INSPECTIONS

Studies have shown that defects cause from 5 to 18 percent of all accidents. Periodic safety inspections are designed to catch defects and reduce accidents. Many urban areas require inspection of the car's emission control system; this could be done at the same time as safety inspections. Emissions inspections not only help reduce air pollution, but also improve fuel economy by catching improperly tuned vehicles that waste energy.

When Carol Thomason of Atlanta, Georgia experienced sudden stalling out while driving her 1986 Buick, she returned the car repeatedly to her dealer for diagnosis and correction. The dealer could not find the problem. Mrs. Thomason then tried other Buick dealers for a total of eight unsuccessful trips. Rather than give up, she went to Auto Chek, an independent diagnostic center in suburban Atlanta. Auto Chek found that the elusive stalling in Mrs. Thomason's Buick was caused by a faulty throttle position sensor.

Facilities like Auto Check, and the AAA Diagnostic Clinic in St. Louis, both of which are independent of any repair facility, rely on computer diagnosis to track down defects. Diagnostic inspections run a series of tests on a car, giving the consumer a status report on the car's overall condition or on a specific problem. A diagnostic report serves as a prescription for getting proper repairs.

The most impartial diagnostic inspections can be obtained from independent centers or clinics like the St. Louis Diagnostic Car Clinic and Auto Chek in Atlanta. In most large cities, you can find shops that have diagnostic lanes, but since most of these operate in conjunction with repair shops, they can't offer the same type of objective, disinterested advice as do government-operated or otherwise independent centers. In many cases, diagnostic clinics help consumers spot needed repairs, as in Mrs. Thomason's case. Consumers can have more confidence in results from independent clinics, since there is no profit-making incentive to find unnecessary repair jobs.

At present, there are only a handful of independent diagnostic centers. The St. Louis Diagnostic Car Clinic provides a good example of how such clinics operate; it is run by the American Automobile Association (AAA) of Missouri for its members and the general public. According to Michael Right, Director of Public Affairs for the Missouri AAA, consumers at the clinic pay a moderate charge ($49 members, $65 non-members) to have their entire vehicle diagnosed. For $5, the consumer can return the car to the clinic to verify that all repairs were done correctly. If repairs have been made improperly or not at all, the Club will mediate complaints on the consumer's behalf with the repair shop.

Maintaining and Repairing Your Car

The Automobile Club's former Director of Membership Services, John N. Noettl, described the club's ten years of experience with diagnostic inspection:

> Our own conclusions on the benefits of diagnostic clinics that give an unbiased appraisal of one's car, seem to be supported by reports from DOT, EPA and other organizations. Namely: (1) lower repair costs; (2) more safe cars; (3) less polluting cars; (4) more safety consciousness on the part of the motorist; and, (5) information feedback to the government regulatory agencies and the manufacturers concerning the "real world" benefits of safety regulations and design changes.
>
> We completed a study for the DOT in which 288 collision-damaged vehicles were inspected for damage to their safety and engine exhaust emission systems, as well as for precollision non-compliance with established standards.
>
> The program data revealed that many types of information are accessible and a thorough evaluation of vehicles involved in accidents is available from this type of program. It appeared that a statistically large number of accident-involved vehicles had poor components in their brake system. The brake pads and linings were thinner than considered a safe level on 27% of the vehicles; 31% had low brake fluid. Also 33% of the vehicles exhibited alignment problems.

Testifying before the U.S. Senate Commerce Committee, Noettl advocated making independent diagnostic centers available nation-wide to the motor public at low cost, and with government assistance if need be. According to Noettl, the clinics are usually self-sustaining, since the cost of operations is supported by fees paid by car owners. "Aside from the benefits to individual motorists, the societal benefits in cleaner, safer, more economical, and energy efficient cars would be incalculable."

The National Highway Traffic Safety Administration (NHTSA) found that national diagnostic motor vehicle inspections would save consumers $1.4 billion. NHTSA's report, "Motor Vehicle Diagnostic Inspection Program," concluded that car owners can achieve greater safety, lower pollution, improved gas mileage and lower repair and maintenance costs for their cars by using diagnostic inspections. This report was based on pilot diagnostic inspection programs set up in

Alabama, Tennessee, Arizona, Puerto Rico and Washington, D.C. The projects carried out 125,000 in-depth diagnostic inspections of safety-related and exhaust emissions systems of cars.

In the NHTSA project, consumers whose cars were diagnosed as defective had the repairs performed at a repair shop. After repairs, a car owner would return to the inspection station with repair bills to see that the proper repairs were made. Consumers relying on the diagnostic inspections achieved better quality or lower-cost repairs than owners of cars going through non-diagnostic (pass/fail) inspections, particularly where more complex repairs were involved. For example, the diagnostic group spent an average of 5.7 percent less on emission-related repairs than the non-diagnostic group for the first periodic inspection. The diagnostic group had a 40% lower failure rate on reinspection, indicating that they were getting better quality repairs than the non-diagnostic group. NHTSA specifically found that owners of diagnostically inspected cars had an average improvement in fuel economy of 4.7 percent right after repairs. The failure rates for safety systems like brakes dropped by 50 percent.

NHTSA reported that consumers reacted positively to the diagnostic inspection program—93% said that they would pay $30 or more for the service and a third said they would pay $45 or more adjusted for inflation. Inspection helped auto repair shops near the diagnostic center, too. Aided by a diagnostic status report on the car, the shops could fix only what was needed and do it right the first time.

One of the NHTSA projects included an analysis by the University of Alabama which further corroborated the value of diagnostic inspection. Alabama found that its inspected cars had 12 percent fewer accidents than uninspected cars, after adjusting data for owner sex, age and income.

Other diagnostic clinics are not so helpful to consumers. As noted above, most diagnostic clinics also perform repairs so they profit from the problems they find. Other clinics are simply incompetent. Studies by consumer groups, government agencies and other clinics affiliated with repair shops have reached the same conclusion as did the Center for Study of Services. It examined garages in the Washington Metropolitan area that were licensed to do safety and emission inspections and found that licensed inspection garages had more repair complaints.

You might think that shops that qualify as inspection stations would have more satisfied customers than other shops. Not so . . . Many good shops choose to stay out of the inspection business and some second-rate shops make an effort to qualify as an easy way to get more customers.

Washington Consumer's *CHECKBOOK*: Summer 1988.

But this is not to dismiss the value of competent diagnostic centers which happen to be affiliated with repair shops. Despite the bad experiences with diagnostic centers as reported by various studies and consumers, many car owners have saved money by using clinics before getting repairs. One precaution can help you avoid being "taken" by clinics connected to repair shops. When you want a diagnosis to help you decide what repairs to get at a repair shop, let the diagnostic center know, in no uncertain terms, that any recommended repairs will be done elsewhere.

In the following situations, a repair-connected diagnostic clinic will see no incentive to over-prescribe repairs:

1. When the car's warranty is running out, a diagnosis can catch major problems before the warranty actually expires;
2. When checking out a used car before purchase;
3. When taking delivery on a new car;
4. Before settling an insurance claim for damage to a car.

DO-IT-YOURSELF MAINTENANCE

Some consumers regularly perform their own maintenance, such as changing the oil and filter in their cars and performing tune-ups. However, the number of "do-it-yourselfers" or "shadetree" mechanics is getting lower as cars get more complex. After consulting the manufacturer's owners manual and other guide books, many of these consumers are successful at performing proper maintenance. Then again, others are not, wasting time and money. The major advantages of performing your own maintenance are: (1) you save money and (2) you eliminate time required to go to a repair shop. The major disadvantages of self-maintenance are: (1) you might make a mistake which can be expensive and time-consuming to correct; (2) your mistake may constitute "owner abuse," thus eliminating otherwise guaranteed warranty repairs; and (3) you may not have the skill or tools to maintain the sophisticated electronic gadgets or perform complex repairs on your new car.

Familiarity with auto maintenance and repair can best be developed by learning from an experienced friend who does his or her own maintenance, studying repair manuals and attending consumer car repair courses. Some consumer groups, YMCA's and YWCA's, community centers, local colleges and recreation departments conduct courses like "Auto Awareness," "Driveway Mechanics" and "Basic Auto Repair" to educate car owners on automobile maintenance and repair. You can select from several do-it-yourself books, covering such topics as auto tune-ups for beginners and the mechanics of specific auto models. See Appendix O for a list of some titles.

Before rolling up your sleeves and buying your own supplies, carefully weigh the disadvantages and advantages of self-maintenance. For example, one consumer found himself in a warranty dispute with Honda after changing his car's oil. G. DeBoer of Portland, Oregon regularly changed the oil and filter on his 1983 Honda Accord. When his automatic transmission failed at 13,000 miles, Honda refused to pay for repairs under warranty because there was no oil in the transmission. Honda blamed the lack of transmission oil on the consumer, saying that the transmission oil must have been drained out when the engine oil was changed. Even though the engine and transmission oil cases have separate drain plugs and Mr. DeBoer insisted he did not drain the transmission, Honda refused to pay the $1,000 + repair bill.

NEW REPAIR EXPERIENCE

Proper repairs are vital to vehicle safety, reliability and cost of operation. Yet auto repairs rank number one on almost every complaint list across the country. Testifying at hearings on auto repair problems held by the Consumer Subcommittee of the U.S. Senate Commerce Committee in March 1978, Joan Claybrook, NHTSA Administrator estimated that consumers lost over $20 billion in 1977 on inadequate, incompetent, unnecessary or fraudulent auto repairs and maintenance. Claybrook reported that almost 40 cents of every dollar spent on car repairs is wasted. Most witnesses at the hearing agreed on the extent of the auto repair problem. The controversy lay in what to do about it. NHTSA's findings of waste in auto repair are still true today.

Another cause of wasted consumer auto repair dollars is the "flat-rate" system of charging for repairs, used by most repair shops around the country. Under the flat-rate system, the service shop sets repair charges by consulting a manual that specifies the amount of time needed for each job, even if that amount exceeds the actual time spent on repairs. According to a study by a subsidiary of the National Automobile Dealers Association, mechanics can beat the time listed in flat-rate manuals on 75 percent of all jobs.

STATE AUTO REPAIR LAWS

A number of state and local governments have attempted to reduce auto repair problems through one of three basic types of auto repair laws: (1) disclosure, (2) shop licensing and (3) licensing of mechanics. Disclosure laws give the consumer a right to certain information about the auto repair being performed. Shop licensing laws require auto repair shops to avoid fraud, deceptive practices and gross negligence or face losing the license which permits them to do motor vehicle repairs. Licensing laws for mechanics require that persons performing repairs meet certain competency standards before being permitted to repair motor vehicles.

Disclosure and shop licensing laws may help decrease the number of fraudulent repairs, but they are not directed specifically at competence, as are mechanics licensing laws. Many states and two counties now license mechanics. They are: Colorado, Connecticut, Washington, D.C., Florida, Hawaii, Maine, Michigan, Minnesota, Nevada, New Hampshire, New Jersey, New York, Oregon, Pennsylvania, Virginia, Washington, Wisconsin, Montgomery County, Maryland, Dallas County, Texas, and New York City. To find out if your state is planning to legislate in this area, you may contact the Motor Vehicle Manufacturers Association in Detroit.

There are other types of auto repair laws which help the consumer. These laws vary in approach and scope among states. On the whole, the best auto repair law is in California. This law requires written estimates before the repairs are performed, return of replaced parts to the consumer after the completion of repairs (only if the consumer requests them) and a sign placed in a conspicuous place at the repair shop containing the address and telephone number of the state agency which handles consumer auto repair complaints. The act provides for state enforcement of the auto repair laws.

FINDING A RELIABLE REPAIR SHOP

A reliable garage performs only those repairs that are necessary, performs them properly the first time, and does not overcharge. Finding a repair shop that fits all three criteria is not easy. For example, Reader's Digest conducted a survey of 225 repair garages across the nation. They set out in a 1984 Olds Cutlass Ciera which they had tuned, repaired, and adjusted to good-as-new condition. From New England to Arizona they stopped in big city and small town garages for the same problem—a spark plug wire which they loosened before each stop.

At the end of the study, Robert Sikorsky, the driver and veteran of numerous road tests remarked, "auto repair still involves a disturbing amount of flimflam." This problem, he said, exceeded the gap created between increased technology and mechanical know-how. Sikorsky experienced phony repairs, sabotage, and false diagnoses. In Beaumont, Texas he was charged for replacing the plug wire when all the mechanic had done was reconnect the original one. This "fix" was common along interstates where there is little chance of the customer returning. In Salt Lake City the plug wire was actually cut so that a new one was necessary. A mechanic in Connecticut went to great lengths to demonstrate the gravity of Sikorsky's problem. Lowering a long screw driver into the oil well, he listened and then carefully explained by use of another's discarded parts, that the problem was the rocker arm. Five repair shops in Jacksonville, Florida offered five different diagnoses with appropriate remedies.

Many experts on consumer auto repair abuses agree that small, independent garages that pay their mechanics a straight salary, as opposed to following the "flat-rate" manual, often offer the best repair work. Since, on the whole, independent shops are usually the most reliable, consider one even if the mechanics are paid by "flat-rate." The reliability of independent garages is increased because they usually survive on reputation only, as opposed to a "big-name" shop like Sears or Goodyear or a car dealership which attracts many customers on the basis of its name alone.

Most surveys show greater consumer satisfaction with the performance of independent shops when compared to dealerships. A 1988 survey by the Center for Study of Services in Washington, D.C. found that 88 percent of customers at the average independent shop were satisfied with the way the shops fixed their cars, compared to only 65 percent at the average dealership. Large retail outlets such as Sears Roebuck and Montgomery Ward received a 74 percent satisfactory rating.

NHTSA offers the following helpful tips on choosing an auto repair shop:

1. Reputation
    —Consult with your friends and neighbors.
    Check with your local consumer office,
    Better Business Bureau and voluntary consumer groups.
2. Qualifications
    —Are the mechanics certified or licensed?
3. Facilities
    —How long has the shop been at its present location?
    —Does the shop appear to be well equipped?
    —Is it clean and organized?
4. Repair Practices
    —Will the shop give you a written estimate?
    —Will it advise you on additional costs?
    —How does it handle complaints?
    —Does it guarantee its work in writing?
5. Cost
    —Do the shop's prices seem competitive?
6. Convenience
    —Is it close to where you live or work?

Also consider these guidelines for distinguishing the types of repair shops available:

INDEPENDENT SHOPS—Independent garages are usually the best place for consumers to get their cars serviced because they do not sell anything but service. They depend on the customer's coming back and, often, word-of-mouth to get new customers.

MASS MERCHANDISERS—Many repair shops are operated by mass merchandisers with branch operations such as Sears, Penney's, Montgomery Ward, and the major tire manufacturers. These shops push fast moving and profitable items such as tires, batteries and accessories. They are usually interested in selling parts—not service. Although the price may be right for tune-ups, alignment, brake jobs, and the like, watch out for unneeded repairs or more repairs than you anticipated.

FRANCHISE OPERATIONS—Some repair shops are operated under a franchise with a controlling company, such as AAMCO Transmissions, Midas Muffler and General Tire. When dealing with one of these franchise shops, make sure to check complaints lodged at local consumer affairs offices; another of the franchise's shops in your area may have a better record. Be careful with advertised specials. They often attempt to sell you more expensive repairs.

GASOLINE STATIONS—If you can establish yourself as a regular customer at such a service station, your chances of being satisfied increase—if there are competent mechanics employed there. With the advent of self-service, the number of "service" stations that perform mechanical repairs on the side has dwindled. Friends may be able to recommend a good service station to you.

NEW CAR DEALERS—Most car dealers sell cars, not service, to make money. The service department primarily supplements the car sales business. But where a relatively new car requires complicated repairs to the engine, transmission or electrical system, often the dealer's service department has the most expertise. A dealer's service department generally has the right equipment, as well as familiarity with manufacturer service bulletins and circuit diagrams not always available to non-dealer shops. If you suspect that your car's problem is the subject of a "secret warranty," you will find it difficult to take advantage of that policy unless you go to a dealer.

In judging the competence of a repair shop through its mechanics, you can be somewhat assured if the mechanic has been certified by the National Institute for Automotive Service Excellence (ASE). ASE was established in 1972 by the domestic auto manufacturers and auto dealers to improve the competence of mechanics. The ASE program gives voluntary tests and certifies mechanics who pass. But just because mechanics are not certified with ASE does **not** mean they are incompetent. If the mechanic does wear the ASE seal of approval, then you know that the mechanic at least passed a competency test. Since 1972, over 100,000 mechanics have been certified in at least one area of automotive repair. ASE publishes a list of repair shops employing ASE-certified mechanics. The booklet, "Where to Find Certified Mechanics for Your Car," is available for $1.95 from ASE, 13505 Dulles Technology Drive, Herndon, Virginia 22071. Or you can request a free list of only the shops in your state.

One helpful aid is available to consumers in the Washington, D.C. and San Francisco areas and could be adopted by consumer groups in other areas. The Center for the Study of Services, a private, non-profit consumer organization, researches the quality and price of auto repair services in these metropolitan areas. Then the Center publishes the results in books called *Consumers' Checkbook* mentioned earlier in this chapter, which rates different repair shops in the Washington and San Francisco areas. The ratings are based on consumer surveys, Better Business Bureau complaint records, local consumer office files and investigations of repair facilities' equipment and personnel. For information write the Center for the Study of Services, 806 15th Street NW, Suite 925, Washington, D.C. 20005.

HOW TO TALK TO A MECHANIC

> The best customer is the fellow who comes in with a list of work to be done, leaves the car for three days while he's out of town and tells the service writer to drive the car home several evenings to make sure everything works right.
>
> "How the Customer Looks to a Service Writer,"
> by Charlotte Slater,
> The Washington Star, Jan. 22, 1977

Although it is not always convenient to leave a car for three days at the repair shop, there are other ways to help the shop employees. If you know what needs to be done, such as a wheel alignment, new brake linings, or an oil change, simply give the mechanic or service writer a written list of the work to be done. Taking the car to an independent diagnostic clinic first is a good method of finding out just what needs to be repaired. Communication is the key to getting your car fixed right and avoiding unnecessary repairs.

If you do not know what repairs are necessary and have been unable to find a good diagnostic clinic, do not guess. Simply describe the symptoms. If the symptoms are difficult to describe, ask a friend who knows about cars or the mechanic at the shop to take the car for a test drive. If the vehicle makes a tell-tale noise, say, while the car is at 35 MPH, try having a friend tape-record the noise for playback to the mechanic. The more you are able to narrow down the symptoms, the better are your chances of getting the car fixed right the first time. Give details and description of the symptoms as precisely as possible:

1. What are the sounds or smells? (clunking or burning, etc.)
2. Where are they coming from?
3. When do they occur? (Hot or cold weather: right after starting the car; at 55 MPH?)
4. How does the car feel to drive?
5. How long has the problem occurred?

Write down each repair to be performed and all the symptoms of problems to be fixed before going to the shop. Keep a copy for yourself for later reference.

As mentioned above, consumer auto courses are frequently given by community colleges or local community groups. These courses are not held for auto mechanics, but are aimed specifically at teaching auto consumers more about their cars. Such training can be especially valuable for consumers who want to know more about the upkeep of their cars in order to avoid being "taken" by a repair shop.

HOW TO AVOID GETTING GYPPED

Always request a written estimate. The value of an estimate is that it prevents a dishonest shop from running up a bill for unnecessary items. If you are overcharged, you can hold the repair shop to the figure in the estimate, taking the written estimate to small claims court to recover the overcharge if necessary.

Ask the shop what kind and length of warranty covers your repair work. Be sure that the terms of the warranty are spelled out in writing on your copy of the repair order.

Never sign a blank repair order. Unless you completely trust the mechanic, never tell him simply to "do **whatever** needs to be done to repair the car." Find out how long the repairs will take and how much they might cost. Leave a phone number where you can be reached.

Ask that replaced parts be returned to you after the completion of repairs. Most good shops will agree to return replaced parts unless the parts must be returned to the manufacturer for warranty reasons.

Where the car needs a major repair, such as a transmission overhaul, call a few shops ahead of time to compare prices. Beware of bargain advertisements, especially for transmission work, tune-ups or brake repairs. Many unscrupulous shops use these gimmicks as "bait" to get your car up on the lift so the service writer can talk you into unnecessary repairs.

When picking up the car, check over the repair order to see that everything was done and make sure no extras were added. Test drive the car to make sure all the work was done correctly. Keep copies of all repair orders, as discussed previously in this book. If the repair was not done correctly, discuss the problem with the repair shop first. If necessary, talk with the shop manager or owner. Many problems caused by a lack of communication can be resolved by talking to a person in authority at the shop.

Avoid having major repairs performed on auto trips, unless the car has "broken down" and you have no choice. Consumers who are away from home and anxious to be on their way are often victimized by a number of unethical repair shops that are located right off major highways. These highway bandits stock up on parts like air filters, tires or batteries, and will try to sell the traveling consumer a new one whether necessary or not. For example, the mechanic may tell you how lucky you are that you stopped, because the air filter is too dirty and in need of replacement. Or the gasoline attendant may cut the fan belt, puncture the tires or disconnect the battery cables and then try to sell unneeded part and repairs. One segment of CBS's *60 Minutes* secretly filmed attendants at a service station along a major highway tampering with consumers' cars to make them appear as if they needed major, expensive repairs.

To avoid becoming a victim of such tactics, get out of the car and watch the attendant carefully. Always take the name and shop address of the salesperson who tries to sell you a new tire or battery, and if he or she seems hesitant, take your business elsewhere. Consumers who do get swindled by a service station connected to a big oil company may have some recourse against the oil company that franchises the station. One way to prevent this form of highway robbery is to have a trusted mechanic thoroughly check your car before leaving on a long trip.

Following these tips should help avoid the trouble H. Cherry, a West Virginia consumer, found herself in when she brought her VW to an independent shop for repair. She did describe the problem, but no repair order was written up, no written estimate was provided, no request to keep any replaced parts was noted, and no authorizing statement was signed. Ms. Cherry arranged to have the car repaired when she was scheduled to be in the hospital for three weeks. When she picked up the car, it had an additional 3,000 miles and the repair bill was over $800. To make matters worse, the problem was not fixed.

Not only did the mechanics know that Ms. Cherry would be in the hospital while the repairs were being made, they called her there on several occasions to inquire as to her well being. At no time did they inform her about their lack of progress in diagnosing and repairing her car.

When she protested she was simply told to document her complaint. The Volkswagen dealership where she took the car for a second opinion said that it was inconceivable that all four fuel injectors would need replacement simultaneously. If so, they pointed out, other parts would have had to be replaced. Ms. Cherry sent this and further statements to the first shop and threatened to take the matter up with consumer groups if they did not reimburse her. While she ultimately prevailed, she could have avoided this difficulty by getting a written estimate.

HOW TO COMPLAIN

If the repair shop refuses to resolve your complaint, follow the suggestions in Chapter 4, "How to Complain," which discusses federal, state and local agencies that may take an interest in your complaint.

If further help is needed in solving the problem, consider using small claims courts and other strategies discussed throughout the book. If your complaint is based on incompetence and the mechanics are certified by NIASE at the repair shop, send a copy of your complaint to ASE, 13505 Dulles Technology Drive, Herndon, Virginia, 22071.

If you disagree with the repair bill, it is normally advisable to pay it first in order to get the car back, then pursue your complaint. Most states have what are called "mechanic's lien" laws; if a consumer refuses to pay a bill, no matter how outrageous, the shop can keep the car. In some states, you do not have to pay the bill to get the car back under a mechanic's lien. In those states a consumer can post a bond in court for twice the amount of the disputed bill. The consumer can recover the bond by taking the case to court and winning. Consumers in states where no bond is permitted can pay and then sue to recover the overcharge. In cases of blatant overcharge by the repair shop, a consumer can pay by check and then drive away, stopping payment on the check that day.

Some states require written estimates and authorization for repairs. In those states, a mechanic's lien would be invalidated where the shop has failed to comply with these requirements. Check with a local consumer organization or agency, or a lawyer to find out the law on mechanic's liens in your state.

Whatever your gripe against a repair shop may be, you have to file a complaint before you can successfully resolve the dispute.

CHAPTER 15

WHAT USUALLY GOES WRONG

Breakdowns can be caused by defects, abuse, or plain wear and tear, but in a new car practically any malfunction can be called a defect. As a general rule, all parts of a car except routine maintenance items such as oil filters should last at least as long as the period of any written warranty. If, with normal wear and tear, a part breaks down during this period, then according to the warranty it is defective. Major items such as the engine and transmission should last for the life of the car which is 12 years and 120,000 miles on average. In no event should an engine or transmission fail in less than 7 years or 70,000 miles.

Certain breakdowns are more common in new cars, others in particular makes and models, while some are very common in all cars. This chapter will describe the most important defects and the ways in which they affect the safety of the car, and provide you with enough knowledge to develop a sense of whether they are repaired properly.

1. Tires

Tires tend to be one of the more defect-ridden components on cars, and their failures generally have more disastrous consequences than do other car defects. You can see evidence of how frequently they fail along any major highway—chunks of rubber and damaged guard rails are left behind, although the rest of the debris has been removed.

Until radial tires became standard equipment on U.S. cars during the 1970's, owners were lucky to get as many as 20,000 miles on a set of bias-ply or bias-belted tires. The radial, with its more efficient design, eliminates much of the friction within the tire's construction, prolonging tire life and increasing gas mileage. Because of increased demand and the effects of competition in the tire industry they now constitute the lion's share of U.S. tire sales. Treadwear ratings, which appear on tires as the result of a successful suit by the Center for Auto Safety against the National Highway Traffic Safety Administration (NHTSA) demonstrate that the tread life of radials is generally superior to that of bias-ply and bias-belted tires.

In addition to treadwear ratings, passenger tires have traction and temperature (high-speed) ratings molded into their side walls as part of the Uniform Tire Quality Grading System mandated by Congress. For information, write NHTSA or call the Auto Safety Hotline and ask for information on tire ratings **plus** a list of the ratings. (See Appendix P for address and number.) All tires also have identification numbers molded into the front sidewall. The ID number is preceded by the symbols DOT #. The first two digits of these numbers identify the plant where the tire was made while the last three digits identify the week and year the tire was made just like a date code for food in the supermarket. Thus 409 at the end of the ID number means the tire was made in the 40th week of 1989 while 220 shows the tire was made in the 22nd week of 1990. When complaining about tire defects, it is very important to include this number. These ID numbers are also used to identify tires included in a recall.

Defective tires—whether radial or bias—can disintegrate at any time, regardless of the age, price, or general quality of the brand. Failure can be sudden and often total. Chances of failure are greatest at the precise moment when an accident would be unthinkably disastrous—when the car is filled with passengers and traveling at high speed.

If the tire is properly loaded and inflated, it is safe from disintegration only if there are no serious defects in the cords or other parts of the tire. To inflate a tire properly, you **must** check with your own, pretested pressure gauge. A pressure gauge, treadwear gauge, valve caps and safety booklet are included in a "Tire Safety and Mileage Kit" available for $3.00 from the Tire Industry Safety Council, PO Box 1801, Washington, D.C. 20013 for $3.00. See the February 1987 issue of *Consumer Reports* for comparative ratings of tire gauges.

The rubber tread and sidewalls of tires are laid over layers of heavy cord which form the plies of the tire. The plies give a tire its strength, so when the cord breaks or fails, the tire usually loses its air. On some tires the cord is poorly bonded to the rubber, and cord separation occurs. Cord separation causes heat to build up and may lead to ply or tread separation. You can easily spot thread separation: pressurized air from inside the tire escapes through the plies of cord and forms a bubble beneath the stretchy rubber tread or sidewall.

Ply separation, or disintergration for which a single cause is not apparent, usually occurs when the tire is subjected to high speed or heavy loads for sufficient time to built up heat. Other common defects include "out-of-round" tires (which ride roughly and wear unevenly), tires that are simply too weak to withstand normal road hazards, and tires which are so far out of shape or size they do not fir properly on the wheels.

All of these defects have been found on tires bought and tested by NHTSA. This is particularly disturbing since the workout given to tires in NHTSA's tests is mild compared to the more strenuous use the tires get on the highway.

Defective tires have been recalled in increasing numbers since the introduction of longer-life radials which enabled NHTSA investigators to catch up with defective tires before they were off the road. The Firestone 500 steel-belted radial, with its chronic tread separation tendency, represents the classic "bad tire." Of over 50 million made between 1972 and 1978, NHTSA ordered some 15 million recalled. Millions more would have been recalled, but the short three-year statute of limitations from the date of sale had expired.

Consumers who survived a Firestone 500 blowout will never forget the experience. M. E. Pitcher of Phoenix, Arizona wrote:

> I wanted the best tires for my new car and paid extra money to the Ford dealer to have Firestone 500 steel-belted radials. I feel that my family and friends are very lucky to be alive.
>
> My car had less than 5,000 miles on it when the first tire went. Fortunately I was traveling below the speed limit. In spite of that when the tire blew out it completely lifted the rear end of the car off the road and flipped it over. My mother and a young child were in the car with me at the time. We landed upside down in the median between divided highways. By the time we stopped rolling, a tow truck was already there since the driver was at a station across the highway and heard the tire blow. The Highway Patrol even explained about the bad quality of the Firestone tires on my car. There was nothing left of the tire but powder on the road.

Similarly, D. Hance of Durham, Pennsylvania wrote:

> There are no words that could express my feelings toward the Firestone Company. In my opinion they have completely defrauded the American public by supplying an inferior product and then refusing to face up to its shortcomings in the face of criticism.
>
> My family's experience has been with five (5) different sets of Firestone 500 tires. At least two tires of each set developed large bubbles on the sidewalls. Two tires had complete tread separation, one of which caused a major accident. All tires failed between 9,000 and 19,000 miles.
>
> Whenever the Firestone people were contacted they accused us of riding with the tires under–inflated which they say caused over-heating resulting in bubbles and tread separation.
>
> I am glad to see that someone has finally been able to do something for the American public in stopping a large organization like Firestone from cheating them.

After holding extensive hearings on the Firestone 500 steel-belted radial, Congressman John E. Moss of California concluded:

> The record is clear that Firestone had early knowledge of the serious failure propensities of the 500. Its high adjustment rates in the early years, its unusually brisk activity in settling damage claims, and its energetic efforts to improve on the earlier tires all suggest its early knowledge.
>
> These facts lead to but one conclusion. The Firestone Tire and Rubber Co., is and has been for some time in a position to avoid the devastating toll of human destruction which it knew its tire could cause. In the exercise of clear and conscious choice, it nonetheless permitted this destruction to take place.

2. Brakes

No matter what kind of car you buy, the brakes may well either be defective or dangerously inadequate under expected conditions of highway use, even though the car is brand-new. "Even with passenger car disc brakes . . . prolonged braking with a heavily laden car is still a hair-raising experience," writes Karl Ludvigsen of *Motor Trend*. In many new vehicles, the opposite problem occurs: the rear brakes are **too** effective, causing premature lock-up which can throw the car into a sideways spin even under ideal road conditions.

The rear brake lockup problem particularly affects cars with front-wheel-drive, such as the defunct General Motors "X-car," or rear-wheel-drive cars which have roughly 60% or more of their weight on the front wheels, such as Ford Mustangs with V8 engines. On the X-car and other cars with rear lockup problems, poorly chosen rear brake lining materials and improper front–rear distribution of brake fluid pressure aggravate the lock-up condition. Use of metallic rather than asbestos brake linings leads to higher friction as brake temperature increases, producing an "aggressive" lining. Careful attention by brake engineers at the drawing board stage can help avert this defect.

In 1988, the Auto Club of Missouri's Diagnostic Clinic in St. Louis conducted state safety inspections on just over 2,800 vehicles and found defective brakes were responsible for 34.4 percent of all rejections. Only exhaust systems and emission controls accounted for greater numbers of failures. Of all vehicles inspected in 1988, 13.2 percent flunked because of brake defects. Brake repairs accounted for the largest percentage (22.5%) of all vehicle repair costs, ahead of tires and wheels (21.9%), in DOT's Motor Vehicle Diagnostic Inspection Demonstration Program.

Brake failure sometimes results from leaks which allow the brake fluid to drain out. Other causes include water in the fluid which vaporizes when the brakes get warm, and (in cars with power brakes) engine stalling which cuts power assist to both brakes and steering. Also, uneven brake drums often wear the brake shoes out quickly, and differences among the braking strengths of the wheels can make the car swerve uncontrollably in a panic stop.

3. Sudden Acceleration

If anything qualifies as the "automotive defect of the 1980's" it's sudden, unexpected acceleration. Before the age of automotive engine computers, most sudden acceleration cases stemmed from defects in the mechanical throttle linkage. For instance, the largest auto recall in history involved nearly 7 million 1965-69 Chevrolets on which a motor mount broke, causing the engine to move upward and pull the accelerator linkage open without any input from the driver.

However, the newest wave of sudden acceleration reports is associated with the introduction of engine control computers on cars in the late 1970's and early 1980's. In a typical sudden acceleration accident, the driver enters the vehicle, starts the engine and shifts from park into drive or reverse. At this instant the car hurtles out of control, often into the nearest solid object, mowing down any people unfortunate enough to be in its deadly swath. Some independent engineers have isolated faults in engine computers and cruise units which have tied those components to sudden acceleration; the only common factors in new and old cases are automatic transmissions and relatively powerful engines. Reported complaints on later model cars number in the tens of thousands, with thousands of injuries and hundred of deaths. Yet by all appearances the problem has perplexed the manufacturers and the federal government. A 400-page report released by DOT in March 1989 blamed the problem on "pedal misapplication" by the driver but provided little substantiation of that theory, since most of the tests run by the agency produced contradictory or unexplained results. However, the study did contain several clues on possible electronic and mechanical explanations of sudden acceleration.

Between September 1966 and March 1989, defects in accelerator systems warranted recalls in 143 separate instances. A failure record this high is unjustifiable and disgraceful. The function of the accelerator system is simple: it transmits the movement of your foot on the gas pedal to the carburetor or fuel injection, and in some cases downshifts the transmission into passing gear. In most cars, the cables, springs and levers making up the accelerator linkage run totally unprotected through the engine compartment. If pieces of debris or other engine parts interfere with this system, the throttle can be held open. A much safer, fully protected system could easily be developed by today's engineers.

4. Engine Defects

The most common engine defects include poor tuning, cooling system defects or overheating, and excessive use of oil.

a. Tuning

Poor tuning (improper adjustments of the fuel controls in the carburetor or fuel injection and of the electrical impulses sent to the spark plugs) can cause inferior performance, stalling, hard starting, or too fast an idle. Also, poor tuning allows partly burned fuel to go out the exhaust, causing air pollution and poor gas mileage at the same time.

b. Overheating

Overheating is a particular problem with air conditioned cars. The air conditioning puts an extra strain on the engine which the cooling system may not be designed to handle. An obstruction may slow down the flow of coolant through the engine and radiator causing repeated overheating; this usually can be corrected by flushing out the cooling system or by ordinary replacement of parts. In any case, the repairs are covered by the warranty, and should be done immediately, before overheating can lead to serious engine damage. The 1984 Pontiac Fiero developed such chronic overheating and engine fire problems that General Motors set up a "Fiero Thermal Distress Task Force" within the company's bureaucracy in a futile effort to combat that car's maladies. When Lisa Lima of Kankakee, Illinois experienced an engine fire that destroyed her 1984 Fiero, she created the "Fiero Fire Fighters," a network of owners who became fed up with the car's overheating and engine fire problems.

c. "Burning" Oil

Leaking gaskets often cause heavy oil consumption in new cars. If no leaks can be found, a dealer may doubt that you are burning excessive oil and will insist on proof of oil purchases before he checks any further for causes such as faulty piston rings. As a general rule, a fully broken-in car in good condition should get at least 1000 miles for every quart of oil added. A quart of oil should last 2000 miles on average.

The issue of what constitutes excessive oil consumption brought one major automaker, Ford Motor Co., into conflict with Arizona Attorney General Robert K. Corbin during the summer of 1981. For over two years his office had investigated complaints that Ford denied warranty claims on engines which consumed excessive amounts of oil. Ford policy deemed a consumption rate as low as 400 miles per quart of oil "acceptable" for a car with 7500 miles on the odometer. On August 4, 1981 Corbin secured a settlement in which Ford agreed to increase the threshold for acceptable oil consumption to 900 miles per quart and to repair engines that consumed more oil. Two months later, Ford set that figure as nationwide policy.

5. Fires Without Crashes

FIRE! is the last cry made in many automobiles. A brief tour of any junkyard will show how completely fire can sweep through an automobile. Occasionally a gutted hulk will show no signs of having been in an accident. Most "accident-caused" and non-accident fires could be prevented.

What Usually Goes Wrong

Two of the more common causes of non-accident fires are electrical short–circuits and gasoline leakage near the hot engine where it easily catches fire. Other flammable fluids that circulate under the hood include engine oil and antifreeze. Any type of fire can result in a dangerous situation—the car can easily explode like a bomb if the fire is not quickly extinguished. Ironically, in many cases where a defect causes the fire, the burnt-out car is often junked with the consumer being reimbursed by the insurance company rather than the responsible party—the manufacturer. To make matters worse, the depreciation deducted by the insurance company often requires a consumer to shell out more money in replacing the car with a new one.

When the engine caught fire on an almost-new 1981 Renault 18i owned by Mr. and Mrs. Parker of Washington, D.C., they contacted the dealer and manufacturer but were only offered repair costs. At that point the Parkers hired an attorney who advised them to return the car to the dealer and formally revoke acceptance of it. Only after filing suit for breach of warranty were the Parkers able to recover the purchase price of their car plus expenses, damages and attorney fees totaling $41,000.

As if consumers didn't have enough to worry about, one additional factor has crept into the sorry picture of non-crash fires, namely, the volatility of gasoline being supplied by petroleum refiners today. Addition of extreme exhaust-system heat to a fuel tank containing high-volatility gasoline or gasoline-ethanol blend causes overpressurization within the tank. This excessive pressure forces fuel out from even a tightened filler cap; if the cap is then opened, a gusher of fuel douses the area and any bystanders. Introduction of a spark or other ignition source creates the potential for an inferno.

In 1987-88 Ford was forced to recall over 200,000 1983-87 Econoline vans and ambulances for fuel spurting and fires. Before they were recalled, over 80 of these vehicles had caught fire with 31 injuries and 1 death. In many instances, owners had removed the filler cap only to be drenched with gasoline and terribly burned when the gasoline caught fire.

Accident fires often result from ruptures in the gas tanks. Most gas tanks are made with only a single layer of steel, which can rupture in a serious collision. If the tank is placed between the bumper and rear axle as in the infamous 1971-76 Ford Pinto, fires can and will occur in low speed rear impact crashes. Fortunately, as manufacturers have converted to front-wheel drive, they have moved the fuel tank to a position ahead of the rear axle, thus making the tank much less vulnerable to impact damage. Check this feature on any car before you buy.

6. Transmission Failures

Whether it's an automatic or manual, manufacturers usually blame transmission failures on owner abuse and refuse to pay for the repair. Both types of transmissions have clutch plates that quickly wear out if misaligned in the case of a manual transmission or inadequately lubricated in case of an automatic. Either will subject consumers to expensive repair bills.

Another common transmission problem results when the manufacturer puts an undersized or poorly designed transmission in a car, leading to failure under moderate loads. For nearly fifteen years, defects have plagued GM's automatic transmissions, from the "Type 200" of the late 1970's through the present "automatic overdrives" that GM has installed on larger vehicles to help their gas mileage. Failures can occur at mileages of 20,000 or less and repair costs can range from $400 to over $1,000. A properly designed transmission should last 120,000 miles if properly maintained. If you want to pull a trailer or other load with a new car, tell the salesperson and ask for an adequate transmission. Even if you don't get a larger transmission, the salesperson's representation can create an implied warranty that will be the basis for recovery if the transmission fails.

7. Steering, Tire Balance and Alignment

Faulty steering, poor tire balance and/or improper front end alignment occur to some degree in practically every new car. Often they can conspire to make handling both unsure and unsafe. Vibrations develop which allow tires to shimmy on the road, ruining traction and rubbing off tread in uneven patterns. The resulting lumpy tires make the vibration even worse. In extreme cases the tire may overheat and eventually blow out.

Some cars with steering or alignment defects wander sideways on the road or consistently pull to one side, while others fail to straighten out promptly after turns. Some, running as if pigeon-toed, quietly erase the rubber form the tire within a few thousand miles. A chronic alignment problem on many 1985-86 GM models caused "cupping" and premature wear on tires installed on the non-drive axle. Wayne Orel of Lake Arrowhead, California replaced eight front tires on his Chevrolet Astro van within the first 23,000 miles. In response to complaints, GM authorized a policy extension to replace tires, install "shim kits" and perform alignments at no charge, but failed to contact owners directly. Since tires are warranted by the tire maker, not GM, most owners did not complain to GM dealers. Even the free repairs often would not cure the problem: some owners had to make several visits to the dealer to get the problem corrected. Because a given symptom could indicate any of several front-end problems, only painstaking measurement and observation can pinpoint the cause. As a result, the problems often outlive the warranty.

Alignment of the wheels and steering involves adjusting all parts of the steering mechanism and suspension so that the front wheels stay parallel to each other and flat on the pavement at all speeds with no scuffing or other unwanted action, the feel and balance of the steering are even and the ride is stable.

The cost of a shimmy or vibration can be high if the problem is not corrected immediately. Along with the front tires, parts of the steering mechanism and the front suspension may have worn out. The cause is usually faulty alignment or wheel balance, both of which are supposed to be checked in the pre-sale dealer preparation of the vehicle. In cars with independent rear suspensions, the rear wheels may also need to be aligned, so make sure that the dealer has done that on your car.

Since alignment and balance are not normally covered by the warranty, the dealer has a financial incentive to do the adjusting after you buy the car rather than before. By skimping on the alignment and balancing, the unscrupulous dealer also misses an opportunity to correct any loose or defective parts which then may lead to failure and a possible accident.

You can detect poor alignment yourself in a new car by measuring the wear of the front tires. Insert a tread-wear gauge into the grooves nearest the inner and outer edges of the tread on both wheels. If your measurements indicate any noticeable differences in the depth of the tread, the alignment or wheel balance may be off. If your car has independent rear suspension, check the rear tires too.

Power steering on new cars sometimes fails when the rubber hoses which carry the fluid are cut or abraded by fan belts, tires, or other parts. This happens when hoses are placed too close to moving parts by sloppy designers or assemblers and the defect slips through inspection.

Sudden loss of power steering assist due to fluid leakage or stalling of the engine does not make steering impossible—unless the surprise leaves you frozen and bewildered. But power failure does make steering so much harder that drivers may think that there is no steering at all; and even if they do realize what is wrong, the needed force may be more than they can muster.

Even more dangerous is jamming of the power steering spool valve because of particles in the fluid causing the car to turn sharply to one side or the other. Such hidden defects in the steering system can precipitate accidents for which the true cause is never determined. Some manufacturers have used fine porosity in-line filters in the power steering hydraulic system to eliminate this danger.

Some cars also have steering columns that can lock-up in any gear when the ignition is turned off. Other cars have safety devices that require automatic transmissions to be in park or manual transmissions to have a separate button to be pushed before the ignition key can be removed and the steering locks. Cars without this safety feature can have steering lock-up while in motion if the key is inadvertently turned or the ignition lock malfunctions. Such cars have an unacceptable safety risk. After a serious accident in his Nissan 280Z caused by steering column lockup, Wilson Sherman of Encino, California got California's DMV to include a warning in its Driver Handbook and the NHTSA to issue a notice of proposed rulemaking to change this system.

Power-assisted rack and pinion steering units often develop leaks and lose their power assist in cold weather before warming up. These units incorporate a spool valve, which directs hydraulic fluid within the steering system whenever the steering wheel is turned. The valve rotates on flexible plastic rings inside an aluminum housing. Problems occur when the rings age and lose their seal; as a result, steering effort increases significantly. This condition is often called "morning sickness" by mechanics. Ford was the first major auto company to admit this problem when it extended its warranty to 5 years/50,000 miles for power steering failure on 1978-83 models. General Motors had the most widespread case when 16 million front-wheel-drive 1980-88 vehicles developed this defect. Under pressure from the Center for

Auto Safety, GM was also forced to extend its warranty to 5 years/ 50,000 miles.

8. Suspension

The suspension consists of the springs, shock absorbers, and other parts which are designed to support the car and give it a comfortable, yet stable ride. The suspensions of most American cars used to provide plenty of comfort, but were so soft that control of the car became very difficult in many emergency situations. Newer domestic cars tend to handle more precisely, but some models still emphasize ride over handling. Sudden swerves or bumps can throw such a car so far off balance that it will go out of control. Suspension inadequacies frequently cause single-car crashes where no one lives to describe what happened, and where the police report often attributes the crash to reckless driving.

What stability a car has deteriorates rapidly with age. Shock absorbers often become useless after a few thousand miles, and the soft springs become even softer when they age. To reduce these problems, a consumer can specify a heavy-duty suspension when ordering a new car. When buying, test both types of suspension to see which offers better handling. In an advertisement, Mercedes-Benz stated the problem well:

> A passenger doesn't **need** suspension fit for a racer, argue some critics . . . For everyday city driving, this is sheer engineering extravagance.
>
> But some day you **might** have to get off the pavement, onto a stretch of potholed back road. You **might** have to enter a sharp curve or a turn-off faster than you intended. You **might** have to change course quickly while cruising on a busy turnpike.
>
> And suddenly, you realize this engineering extravagance is no extravagance at all.

9. Electrical and Electronic Systems

Once the "electronics" in your car were almost entirely confined to the transistorized radio. Now, talented electrons set the speed at which your car travels, adjust engine operation to suit driving conditions, give you readouts on vehicle speed, oil pressure, time and engine temperature, and in some vehicles shift your automatic transmission from one forward gear to another.

If all this electronic wizardry functions correctly, fine—but what happens when something goes wrong? As noted in the section above on Accelerator Systems, electronic engine control computers and cruise control units can malfunction and lead to unintended episodes of sudden acceleration. The section below on "Gauges" details some of the problems with electronic dashboards.

The wiring, switches, and sockets of modern automotive lighting systems are generally so cheaply constructed that failure is frequent. The plugs and sockets which connect the various parts of the lighting system are made of plastic which melts whenever the overloaded wires and connections inside heat up. Inadequate moisture protection allows water to get in the sockets and corrode the metal contacts. As a result your headlights may go out when you hit the dimmer switch, your taillights may fail repeatedly, or your car's entire electrical system may short out with no warning at all.

10. Headlights

Since the government relaxed headlight standards in 1982, the auto makers have concocted a virtually infinite variety of "aerodynamic" or "designer" headlights for their cars. When an old-fashioned round or rectangular lamp burned out, you could find cheap replacements even in supermarkets and drug stores. With the new-age lamps, however, auto makers force you to go back to a dealer—at "eye-opening" costs of up to $245 on these photometric marvels. What's worse, the aero lamps often provide a dimmer view of the road than the old standardized units.

With the trend toward aero headlamps, at least manufacturers are turning away from the fad of the 1960's-1970's—"hidden headlamps," often called "eyelids" or headlight covers. Hidden headlamps cost a small fortune yet serve absolutely no useful purpose, require expensive repairs, stick shut so often that the auto manufacturers give instructions in their owner's manual on how to rip them open by hand, and have been the subject of recall campaigns.

11. Air Conditioners

Air conditioners are not only the most expensive of all options, but also one of the most popular. Given the high frequency of repair and increased service costs and fuel consumption, air conditioning is an option that many consumers would do well to avoid if they live in a climate that doesn't require it. Because an air conditioner takes so much power to run, it invariably cuts down on gas mileage. Some air conditioners are prone to growing mold in areas where condensed water accumulates, so you should be particularly alert to this problem if you are allergic to molds. Watch out for dealers who attempt to cure this problem by dumping hazardous chemicals into the air conditioner.

Air conditioning cuts gasoline mileage by as much as 4 mpg when operated on a hot summer day. Much of the heat pulled out of the occupant area by the air conditioner is dumped under the hood. Also, the car's engine, which must supply extra power, heats up more as it runs harder. The engine's cooling system is sometimes not beefed up enough to remove this extra heat, so the engine can be damaged by overheating. Manufacturer-installed air conditioning tends to come with heavy duty electrical and cooling systems to handle the extra load. Check with the salesperson to see what type comes on your car; if dealer-installed, ask the dealer what steps have been taken to insure adequate engine and cooling system performance.

Freon leakage is a common problem, and studies have now conclusively shown that freon and other chlorofluorocarbons (CFC's) that escape into the stratosphere are destroying the earth's ozone layer, which shields the planet from excessive ultraviolet radiation. Venting of freon from automotive air conditioners causes about 16% of the destruction to the earth's ozone layer. If you do purchase an air conditioner and need to have it serviced, be sure to deal only with a shop that uses equipment which can capture used refrigerant and recycle it. Have any freon leaks repaired promptly, and don't use "do it yourself" freon kits to refill a leaking air conditioning system, since the chance of accidental escape of freon is high. Less frequent but more expensive failures occur when the air conditioner's compressor bearings seize up and stop the compressor.

12. Gauges

Operation of all gauges, especially temperature, oil pressure, amperage, and fuel level, is vitally important for your safety and for prevention of unnecessary damage to your car's engine. Now that warning lights have replaced many needle gauges, the problem is that you can't always tell if the lights are out of order. The best way to be sure they are all working is to have them checked periodically by a mechanic or diagnostician.

Between checkups you can get a rough idea of how the warning lights are doing by watching for them when starting the car. For example, the oil pressure and charging system lights should glow when you turn the ignition key. The light should go out shortly after the engine is started. Many new cars feature space-age "digital readouts" for the speedometer and other gauges; the newest types feature displays right on the windshield. Rest assured that these expensive "light shows" malfunction regularly, and when they fail, you can count on shelling out a lot of money for repairs. Stick to a full set of needle gauges, which are often standard or available as a reasonably-priced option.

Speedometers and odometers are notoriously inaccurate. An inaccurate odometer which over-registers mileage can reduce your warranty by a thousand miles, and an inaccurate speedometer can get you arrested for speeding. The best way to test these instruments is to use the mileage markers on some highways. At an even 55 MPH you should go a mile in one minute and five seconds.

13. Cruise Controls

The automatic cruise control which is available on many cars, may well be one of the most dangerous luxuries available today. Cruise control units have been linked by some engineers to the sudden acceleration defect described above.

Like other vehicle components, cruise controls can succumb to defects. In July 1989, GM recalled almost two million 1984-88 cars with V8 engines to repair the cruise control units due to a small plastic part in the cruise control unit that could dislodge and prevent the accelerator from returning to idle. Even when a cruise control functions correctly, it can lead to driver error and accident by lulling you into inattentiveness.

14. Body Leakage

Water leakage around the windows, doors, or other parts, while not as dangerous as most defects, can be more difficult to get repaired. Windshields that leak around the edges should be taken out to cure the problem, but few dealers do this. Other leaks around fittings or through missing plugs are difficult to spot. Even when a leak is "corrected," dealers often don't check their repair by hosing it with water, so you may have to make several return trips to get the job completed.

15. Loose Parts

Loose parts are so common that they are almost taken for granted. While most loose parts cause only rattles, some, such as loose glove compartment doors, can cause serious injury in an accident or sudden stop and must be fixed immediately. Once loose parts are diagnosed, they can usually be fixed quickly, and a good dealer will fix them while you wait.

Since even the best-maintained vehicle may still cause an emergency, it helps to know what to do when a malfunction occurs. A government pamphlet, "How to Deal with Motor Vehicle Emergencies," can be obtained free by writing:

National Highway Traffic Safety Administration
Office of Public Affairs and Consumer Services
Washington, DC 20590

CHAPTER 16

AUTO SAFETY

Fatalities occurring in motor vehicle accidents are one of our nation's leading causes of death. Motor vehicle accidents are the leading cause of death up through age 40. Two out of every three Americans born today will be injured in a vehicle accident during their life. In 1989, more than 47,000 people in the United States met violent deaths in motor vehicle collisions while almost 2,000,000 more suffered disabling injuries. The total costs arising from motor vehicle accidents in 1989 was nearly $100 billion. This figure reflects lost wages and productivity, medical expenses, ambulance and police services, funeral costs, insurance and administration, rehabilitation expenses and property damage from motor vehicle accidents.

Economic losses are only one aspect of motor vehicle accidents. Persons injured in crashes often suffer physical pain and mental and emotional anguish which is beyond any economic recompense. Permanent disability such as paralysis, loss of eyesight or brain damage can deprive individuals of the ability to achieve even minor goals and aspirations and leave them dependent on others for economic support and routine physical care. While accident victims bear the most severe consequences from the injuries, serious repercussions are felt by those around them. Caring for a disabled person places a considerable burden on the family, both economically and emotionally. The emotional consequences of the victim's physical problems often affect family relationships and may even affect the family bond. Effects on family members can be particularly devastating when the accident leads to death. Sudden, unexpected and permanent separation from parent, child or sibling can create feelings of grief, anguish, guilt, fear, insecurity and a sense of loss that affect a person's emotional state for years after the accident.

Enormous as the highway traffic toll is, it would be even larger but for the passage of the National Traffic and Motor Vehicle Safety Act in 1966 and the imposition of vehicle safety standards in 1968. In 1966 the death rate per 100 million miles traveled was 5.5. With the incorporation of safety standards in all vehicles on the road and imposition of highway safety programs such as mandatory seat belt laws and the 55 MPH speed limit, the fatality rate per 100 million miles dropped to 2.3 in 1989. If the fatality rate had stayed at 1966 levels, then 107,000 Americans would have been killed on the road in 1989. In the first twenty years after creation of NHTSA, at least 150,000 lives have been saved by the imposition of vehicle safety standards alone.

One program which has saved thousands of lives was instituted not as a safety standard, but as a measure to conserve energy. The 55 MPH national speed limit was established in late 1973 in response to the oil embargo and ensuing shortage of gasoline. At first, both speed of travel and the number of fatalities went down noticeably, with more than 5,000 lives saved each year in 1974 and 1975 which were directly attributable to the reduction in speed. But average speeds began inching up over 55 MPH in 1976 with a corresponding change in the fatality rate. As more motorists disobeyed the 55 MPH speed limit and as Congress raised the limit to 65 MPH on rural interstates in 1987, the lifesavings dropped to 2,000 per year.

The years ahead present various safety challenges and opportunities. As we move to lighter cars to conserve energy, we must build more safety into them. As more people substitute light trucks and vans for cars, we must require them to meet the same safety standards as cars. Just the increased numbers of vehicles and miles traveled will mean more deaths and injuries unless more safety measures are put into our vehicles and road systems. Without improving safety, traffic fatalities will climb to over 60,000 by the year 2000. But by improving safety, we can lower the toll to 40,000.

NATIONAL HIGHWAY TRAFFIC SAFETY ADMINISTRATION

The Federal regulatory agency responsible for the development and introduction of safety standards and the duty to get the auto companies to build products with fewer safety related defects is the National Highway Traffic Safety Administration (NHTSA). The NHTSA was established by the National Traffic and Motor Vehicle Safety Act of 1966. The agency was empowered to establish motor vehicle safety standards, to undertake and support necessary safety research and development, and to investigate and recall motor vehicles and equipment with defects.

FEDERAL SAFETY STANDARDS

Most of the federal safety standards first became effective for 1968 model year automobiles. These standards governed the strength and quality of seat belts and anchorages, safety glass, impact-absorbing steering columns and its rearward displacement in a frontal collision, safety door latches and hinges, location of dash instrumentation, padded dash and visors and mounting of fuel tanks and filler spouts. Standards were also implemented setting performance criteria for brakes, tire tread, lights, windshield wipers and other features.

From 1968 to 1989, only a few additional standards have been issued. These include standards governing windshield mounting, performance requirements for optional child restraints, strengthened side doors to better resist side impact, improved crush resistance of vehicle roofs for better occupant protection in rollover accidents, the flammability of materials used in car interiors, protection of the fuel tank in rear and side impacts, and high-mounted brake lights.

The 1990's promise to be the auto safety decade. After 20 years of delay, the most lifesaving safety standard, Standard 208—Occupant Crash Protection, is finally going into effect for all 1990 model year cars. This standard specifies that all passenger cars manufactured for sale or use in the United States must be equipped with front-seat airbags or automatic seat belts to protect occupants from injury in crashes up to 30 mph into a barrier or 60 MPH into a parked car. Other standards planned for the 1990's include improved side impact protection, safety standards for light trucks and vans equal to cars, rear shoulder belts, better bumpers, pedestrian protection and anti-lock brakes for all cars and trucks.

For livesaving potential, nothing beats the airbag. Once they are installed in all passenger vehicles, they will save 12-15,000 lives per year and prevent over 100,000 serious injuries. The airbag system has been extensively tested both on the road and in laboratories. The concept of the airbag is simple: in a collision, airbags inflate within 30 milliseconds inside the vehicle—so that the occupant collides against the bag instead of metal or glass. The airbag cushions the occupants and distributes the crash forces more evenly so that occupants can survive crashes at speeds up to 50 MPH into a wall with an advanced airbag system.

The benefit of airbags was graphically exhibited to Denise Brodie who was driving on Route 3 in Lancaster county, Virginia in a 1988 Chrysler LeBaron convertible on September 22, 1988. Suddenly an on-coming 1985 Ford Country Squire station wagon crossed over into her lane and struck her car head-on at a closing speed of over 70 MPH. Her mid-size 2,600 pound car was driven backward by the massive 4,000 Ford. The airbag inflated so fast she never saw it. Denise Brodie suffered only moderate injuries but the driver of the Ford died, despite wearing a seat belt and shoulder belt. According to NHTSA investigators, "The airbag provided the driver of the LeBaron with the additional restraint [over her 3-point belt] to reduce her level of injury, thus saving her life."

CRASH TEST RATINGS

Beginning with the 1980 model year, NHTSA began crash testing vehicles into fixed barriers at 35 MPH to compare the occupant protection by one car versus another. Each car has electronically monitored dummies in the driver and passenger seats which record injury criteria that determine whether occupants in similar crashes in the real world would be killed or seriously injured. The crash speed is 5 MPH higher than the 30 MPH used to determine compliance with federal occupant protection safety standards. This represents a crash one-third more severe than the safety standards require since crash energy goes up exponentially with speed.

The purpose of the New Car Assessment Program (NCAP) is to not only provide buyers with comparative safety information to buy more crashworthy cars but also to encourage car makers to build more safety into future cars so they perform better on the tests. NCAP is an unqualified success in both regards. When NHTSA first released ratings for the 1980 models, only 5 out of 32 models tested passed all the test criteria. Not a single Japanese car came close to passing. The manufacturers began to improve the crashworthiness of their vehicles so that now more than half the vehicles tested each year achieve passing scores. For companies such as Toyota, a failing model is the exception and not the rule. To obtain the latest crash test information, consumers can call the NHTSA Hotline as explained in Chapter 4.

DEFECTS INVESTIGATION AND RECALLS

Another primary mission of NHTSA is to investigate safety defects unknown to, overlooked by, or covered by the vehicle and vehicle equipment manufacturers. Between 1967 and 1989, over 1,000 defect investigations were conducted. During a defect investigation, the NHTSA checks consumer mail it has received, requires data on failures and other information from the automobile manufacturers, checks with consumer groups and repair facilities for further data, and issues Consumer Protection Bulletins or Public Advisories to the media to generate further reports of failures from the public at large.

After gathering all the information pertinent to the defect, NHTSA makes an initial finding of whether there is or is not a safety defect. The manufacturer is informed of the finding and given notice of the time and place when a public meeting will be held so that the manufacturer and other interested parties may present their views. A notice is published in the Federal Register and released to the media to inform the public of the meeting.

After the public meeting, NHTSA reviews the material presented and makes a final determination. If the administrator determines that a safety defect does exist, a final letter is written to the manufacturer requiring the recall of all other vehicles, tires, or vehicle equipment affected. Should the manufacturer refuse, the administrator can go to court to compel the recall action and impose a fine of up to $800,000.

CITIZEN PETITIONS

As explained in detail in Chapter 4, consumers may petition NHTSA to begin investigations into safety related defects which the consumer believes may also occur in other vehicles. In 1988, NHTSA received eighteen petitions from consumers urging that defect investigations be conducted. Six of these petitions resulted in defect investigation. In response to all the petitions, NHTSA obtained and examined all available information before notifying the consumer whether or not the petition for a defect investigation was granted.

NEED FOR FURTHER IMPROVEMENTS

The need for further improvements in motor vehicle safety is abundantly clear. For example, passenger safety for light trucks and vans needs to be improved because these vehicles are being used more and more as substitutes for cars. As the population of these vehicles has increased, so has the number of deaths to their drivers and passengers and to occupants of other vehicles. Light truck, van and multipurpose passenger vehicle occupant fatalities rose from 4,332 in 1975 to 6,935 in 1987—a 60 percent increase. During that same period, by comparison, there was a three percent decrease in passenger car occupant fatalities.

Currently, most vans, pickup trucks, and jeep-type vehicles are not required to meet many major federal safety standards for passenger cars, and the automobile manufacturers have done little to provide protection for light truck and van occupants. These vehicles do not have to meet the federal safety standards for head restraints, side impact, roof strength, passive restraints, bumper damageability, and rear mounted brake lights that passenger automobiles must meet. To make matters worse, these vehicles are more unstable and rollover more often than passenger cars. Under prodding from Congress and safety groups such as the Center for Auto Safety, NHTSA has proposed to extend passenger car standards to light trucks and vans in the 1990's. Until these standards are actually extended to light trucks and vans, consumers will be getting less safe vehicles.

To date, NHTSA and the automobile companies have done very little to reduce the likelihood of injury or death in pedestrian-automobile collisions. Many domestic and foreign automobiles have numerous exterior protrusions such as hood ornaments and bumper guards that localize the impact and cause extensive injuries. Each year, approximately 100,000 pedestrian accidents kill nearly 8,000 people and injure many thousands more. Pedestrian accident statistics indicate that 77 percent of pedestrian impacts involve the front end of the car and that a majority of these impacts occurs at speeds less than 20 MPH. Research has shown that at 24 MPH, the human body can survive the impact if the front end of the car collapses one foot. Calspan, an automobile safety research corporation working under contract with NHTSA, developed a soft bumper covering the full front face of an automobile that will pick up the pedestrian and carry him along until the vehicle stops, without throwing the pedestrian under the wheels or into the windshield. The bumper developed was designed to recover its original shape after impact. The introduction of similar bumpers would prevent a large number of fatalities and reduced the costs of low speed two-car collisions.

Occupant crash protection in higher speed impacts must be improved if we are to further reduce our highway losses. Current automobiles provide impact protection of 30-35 MPH in a barrier collision or 60-70 MPH in an impact with a stationary vehicle of the same weight. Side impact protection is even worse, protecting only up to 12-15 MPH. The technology is available to significantly improve the crashworthiness of today's average vehicle. Automotive safety researchers have developed subcompact-size vehicles that are designed to protect the vehicle occupants in collisions of up to 50 MPH into a solid barrier or 100 MPH into a parked car. These engineers have not used any exotic materials or processes, but have designed their vehicles with safety as their foremost goal. Not only are these vehicles extremely safe, but they are also very fuel efficient, comfortable and stylish.

Thus the 35 MPH protection assured by passive restraints in current motor vehicles can be greatly improved. Passive protection at 50 MPH is easily attainable and will eliminate nearly 80 percent of the societal costs of frontal automobile accidents and 75 percent of the fatalities. Research has demonstrated that the side crashworthiness of vehicles can be significantly improved by the addition of reinforcements, increasing the thickness of the sheet metal, substituting high strength, low alloy steel for mild steel, using laminated glass in side windows, and padding the door and roof pillars. These improvements would increase the protection from the current 12-15 MPH to a safer 40-50 MPH in side impacts.

LARGE CAR versus SMALL CAR

The adoption of strict fuel economy standards and the increasing cost of gasoline that will insure more fuel efficient and necessarily lighter automobiles have spurred a growing concern over the safety of small cars. If large and small cars are constructed in the same way, larger cars are safer when they strike a smaller car. But as the Tidewater, Virginia airbag crash described above shows, small cars can be made safer than large cars. In addition, large cars pose a greater threat to pedestrians, motorcyclists and bicyclists so that reducing their weight would reduce the 13,000 non-occupant fatalities they cause each year.

Small cars **can** be designed to be as safe as or safer than present large passenger cars. Contractors working for the Department of Transportation's Research Safety Vehicle Program designed and built 2,250 pound subcompact vehicles that have a higher level of occupant protection than is currently available in even the largest 4500-5000 pound automobiles. These cars are able to withstand frontal barrier impacts in the 40-50 MPH range while current automobiles are able to withstand only 30-40 MPH barrier impacts without massive intrusion into the passenger compartment. Minicars, a California company which designed one of the Research Safety Vehicles, also altered a number of 1974 Ford Pintos with readily available techniques that could be used to make current small cars safer than current large ones. Similar results have been obtained by small foreign companies such as Volvo, Volkswagen and Datsun on their own Experimental Safety Vehicles (ESV's). When Volkswagen introduced the Rabbit in 1975, it included many features from their ESV so that the 2,000 pound Rabbit with the automatic seat belt had a lower injury severity rating than the 4500-pound Ford LTD.

Since there is considerable difference in crashworthiness between cars of similar size, it is important for consumers to pick out the best performing vehicles. In addition to relying on the NCAP crash ratings discussed above, consumers can obtain safety ratings based on insurance injury claim frequency for recent model years from the Highway Loss Data Institute (HLDI). Each year, HLDI releases a report which contains ratings for most passenger cars and vans and identifies the best and worst. To obtain the latest ratings, write HLDI at 1005 N. Glebe Road, Arlington, Virginia 22201.

The improved crashworthiness of any automobile is worthless to its occupants unless proper restraints are used—either "active restraints" such as seat belts or "passive restraints" such as airbags or automatic belts. The use of restraints greatly improves the safety of any vehicle. Researchers at the University of North Carolina have shown that lap and shoulder belts were 57.4 percent more effective at preventing or lessening serious or fatal injuries than cars without these restraints. In automobiles under 3,600 pounds, lap and shoulder belts were 51.9 percent more effective; in larger cars, 64.5 percent. For airbag-equipped automobiles, the protection offered in frontal collision is even greater.

Although government safety programs are necessary to reduce the mounting toll of motor vehicle-related deaths, injuries and property damage, the cooperation of the auto industry and individual motorists is also essential to decrease these losses. Human carnage on the highway would be reduced if the industry would put a greater emphasis on auto safety than on cosmetic styling and annual design changes. More lives would be saved if individual motorists would follow the 55 MPH speed limit, wear seat belts or use other available restraints, and avoid speeding, drinking-and-driving and other unnecessary driving risks.

CHAPTER 17

FUEL ECONOMY &
ENERGY CONSERVATION

While environmental problems are still very much with us, we are now confronted as well by an energy crisis which continues to worsen and which threatens the security and economic stability of the country. And once again the automobile is front and center as the single largest source of energy waste in our society.

> Russell E. Train, Former Administrator
> Environmental Protection Agency

This summer, we have seen many reports about the so-called "greenhouse effect." As the nations of the world grow, they burn increasing amounts of fossil fuels that give off carbon dioxide, which acts as a blanket and thus could contribute to an increase in the temperature of the atmosphere. One critical answer to this problem is conservation—and that will be a priority of my administration.

> George H. Bush. President
> United States of America

The Arab oil embargo of 1973–74 demonstrated to the nation the great dependence of automobile transportation on the availability of petroleum sources. The hot summer of 1988 demonstrated to the nation the dangers of global warming due to the "greenhouse" effect of carbon dioxide emissions from fossil fuel combustion. The Arab oil embargo led to a doubling of auto fuel economy. Despite this major accomplishment gas mileage needs to be redoubled again by the year 2000 to lessen global warming.

Almost all fuels used in transportation are derived from petroleum. The amount of energy used by motor vehicles each year in the U.S. grew from 13% in 1950 to 49% in 1987 with 10.5 million barrels per day, more than 60% of total U.S. petroleum consumption, being used in transportation. More than 60% of this amount was used by automobiles. Despite serious adverse effects on our balance of payment and national security, we import nearly half the petroleum we consume at a cost of over $40 billion annually. Each gallon of gasoline burned produces 20 pounds of carbon dioxide with total annual emissions of over 250 million tons from cars alone in the U.S. each year.

Recognizing the need to reduce energy consumption and the refusal of car companies to voluntarily improve gas mileage, Congress mandated fuel efficiency improvements. In 1975, Congress enacted the Energy Policy and Conservation Act (the Energy Act) requiring a 1985 average new car fuel economy standard of 27.5 MPG that effectively doubles the average fuel economy of new cars from 1974 levels. The Energy Act gave the U.S. Department of Transportation (DOT) authority to set fuel economy standards for light trucks and vans and to increase new car standards above 27.5 MPG for post-1985 model year vehicles.

The government's task of setting standards for fuel economy has not been an easy one. One hurdle in promulgating stringent fuel economy standards had been the motor vehicle manufacturers' resistance and misleading excuses as to why one type of vehicle should be exempted, a special class be set up for another, and a lower standard be set because lead time and cost prohibit use of one technological development or another. Ford and GM even claimed plants would have to be closed and workers fired if higher mileage standards were imposed. In truth, stringent gas mileage standards save U.S. jobs by requiring small cars to be built here rather than imported from foreign countries.

The gas mileage standards mandated by Congress in the Energy Act represent the most significant energy conservation program in this country. Despite some relaxations in the late 1980's, motor vehicles will save over 2.5 million barrels per day of gasoline in 1990 as a result of improvements in fuel economy since 1975.

Besides saving the country valuable petroleum, stringent fuel economy standards also benefit consumers by saving them money over the long term with more fuel-efficient automobiles. A new car that gets 30 MPG in 1990 will save $2,500 in gasoline at $1.25/gallon over its life compared to one that gets 20 MPG, the standard for 1980, and $6,000 over the average 14 MPG car when Congress passed the Energy Act in 1975.

To alleviate the greenhouse effect and help avoid global warming that could make deserts of large portions of America and flood coastal areas as polar icecaps melt, we must again double fuel efficiency by the year 2000 and even look to vehicles that don't burn fossil fuels. The car companies say it can't be done just as they said doubling fuel economy couldn't be done in 1975 when Chrysler, for example, told Congress:

> This bill [mandating 27.5 MPG by 1985] would outlaw a number of car models including most full-size sedans and station wagons. It would restrict the industry to producing subcompact-size cars or even smaller ones.

Congress stood fast in the face of these dire predictions and the car companies met the 27.5 MPG standard without any restriction of large car sales or any of the other consequences they predicted. The predictions that car companies make today are no more true than the ones they made in 1975. The U.S. can and should again double fuel economy standards.

GOVERNMENT ROLE IN AUTO ENERGY USE

In requiring the Department of Transportation to set fleet average passenger and non-passenger automobile fuel economy standards, Congress's primary goal was "the need of the Nation to conserve energy." In enacting the Energy Policy and Conservation Act, Congress weighed various alternatives and settled on requiring standards that represented the "maximum feasible average fuel economy." This is not geared to any one manufacturer but the industry as a whole. For those manufacturers unable to meet the standards, Congress carefully delineated an economic penalty system that would enable the manufacturer to stay in business by paying a civil penalty based on the magnitude with which the company missed the standards.

With this in mind, Secretary of Transportation Brock Adams challenged the auto industry to "reinvent" the automobile—leading to 50 MPG by the year 2000. After studying the recommendations of three panels of technical experts on engines, fuels and powertrain systems, and structures and materials at a February, 1979 conference held in Boston, Adams expressed confidence that "a kind of fundamental breakthrough" in automotive technology is possible—that the auto makers could virtually double the average fuel efficiency before the end of the century. The secretary noted that, "The auto industry over the past 50 years has relied on imitation, not innovation,and evolutionary instead of revolutionary thinking in manufacturing their cars." He added that imitation and evolutionary thinking are not sufficient today in order to "deal with the realities of a worsening energy situation."

Without government regulations setting these fuel economy standards, technology would have remained relatively stagnant and few goals in auto energy conservation would have been met. As is the case in other areas of government auto regulations, such as safety and emission control, the domestic manufacturers' policy seems to be a curious mixture of "wait and see" while not making any voluntary technological improvements. This "wait and see" policy was evident in the domestic industry's hesitation to enter the subcompact car market until spurred by the fuel economy standards and import sales penetration approaching 30 percent.

The government role in auto energy use, through the fuel economy standards for both passenger and non-passenger autos, is crucial to force the domestic manufacturers to produce more fuel efficient and utilitarian vehicles in this country, thus contributing to the fuel savings necessary to meet the goals of the Energy Act as well as increasing domestic employment.

WHY BE AN ENERGY SAVER?

There are many reasons why consumers should become energy savers. If the reasons already discussed are not enough, the practical fact is that the world is going to run out of oil. Long-range projections show that, if present energy consumption trends go unchanged, world oil supplies will be insufficient to meet world demand for oil early in the next century. In these circumstances, prices will rise sharply and available gas and oil may have to be rationed among all users, particularly hitting the auto owner. Conservation-minded consumers will help stretch oil supplies and ease the transition to energy sources other than oil.

EPA FUEL ECONOMY RATINGS

In carrying out the Energy Act, DOT must coordinate closely with the Environmental Protection Agency (EPA) which is supposed to provide consumers with gasoline mileage estimates of individual models of automobiles. The annual "Gas Mileage Guide," published jointly by the EPA and the Department of Energy (DOE), gives the new or used car buyer information on the relative fuel economy performance of cars, station wagons, and light trucks. Each new car dealer is required to have free copies of the booklet in the dealer's showroom. The estimates are given in terms of miles per gallon on standardized EPA fuel economy tests. Cars are grouped into classes according to their interior size. Trucks and vans are grouped by type and purpose, i.e., cargo van, passenger van, 2-wheel-drive small pickup, and 4-wheel-drive large pickup.

The guides give fuel economy estimates for both city and highway driving. When the EPA ratings first came out in 1975, they were good estimates of consumer fuel economy. But by 1979, the auto companies had learned how to beat the rating system so well that EPA deflates the **highway** and **city** ratings by 10% and 22% respectively from the gas mileages actually determined on its test procedures.

However, the inflated fuel economies are used for purposes of determining compliance with the gas mileage standards discussed above. Thus the gasoline savings under the fuel economy standards would be almost 20% higher if cars actually achieved the fuel economy projected by EPA certification tests. Thus a car which is required to get 27.5 MPG by law only gets 23.4 MPG in the real world. The inflated ratings are also used to determine whether a car is a gas guzzler so that many gas guzzlers avoid the tax through the higher ratings.

GAS GUZZLERS

Manufacturers can make cars which do not meet the gas mileage standards but they are subject to a "gas guzzler" tax if the fuel economy rating falls below 22.5 MPG for 1986 and later model years. The tax is $500 if the gas mileage is between 21.5 and 22.5 MPG but increases to $3,850 if the gas mileage is less than 12.5 MPG. In 1987, auto makers paid $125 million in gas guzzler taxes.

Since the fuel economy standards do not prevent auto companies form making cars that do not meet the standards, the gas guzzler tax is intended to discourage the productions of fuel inefficient cars by subjecting them to a sizable tax. Thus a consumer may buy a luxury gas guzzler but they must pay for the privilege of doing so. To maximize the deterrent effect of the gas guzzler tax, all cars subject to the tax must have a window label showing the amount of the gas guzzler tax at the time they are sold.

55 MPH SPEED LIMIT

Another government program to reduce energy consumption is the 55 MPH maximum national speed limit. The 55 MPH speed limit, enacted in 1975 by Congress, was originally adopted as a temporary measure under the Emergency Highway Energy Conservation Act. It is saving fuel at the rate of about 200,000 barrels of gasoline a day. One sure way to save costs in operating an automobile is to observe the 55 MPH speed limit. The Department of Transportation had estimated that the nation's consumers as a whole would save about $380 billion a year (at $1.25 per gallon) if all drivers observed the 55 MPH limit.

VANPOOLING & OTHER ENERGY SAVERS

The federal government in cooperation with the states has developed another potentially useful energy saving program—"vanpooling," which is becoming more widespread around the U.S. as a means of commuting to and from work. Vanpooling is an arrangement where up to 15 persons share commuting costs and save fuel by riding together in a passenger van. According to a Federal Highway Administration estimate, one vanpool provides about 120 person miles of transportation per gallon of gas used. Over one year, each vanpool can save 5,000 gallons of gasoline.

Other suggestions for a government role in encouraging more fuel-efficient motor vehicles and consumer fuel conservation include:

1. NHTSA, EPA and DOE should make impartial government testing available for a significant number of fuel saving devices proposed by inventors outside of the auto industry;
2. Development of inherently cleaner and more fuel-efficient alternative engines than the present internal combustion engine;
3. Increased construction of bikeways in urban areas; and
4. Improvement of the quality and quantity of mass transit services.

FACTORS THAT AFFECT FUEL ECONOMY

Consumers can increase their fuel economy savings in many ways. For example, since summer temperatures over 70 degrees Fahrenheit are better for fuel economy than winter temperatures, long trips can often be planned for the spring or summer rather than the winter. More important in saving gasoline is how you drive and the condition of the vehicle. For example, a vehicle which had been properly tuned gets approximately 3-9% better fuel economy than one that has not been properly tuned. Underinflated tires can cause a fuel economy loss of up to 10% so check tire pressure often. Trip length also affects fuel economy. Trips under five miles do not allow the engine to reach its best operating condition, while longer trips do. Try to combine numerous short trips into a single, longer trip.

When purchasing a new or used car, remember that its size and weight affect the fuel economy. Use the EPA Gas Mileage Guide as a means of comparing relative fuel economy ratings. Normally, the smaller and lighter a car, the better the fuel economy. Thus the gas mileage winner in 1990 was the Geo Metro by General Motors at 53 MPG in the city and 58 MPG on the highway.

Other suggestions on saving gas:

DRIVING TIPS

1. Avoid rapid starts. Accelerate gently. Smooth driving improves fuel economy. Try to avoid constant stops and starts.
2. Anticipate stops. Rather than accelerating and braking right up to

every stop, coast to a stop if you can stay within the flow of traffic.

3. Drive at moderate speeds. Obey the 55 MPH speed limit.

4. Do not weave in and out of traffic lanes. Weaving just increases the vehicle miles traveled and can be hazardous as well.

5. Save gas when changing gears. If you drive a car with a manual transmission, run through the lower gears gently and quickly for maximum fuel economy. Then build up speed in high gear.

6. If you drive a car with automatic transmission, apply enough gas pedal pressure to get the vehicle rolling, then let up slightly on the pedal to ease the transmission into high range as quickly as possible. More gas is consumed in lower gears.

7. Use the brake pedal rather than the accelerator to hold your car in place on a hill.

8. Turn an engine off rather than letting it idle for more than a minute.

TRIP PLANNING

1. Share the ride. Take the bus or schedule your trips to share a ride with others. For short trips, walk or ride a bicycle. Avoid driving to work if you work in a large city. Traffic jams can increase fuel consumption as much as 50 percent as well as increasing air pollution.

2. When possible, drive when the roads are dry. Wet pavement demands more power to reach a given speed.

CAR MAINTENANCE AND REPAIR

1. Use multi-grade low-40 or 30-weight motor oils instead of single grade or 30-weight oils. This helps cut engine drag.

2. Keep the wheels properly aligned.

3. Use radial-ply tires.

4. Avoid or do not overuse fuel guzzling options such as air-conditioning. Air conditioning reduces fuel economy by as much as four miles per gallon.

5. Clean out the trunk. Avoid hauling around unnecessary objects that just add extra weight to the car.

6. Check brakes for dragging—brakes that do not fully release when your foot is off the brake pedal.

For a more detailed discussion of the factors that affect fuel economy, write for:

"Factors Affecting Fuel Economy"
Public Information Center (PM-215)
U.S. Environmental Protection Agency
Washington, DC 20460

For additional copies of the "Gas Mileage Guide," write:

Fuel Economy Distribution
Technical Information Center
Department of Energy
P.O. Box 62
Oak Ridge, Tennessee 37830

(All new car dealers are required to display prominently and have available copies of this Guide in their showrooms.)

CHAPTER 18

AUTOMOBILE EMISSIONS AND AIR POLLUTION

By the year 2000, much of our nation will still not meet the air quality goals Congress established in 1970. Almost 20 years after the Clean Air Act became law, about 100 cities housing about half of the American population exceed the standard for ozone, the principal component of urban smog. An estimated 37 new cities were added during the 1988 summer's heat wave. Some healthy adults and children begin to experience coughing, painful breathing, and temporary loss of some lung function after about an hour or two of exercise at ozone concentrations above the standard.

"Catching Our Breath"
U.S. Office of Technology Assessment, July 17, 1989

110 million Americans live in areas that violate air quality standards for ozone while 30 million live in cities that violate air quality standards for carbon monoxide. Automobile emissions are the largest single source of pollutants forming smog, accounting for nearly 50% of all nitrogen oxides and volatile organic compounds emissions that combine to form smog in the presence of sunlight. Automobiles account for 70% of all carbon monoxide, a colorless and odorless gas that causes carbon monoxide poisoning. Some U.S. cities, such as New York and Los Angeles which violated the ozone standard on 180 days in 1988, face even more severe air pollution situations. Automobile-related air pollution is an area of utmost concern for residents of most major urban areas around the country.

The problem of air pollution is not limited to big cities since plumes of ozone travel 100 miles or more from major urban areas. Some of the highest levels of smog are found not in the central cities, but downwind in suburban areas. Ozone generated in New York can travel all the way up to Boston.

As ozone and its precursor pollutants travel outward from urban areas, they damage crops and vegetation which are sensitive to ozone levels well below the human-based standard. At ozone concentrations found in rural areas throughout much of the U.S., ozone depresses yields of crops such as cotton and soybeans by as much as 20 percent. Ozone damages pine trees from the San Bernardino National Forest to the Great Smoky Mountains and Acadia National Parks.

Unlike ozone, carbon monoxide (CO) does not damage the lungs or cause irreversible tissue damage. Rather CO interferes with the ability of blood to transport oxygen by binding with blood hemoglobin. In extreme cases, high levels of CO cause death. In levels associated with air pollution in urban areas, CO poses a threat to the health of people with coronary heart disease and pregnant women. According to a 1988 study by the American Lung Association, 38% of pregnant women and people with coronary heart disease live in urban areas with CO levels in excess of the ambient air quality standard for CO. Elevated CO levels lead to decreased birth weights and various complications or pregnancy. Elevated CO levels lead to earlier onset of angina during exercise and have been associated with higher mortality rates due to cardiovascular disease for tunnel workers exposed to long periods of high CO.

COSTS OF AIR POLLUTION

When the National Academy of Science (NAS) examined the health effects of auto emissions in its 1974 report, "Air Quality and Automobile Emission Control," NAS estimated auto emissions caused up to 4,000 deaths and 4 million days of illness a year. The NAS noted that these figures represent one-eighth of the annual deaths for bronchitis, emphysema, and asthma combined, and one-tenth of the total number of days lost from work each year because of respiratory illness. Later studies indicate that, if anything, NAS underestimated the effects of auto emissions.

The U.S. Office of Technology Assessment (OTA) in its 1989 report,

"Catching Our Breath," found that ozone levels above the national ambient standard caused 8-15 million days of illness each year. A June, 1989 University of California study found that the 12 million residents of the South Coast Air Basin (the area in and around Los Angeles) suffered from excess ozone levels:

Over 120 million days of cough,
Over 190 million days of eye irritation,
Almost 180 million days of sore throat,
Over 100 million days of headache, and
Almost 65 million days of chest discomfort.

Most severely affected by air pollution are the older and younger age groups and those people suffering from or susceptible to heart and respiratory diseases such as asthma, bronchitis and emphysema. The effects of air pollution range from annoying to severe and are experienced by healthy individuals as well. Symptoms include headache, nausea, dizziness, eye irritation, visual disturbances, reduced tolerance for exercise, respiratory tract irritation, and impairment of cardiovascular efficiency. Nitrogen oxides have been statistically related to lung and breast cancer. Auto pollutants also cause damage to trees, crops and other vegetation. Pollutants corrode telephone and other electrical contacts, and cause rapid deterioration in rubber, marble statues and other materials.

Every major study ever done shows the costs of auto air pollution amount to billions of dollars annually. In the most detailed economic analysis done to date, the University of California found that the human health benefits of meeting the ambient ozone standard amounted to $9.4 billion annually and reduced vegetation and crop damage equalled that savings. The American Lung Association projected the national savings from meeting the ozone standard to be $40 billion. As more becomes known about the harmful effects of air pollution and as more efficient technology is developed by the auto industry to reduce emissions, the benefits of tight emission standards to the public become greater.

AUTO INDUSTRY RESTRAINT OF POLLUTION CONTROL DEVELOPMENT

Although auto-related pollution costs the nation at least $20 billion a year, the automobile manufacturers have resisted most efforts to clean up the air. This resistance can be traced back 40 years when the auto industry first began to restrain the development of pollution control equipment for new cars. At that time the U.S. automobile companies conspired to restrain the development and marketing of auto exhaust control systems through collusive, anti-competitive agreements not to compete in the research, development, manufacture and installation of air pollution control equipment. Alternative engines such as the diesel and stratified charge were not developed during the conspiracy even though they had lower emissions, better fuel economy and were more durable. In 1953, the industry announced a pooling of efforts to combat the motor vehicle air pollution problem which had been pinpointed as a major source of smog in 1951 by Dr. Arlie J. Haagen-Smit, a research scientist at the California Institute of Technology. The problem of how to control motor vehicle emissions was turned over by the industry to the Automobile Manufacturers Association (AMA), later renamed the Motor Vehicle Manufacturers Association, of which all the domestic automobile manufacturers were members. In reality the automobile manufacturers engaged only in lip service concerning the health and welfare of severely polluted communities such as Los Angeles. Through AMA, they conspired not to compete in research, development, manufacture, and installation of control devices, and collectively delayed such action to deal with air pollution.

The aggressive delaying of improvement in auto emission control technology by the industry was summarized by Los Angeles chief pollution control officer S. Smith Griswold ten years after the conspiracy took root at the annual meeting of the Air Pollution Control Association in June 1964:

> Everything that the industry had disclosed it is able to do today to control auto exhaust was possible technically ten years ago. No new principle had to be developed, no technological advance was

needed, no scientific breakthrough was required. . . . almost everything Detroit had done with automobiles since World War II had been wrong from the standpoint of smog.

Mr. Griswold more recently noted:

The greatest achievement in air pollution control proffered by General Motors to account for its years of effort is the construction of an environmental study chamber, in which they have been duplicating much of the work that has led to the conclusion that auto exhaust is the basic ingredient of photochemical smog.

The only actual progress in reducing auto emissions during the smog conspiracy came as a result of a 1959 California statute requiring that new cars sold in that state be equipped with exhaust controls one year after the state certified the effectiveness of at least two workable control devices. The auto companies claimed that such controls could not be adopted until the 1967 model year. But when California certified the control devices of four non-automotive companies in 1964 and required the installation of those or equivalent devices on all new cars by the 1966 model year, General Motors, Ford and Chrysler suddenly announced that they could indeed install such devices in 1966 vehicles. Their switch was clearly prompted by the risk of having to use the devices of the non-industry certified companies.

Finally the U.S. Department of Justice brought an anti-trust suit against General Motors, Ford, Chrysler, American Motors and the Automobile Manufacturers Association, accusing the auto industry of conspiring to restrain development of effective pollution control devices. Over the objection of many states, Congressional leaders and consumer advocates, the Nixon Administration settled the case through a consent decree rather than going to trial where the government could have obtained significant anti-trust precedents in collusive trade association activity and "product fixing" as well as substantially eased the burden on those parties bringing private antitrust suits against the auto manufacturers based on the "smog conspiracy."

The consent decree reached between the government and the four major automobile manufacturers plus their trade association was entered on October 29, 1969. The two key provisions of the decree prohibited the defendants from exchanging information on emissions control and safety technology and from submitting joint statements to government regulatory agencies. Under the regulatory pressure of the Clean Air Amendments and National Traffic and Motor Vehicle Safety Acts, the more competitive atmosphere resulting from the decree forced the defendant auto manufacturers to make major improvements in automobile emission control and safety technology. The industry's contention that cooperation (i.e., collusion) is the only way to improve technology has been proven false over and over again since the 1969 consent decree.

Although the decree itself was perpetual, the two key regulatory response provisions had to be renewed after 10 years. In view of their success in improving industry competition, the Justice Department got them extended in 1979 over stiff auto industry opposition. However, in 1981 the Reagan Administration came in and moved to not only drop the regulatory response provisions but also let the whole decree expire in five more years. Despite opposition from public interest groups and the state of California, the court approved dropping the decree in 1982.

AUTOMOBILE EMISSIONS REGULATION

From both an environmental and consumers' viewpoint, auto emissions regulation can only be viewed as a rousing success. Fuel economy is up, maintenance is down and the cost of improved technology is repaid several times over by the reduced operating costs. At the same time, there are significant air quality gains from the reduced emission levels. The striking gains in emissions control and fuel economy are in large part attributable to technological improvements developed under the force of the Clean Air Act.

The tremendous strides of the auto industry since the consent decree and the 1970 Amendments were summed up by Dr. John A. Hutcheson of the National Academy of Science in testimony before the Environmental Protection Agency. (Under the 1970 Clean Air Amendments, the National Academy of Sciences was required to make yearly reports on the progress of the auto companies in meeting the stringent statutory emission standards.)

> The automotive industry, in my opinion, has in the last three years or so learned more about the engine in the automobile they make than they ever knew before.

THE CLEAN AIR ACT

In order to protect the public health and welfare from the effects of air pollution and to get auto pollution control development rolling, Congress in 1970 enacted the Clean Air Amendments to the Clean Air Act. The Amendments gave the U.S. Environmental Protection Agency (EPA) responsibility for setting and enforcing standards on various types of air pollutants, but the Congress set statutory emission standards and time tables for auto emissions. The standards are expressed in terms of grams per mile for the three most dangerous air pollutants: hydrocarbons, carbon monoxide and nitrogen oxides. To provide the auto industry with sufficient lead time to meet these standards, Congress established the model years 1975–76 as the deadline.

Despite the success of more stringent emission standard in improving automotive technology, the original statutory automobile emission standards for 1975–76 were delayed through two separate one-year extensions by the Environmental Protection Agency (EPA) and one year by Congress during the height of the Arab oil embargo. When Congress passed the Clean Air Act Amendments of 1977, it granted an additional two-year freeze of the emission standards, making a total of five years of delay but setting a schedule that resulted in attainment of the statutory emission standards for hydrocarbon of 0.41 grams/mile and carbon monoxide of 3.4 grams/mile in 1981. The original statutory nitrogen oxides standard of 0.4 grams/mile was changed to 1.0 grams/mile by the 1977 Amendments and was also achieved in 1981.

Perhaps the biggest success under the Clean Air Amendments of 1970 was the virtual elimination of lead from gasoline. Between 1975 and 1983, gasoline lead usage dropped by 75%. More importantly, blood lead levels of children who eat lead ladened dust also dropped. From 1976 to 1980, mean blood lead levels in children dropped by 37%. With gasoline lead usage dropping by 99% by 1988 when the maximum lead content of leaded gasoline was only 0.1 grams/gallon and leaded gasoline itself being phased out of the marketplace, children's blood lead levels will drop even further.

More stringent emission standards are needed for the 1990's to keep up with increased vehicle travel. While total vehicle emissions decreased by about 25% from 1975 to 1985, the reduction would have been greater but for a 26% increase in vehicle miles traveled during the same period. By 1986, total transportation emissions began to go up again. Even passenger vehicles emissions will go up in the 1990's as the impact of attainment of the statutory standards in cars after 1981 reached full attainment. Tighter statutory standards for all trucks as well as imposition of 0.4 grams/mile nitrogen oxides and 0.25 grams-/mile hydrocarbon standards for cars must be imposed.

While diesel powered vehicles have low levels of carbon monoxide and hydrocarbon emissions, they have very high levels of particulate emissions, approximately 30-70 times higher than gasoline vehicles equipped with catalysts. Even worse, diesel particulates are so small they can be inhaled directly into the lungs. Diesel emissions are likely to cause cancer and increase mortality and morbidity from respiratory disease. Congress failed to set statutory standards for diesels and the Reagan Administration killed regulatory standards during the 1980's so that needed diesel control standards of 0.08 grams/mile will be delayed until at least 1992.

IN-USE ENFORCEMENT

In addition to setting emission standards, the Clean Air Act gave the EPA responsibility for setting and enforcing standards of motor vehicles in use. This in-use enforcement takes the form of warranties for the emission control systems, recalls when defects are discovered and prohibitions against tampering with or removal of these systems. Strong in-use enforcement is necessary because manufacturers fail to design and build their cars as well as the prototypes which are used for testing. In fact, EPA has found that up to 80% of in-use vehicles fail to meet emission standards where there is no in-use enforcement. After an automobile reaches five years/50,000 miles, there is no effective federal enforcement because this is the defined useful life for emission control even though the average car today lasts for 12 years/120,000 miles. At a minimum, the useful life should be redefined up to 100,000 miles by Congress or the Environmental Protection Agency.

Under the Clean Air Act, every new automobile is required to have two warranties covering the emission control system, as discussed in Chapter 6. The Act gives the EPA the authority to order recalls when defects are found in the emission control system, as discussed in Chapter 4. The Act makes it illegal for manufacturers, car dealers or independent garages to remove or tamper with emission control systems.

CONSUMER PARTICIPATION IN AIR POLLUTION CONTROL

There are many things consumers can do to help control the auto pollution problem. These include cutting down on the overall use of the automobile and keeping the vehicle properly maintained. Take advantage of public transportation where available, form car pools to work, make less auto trips—where possible, walk, or ride a bicycle. Keep your car properly tuned, and support local and state government programs which provide for annual vehicle inspection and mainte- nance to ensure that emissions reductions are being met. Support efforts within your community to develop transportation control programs that do not encourage use of the automobile. For example, many employers subsidize parking for employees but not mass transit. While parking should not be subsidized since it encourages use of single passenger vehicles, at the very least employees who use mass transit, bicycles or walk should be given a subsidy equal to the value of the parking.

CHAPTER 19

WHISTLE BLOWING

Corporate employees are among the first to know about industrial dumping of mercury or fluoride sludge into waterways, defectively designed automobiles, or undisclosed adverse effects of prescription drugs and pesticides. They are the first to grasp the technical capabilities to prevent existing product or pollution hazards. But they are very often the last to speak out.

[Yet], the willingness and ability of insiders to blow the whistle is the last line of defense ordinary citizens have against the denial of their rights and the destruction of their interests by secretive and powerful institutions. As organizations penetrate deeper and deeper into the lives of people—from pollution to poverty to income erosion to privacy invasion—more of their rights and interests are adversely affected. This fact of contemporary life has generated an ever greater moral imperative for employees to be reasonably protected in upholding such rights regardless of their employer's policies.

Whistle Blowing. Edited by Ralph Nader,
Peter J. Petkas, and Kate Blackwell

"Whistle blowing" is the act of a person who believes that the interest of the public overrides the interest of the organization he or she serves. If that organization is involved in a corrupt, illegal, fraudulent, or harmful activity, the individual publicly "blows the whistle," speaking out against and informing everyone of the activities of that organization.

Many activities harmful to consumers and the public interest carried out by business and governmental organizations have been uncovered and brought up to light with the help of whistle blowers. For example, since the publication of *Unsafe at Any Speed* in 1965, Ralph Nader and the Center for Auto Safety have often been aided by whistle blowers, whose information and assistance have sometimes been rendered anonymously, sometimes publicly. It was a General Motors engineer, in fact, who first called Nader's attention to the hazards of the Corvair.

HOW WHISTLE BLOWING WORKS

Many people today are alive and healthy due to the actions of conscientious and concerned individuals of both government and industry who blew the whistle on their employers. Risking job demotion or loss of employment, these disgruntled employees have stepped forward to the benefit of the general public. The beneficiaries of whistle blowing often include the owners of motor vehicles as well as innocent bystanders. Among these whistle blowers have been design engineers who were working for the auto industry and spoke out against the company's production of unsafe vehicles. Employees of auto dealers and factory workers have also blown the whistle on callous manufacturers.

Whistle blowers usually hand over their "inside information" to the press or consumer groups. For example, the Center for Auto Safety frequently receives such information from industry "insiders" which may lead to a recall of the unsafe vehicles. Many "insiders" send the information anonymously to protect themselves from job loss or demotion. Some insiders are known only to the consumer group which protects their anonymity but uses the information to benefit consumers.

In 1972, the Center for Auto Safety received revealing internal General Motors documents from an "insider" whose name was never made public. The documents revealed that pitman arms in 1959-60 Cadillacs were failing with great frequency. (The pitman arm is a vital steering assembly component. When it fails, total loss of steering control results.) The Center released the information to the public, petitioning the National Highway Traffic Safety Administration (NHTSA) to order a recall of the vehicles. In 1973, NHTSA did so, declaring the vehicles defective. The government based its case in large part on the whistle blower's information submitted by the Center. NHTSA ordered GM to notify affected owners and replace the pitman arms and went to court to enforce the order.

GM lost in the courts and had to recall the cars when the District of Columbia Court of Appeals ruled the evidence was:

> . . . uncontradicted that GM sold six times as many replacement pitman arms for 1959–60 Cadillac models as for adjacent years, that steering pitman arm failures have occurred while these models were being driven, and that, when the steering pitman arm fails, the driver loses control of the car. . . .

The court stated that these facts demonstrate "unreasonable risk of accident" stemming from the defect. *United States v. General Motors*, 561 F.2d 923, 924 (D.C. Cir. 1977). The U.S. Supreme Court refused to review the decision even though GM was supported by legal briefs from Chrysler Corp., Volkswagen and the Automobile Importers of America.

The Cadillac case also established the Center's right to protect the confidentiality of whistle blowers. GM brought legal proceedings against the Center to compel its Director, Lowell Dodge, to reveal the name of the whistle blower who had provided the Center with the internal GM documents. The Center refused on the ground that the identity of the whistle blower was privileged. The Center told the court that its ability to protect the public interest would be seriously jeopardized if forced to reveal the identity of auto company employees who blew the whistle on auto safety defects. The court refused to grant GM's motion to compel disclosure and thus protected the confidentiality of not only this GM whistle blower but all future auto company whistle blowers.

Whistle blowers appear in the small companies too. In 1977, the Center received an insider's report from within British Leyland Motors (BLM). The report revealed numerous specific safety defects in BLM cars and described "the games some automobile importers play with the lives and pocketbooks of consumers." Based on this report and confirming consumer complaints in its files, the Center petitioned NHTSA to recall BLM's Austin, Jaguar, MG and Triumph for dozens of defects. As a result of the Center's investigation and use of the insider's report, British Leyland eventually conducted 13 separate recalls.

One of the best kept secrets of auto companies that are often exposed by whistle blowers are secret warranties where a company finds it had widespread defects that occur after the written warranty expires and sets a secret policy to reimburse consumers who complain loudly enough about the failure. In 1988, a Toyota whistle blower sent the Detroit News a comprehensive list of 41 defects for which it would pay for repair after the warranty expired. Millions of Toyota owners stood to benefit from this courageous whistle blower.

Because of the risks associated with whistle blowing, assisting consumer groups anonymously is a good strategy for some whistle blowers. But there are many activities which affect the public where no consumer group is available to help the whistle blower release the information to the public. In these cases, the whistle blower often has no choice but to step forward individually and publicly speak out through the press. Such individuals, whether employees of the government or industry, can often expect to be fired, cast into some obscure position or otherwise punished.

Congress is beginning to show interest in not only protecting whistle blowers from retribution but also rewarding them for their actions. In 1986, Congress amended the False Claims Act to enable whistle blowers to obtain up to 30% of any recovery from contractors who defraud the government and to provide for damages if they lose their jobs. In one 1989 case under the Act, Industrial Tectronics of Dexter, Michigan paid the government $14.3 million for overcharges with $1.4 million going to a whistle blower who had started the lawsuit.

Efforts to protect whistle blowers also have been made by private organizations. For example, the Government Accountability Project in Washington had provided counseling to many hundreds of workers who have publicly questioned decisions of their bosses. In 1971, the Conference on Professional Responsibility was held in Washington, D.C. Some of the leading exponents of whistle blowing joined individual whistle blowers to discuss the subject. Details of the conference are available in *Whistle Blowing: The Report of the Conference on Professional Responsibility* edited by Ralph Nader, Peter J. Petkas, and Kate Blackwell, Bantam Books: New York (1972). Some strategies for whistle blowers discussed at the conference and reported in *Whistle Blowing* include:

Whistle Blowing

1. Precisely identify not only the objectionable activity or practice, but also the public interest or interests that are threatened and the magnitude of the harm that will result from nondisclosure.
2. Verify the accuracy of your knowledge of the situation.
3. Identify ethical standards as well as laws, rules, and regulations that support your decision to blow the whistle.
4. Develop a plan of action: consider the personal costs and the likely response of allies and antagonists within and outside the organization.
5. Select an appropriate outside contact.

There is no tried and true formula for blowing the whistle effectively and safely. Every person is unique and every situation is different. A strategy which has proved successful in one instance may be totally inappropriate in another. It is imperative that a person considering such a bold action do so with as much forethought as possible. Still, the willingness and ability of insiders to blow the whistle is the last line of defense ordinary citizens have against the denial of their rights and the destruction of their interest by secretive and powerful institutions.

ARBITRATION PROGRAMS BY AUTO COMPANY

Acura—BBB
Alfa Romeo—AUTOCAP & BBB
Audi—BBB
BMW—AUTOCAP
Chrysler—Chrysler Customer
  Arbitration Board
Fiat—AUTOSOLVE
Ford—Ford Consumer
  Appeals Board
General Motors—BBB
Honda—BBB
Hyundai—AUTOSOLVE
Isuzu—AUTOCAP
Jaguar—AUTOCAP & BBB

Mazda—AUTOSOLVE
Mitsubishi—AUTOCAP & BBB
Nissan—BBB
Peugeot—BBB
Porsche—BBB
Rolls-Royce—BBB
SAAB—AUTOCAP & BBB
Sterling—AUTOCAP
Subaru—BBB
Toyota—AUTOSOLVE
Volkswagen—BBB
Volvo—State Mandated
  Program
Yugo—AUTOCAP & BBB

ADDRESSES OF ARBITRATION PROGRAMS

Ford Consumer Appeals Board
Manager, Owner Relations
  Operations
Ford Motor Company
P.O. Box 1805
Dearborn, MI 48121
1-800-392-9292

Chrysler Customer Arbitration
  Board
Box 1919
Detroit, MI 48288
1-800-992-1997

APPENDIX A

Better Business Bureau
Contact your local BBB or
Council of Better Business
  Bureaus
4200 Wilson Blvd., Suite 800
Arlington, VA 22203
(703) 276-0100

AUTOSOLVE
American Automobile
Association (AAA)
Contact your local AAA or
1000 AAA Drive
Heathrow, FL 32746-5063
(407) 444-7740

AUTOCAP
8400 Westpark Drive
McLean, VA 22102
703-821-7144

The National Automobile Dealers Association sponsors the AUTOCAP program in 26 states, listed below. The Washington, D.C. program serves the Washington metropolitan area.

LIST OF AUTOCAPS

AUTOCAPS are located in these states (as of February 1, 1989):

Phoenix, Arizona
Playa del Rey, California
San Diego, California
Denver, Colorado
Jacksonville, Florida
Miami, Florida
West Palm Beach, Florida
Atlanta, Georgia
Honolulu, Hawaii
Springfield, Illinois
Lexington, Kentucky
Augusta, Maine
Rockville, Maryland
East Lansing, Michigan
Helena, Montana
Concord, New Hampshire
Albuquerque, New Mexico

Albany, New York
Binghamton, New York
Rochester, New York
Whitestone, New York
Williamsville, New York
Raleigh, North California
Fargo, North Dakota
Cleveland, Ohio
Columbus, Ohio
Tulsa, Oklahoma
Portland, Oregon
Columbia, South Carolina
Sioux Falls, South Dakota
Austin, Texas
Montpelier, Vermont
Richmond, Virginia
Madison, Wisconsin

APPENDIX B

AUTO COMPANY EXECUTIVES AND ADDRESSES

Mr. Gunter Kramer
Chairman and President
BMW of North America, Inc.
300 Chestnut Ridge Road
Woodcliff Lake, NJ 07675

Mr. Lee A. Iacocca
Chairman and CEO
Chrysler Corporation
12000 Chrysler Drive
Highland Park, MI 48288

Mr. Sota "John" Fukunaka
President
Daihatsu
4422 Corporate Center Drive
Los Alamitos, CA 90720

Mr. Marik Bosia
President
Fiat Auto U.S.A., Inc.
777 Terrace Avenue
Hasbrouck Heights, NJ 07604

Mr. Donald E. Petersen
Chairman of the Board
Ford Motor Company
The American Road
Dearborn, MI 48121

Mr. Robert C. Stempel
President
General Motors Corporation
General Motors Building
Detroit, MI 48202

Mr. K. Amemiyz
President
American Honda Motor Co.
100 West Alondra Blvd.
Gardena, CA 90247

Mr. H.W. Baik
President
Hyundai Motor America
7373 Hunt Ave.
Garden Grove, CA 92642

Mr. Kozo Sakaino
President
American Isuzu Motors, Inc.
2300 Pellissier Place
Whittier, CA 90601

Mr. Graham W. Whitehead
President
Jaguar Cars Inc.
600 Willow Tree Rd.
Leonia, NJ 07605

Mr. Munneo Kishimoto
President
Mazda (North America), Inc.
1444 McGaw Avenue
Irvine, CA 92714

Mr. Erich Krampe
President and CEO
Mercedes-Benz
1 Mercedes Drive
Montvale, NJ 07645

Mr. Kazue Naganuma
President
Mitsubishi of America, Inc.
6400 Katella
Cyress, CA 90630

Mr. Kazutoshi Hagiwara
President
Nissan Motor Corp. in U.S.A.
18501 So. Figueroa Street
Carson, CA 90248

Mr. Pascal Henault
President
Peugeot Motors of America
1 Peugeot Plaza
Lyndhurst, NJ 07071

Mr. Brian Bowler
President
Porsche Cars North America
One West Liberty Street
Reno, NV 89501

Mr. Robert J. Sinclair
President
Saab-Scania of America, Inc.
Saab Drive, P.O. Box 697
Orange, CT 06477

Mr. Graham Morris
President
Sterling Motor Cars
8300 N.W. 53rd Street
Suite 200
Miami, FL 33166

Mr. Harvey Lamm
Chairman of the Board
Subaru of America, Inc.
P.O. Box 6000
Cherry Hill, NJ 08034-6000

Mr. Toshiyuki Arai
President
American Suzuki Motor
  Corporation
3251 E. Imperial Hwy.
Brea, CA 92621-6722

Mr. Yukiyasu Togo
President
Toyota Motors Sales-USA
19001 S. Western Avenue
Torrance, CA 90509

Mr. Hans-Jorg Hungerland
President and CEO
Volkswagen of America, Inc.
888 West Big Beaver Road
Troy, MI 48007-3951

Mr. Bjorn Ahlstrom
President and CEO
Volvo North American
  Corporation
Seven Volvo Drive
Rockleigh, NJ 07647

Mr. John Spiech
President and CEO
Yugo America, Inc.
28 Park Way
Upper Saddle River, NJ 07458

APPENDIX C

MODEL CONSUMER GROUP COMPLAINT

This is the form letter that CEPA uses to initiate its highly successful campaigns on behalf of consumers. A businessman who does not respond constructively to this letter is likely to find himself picketed. The letter-and-picket program is one other consumer groups might emulate.

CONSUMERS EDUCATION AND PROTECTIVE ASSOCIATION
_____ **BRANCH**

Date

To:

Concerning:
(Consumers Name)

_____   _____
_____   _____
_____   _____

To Whom It May Concern:

We have been authorized by the above-named member(s) of the Consumers Education and Protective Association (CEPA) to investigate a complaint against your company. The complaint is as follows:

_____
_____
_____

Appendix C

The consumers request is

_____

_____

We would appreciate hearing from your company within (3) days regarding your intentions in adjusting this complaint.

Please send reply to: And please send copy to:

Name _____   CEPA

Address _____   Grievance Department

City _____   6048 Ogontz Avenue

Telephone _____   Philadelphia, Pa. 19141

Tel: (215) 424-1441

APPENDIX D

GUIDEBOOKS FOR CONSUMER ORGANIZING

Action for Change: A Student's Manual for Public Interest Organizing by Ralph Nader and Donald Ross. New York: Grossman Publishers, 1972.

Available for $4.95 from: Center for Study of Responsive Law
P.O. Box 19367
Washington, D.C. 20036

"A Directory of State and Local Organizations
(Non-government)"
by the State and Local Organizing Project.

Available for $5.00 from   Consumer Federation of America
1424 16th St., N.W. Suite 604
Washington, D.C. 20036

For the People: A Consumer Action Handbook
by Joanne Manning Anderson, introduction by Ralph Nader. 1977.

Available for $5.95 from: Center for Study of Responsive Law
P.O. Box 19367
Washington, D.C. 20036

"Consumer Resource Handbook"
by U. S. Office of Consumer Affairs.

Single copies available free from:
Consumer Information Center
18th and F Streets NW Room 6-142
Washington, D.C. 20405

"A Nader Guide for Establishing Local Consumer Auto
  Complaint Organizations"

Available from: Center for Auto Safety
                    2001 S Street N.W. Suite 410
                    Washington, D.C. 20009
Also reprinted in the Congressional Record (daily edition Dec. 1, 1971)
page E 12794.

Public Citizen's Action Manual
by Donald K. Ross, introduction by Ralph Nader. 1973.

Available for $1.95 from: Center for Study of Responsive Law
                           P.O. Box 19367
                           Washington, D.C. 20036

When Consumers Complain
by Arthur Best. New York: Columbia University Press.

Consumers Guide to Fighting Back
by Morris J. Bloomstein. New York: Dodd & Mead, 1976.

Getting What you Deserve, A Handbook for the Assertive Consumer
by Stephen A. Newman and Nancy Kamer. Garden City, NY: Double-
day, 1979.

The Ultimate Guide to Consumer Self-Defense
by Ralph Charell, New York: Simon & Schuster, 1985.

Regulating Consumer Product Safety
by W. Kip Viscusi. All Enterprise, 1984.

The Expert Consumer: A Complete Handbook
by Kenneth Eisenberger. Englewood Cliffs, NJ: Prentice-Hall, Inc.,
1977.

Consumer Action
by John S. Morton and Ronald R. Rezny. Boston: Houghton Mifflin
Company, 1978.

TYPICAL NEW CAR WARRANTY

1990 GENERAL MOTORS CORPORATION

General Motors Corporation will provide for repairs to the vehicle during the warranty period in accordance with the following terms, conditions and limitations:

WHAT IS COVERED

REPAIRS COVERED
This warranty covers repairs to correct any defect in material or workmanship of the vehicle occurring during the WARRANTY PERIOD. New or remanufactured parts will be used.

WARRANTY PERIOD
The WARRANTY PERIOD for all coverages begins on the date the car is first delivered or put in use and ends at the expiration of the BUMPER TO BUMPER PLUS COVERAGE or other COVERAGES shown below.

BUMPER TO BUMPER PLUS COVERAGE
The complete vehicle (except those items listed under "WHAT IS NOT COVERED,") is covered for 3 Years or 50,000 Miles, whichever comes first. After the first year or 12,000 miles, whichever comes first, repairs are subject to a $100 deductible per repair visit. The sealed refrigerant portion of the factory-installed air conditioning system has no deductible the first year, regardless of mileage.

NEW CAR LIMITED WARRANTY

SUPPLEMENTAL INFLATABLE
RESTRAINT COVERAGE
The Supplemental Inflatable Restraint System (if equipped on your vehicle) is covered for 3 Years, regardless of mileage (with no deductible).

CORROSION (RUST-THROUGH)
COVERAGE
Any body sheet metal panel that Rusts-Through due to corrosion is covered for 6 Years or 100,000 Miles, whichever comes first (with no deductible). Sheet metal panels may be repaired or replaced.

OBTAINING REPAIRS
To obtain warranty repairs, take the car to a Chevrolet dealership within the WARRANTY PERIOD and request the needed repairs. A reasonable time must be allowed for the dealership to perform necessary repairs.

TOWING
TOWING is covered to the nearest Chevrolet dealership, if your vehicle cannot be driven because of a warranted defect.

NO CHARGE
Warranty repairs, including TOWING, parts and labor, will be made at NO CHARGE (except for applicable $100 deductible per repair visit after 1 Year or 12,000 Miles, whichever comes first).

1990 GENERAL MOTORS CORPORATION

WARRANTY APPLIES
This warranty is for GM cars registered in the United States and normally operated in the United States or Canada.

WHAT IS NOT COVERED

TIRES
Tires are warranted separately by the tire maker. See tire warranty folder for details.
NOTE: If tire damage is caused by defects in material or workmanship of the vehicle, General Motors will cover the replacement of the tire under the BUMPER TO BUMPER PLUS (subject to a $100 deductible per repair visit after 1 Year or 12,000 Miles, whichever comes first).

DAMAGE OR CORROSION DUE TO ACCI-DENTS, MISUSE, OR ALTERATIONS
Accidents or damage caused by collision, fire, theft, freezing, vandalism, riot, explosion or from objects striking the car; misuse of the car such as driving over curbs, overloading, racing, or other competition; and alterations to the car are not covered. In addition, coverages do not apply if the odometer has stopped or been altered. Proper vehicle use is discussed in the Owner's Manual.

NEW CAR LIMITED WARRANTY (Cont'd.)

DAMAGE OR SURFACE CORROSION FROM ENVIRONMENT

Airborne fallout (chemicals, tree sap, etc.), stones, hail, earthquake, water or flood, windstorm, lightning, etc., are not covered.

DAMAGE DUE TO LACK OF MAINTENANCE OR USE OF WRONG FUEL, OIL, OR LUBRICANTS

Lack of proper maintenance as described in the Maintenance Schedule; failure to follow Maintenance Schedule intervals; and failure to use or maintain proper levels of fluids, fuel, oil and lubricants recommended in the Owner's Manual are not covered. Proof of proper maintenance is the owner's responsibility. Keep all receipts and make them available if questions arise about maintenance.

MAINTENANCE

Cleaning and polishing, lubricating, replacing filters, spark plugs, clutch, and brake linings as well as performing other normal maintenance services detailed in the Maintenance Schedule and Owner's Manual are not covered and are the owners expense.

EXTRA EXPENSES

This warranty does not cover any economic loss and other extra expenses, including (without limitation), payment for the loss of time or pay, inconvenience, loss of vehicle use, vehicle rental expense, lodging bills, meals, other travel costs, storage charges and other incidental or consequential loss or damage.*

OTHER TERMS: This warranty gives you specific legal rights and you may also have other rights which vary from state to state.

General Motors does not authorize any person to create for it any other obligation or liability in connection with these cars. ANY IMPLIED WARRANTY OF MERCHANTABILITY OR FITNESS FOR A PARTICULAR PURPOSE APPLICABLE TO THIS CAR IS LIMITED IN DURATION TO THE DURATION OF THIS WRITTEN WARRANTY. THE PERFORMANCE OF REPAIRS AND NEEDED ADJUSTMENTS IS THE EXCLUSIVE REMEDY UNDER THIS WRITTEN WARRANTY OR ANY IMPLIED WARRANTY. GENERAL MOTORS SHALL NOT BE LIABLE FOR INCIDENTAL OR CONSEQUENTIAL DAMAGES RESULTING FROM BREACH OF THIS WRITTEN WARRANTY OR ANY IMPLIED WARRANTY.

*Some states do not allow limitations on how long an implied warranty will last or the exclusion or limitation of incidental or consequential damages, so the above limitations or exclusions may not apply to you.

NEW CAR LIMITED WARRANTY (Cont'd.)

WARRANTY SERVICE—
UNITED STATES AND CANADA

For your records, the servicing dealer should provide a copy of the Warranty Repair Order, listing all warranty repairs performed. While any Chevrolet dealership will perform warranty service, we recommend that you return to the Chevrolet dealership that sold you your car because of their continued and personal interest in you. If you are touring or move, visit any Chevrolet dealership in the Unites States or Canada for warranty service.

TOURING OWNER SERVICE—
FOREIGN COUNTRIES

If you are touring in a foreign country and repairs are needed, it is suggested you make your vehicle available to a General Motors dealer, preferably a Chevrolet dealership. Once you return to the United States, you should provide your dealer with a statement of circumstances, the original repair order and any "paid" receipt indicating the work performed and parts replaced for reimbursement consideration. Please note that repairs made necessary by the use of improper or dirty fuels are not covered under the warranty. See Owner's Manual for additional information on fuel requirements when operating in foreign countries.

THINGS YOU SHOULD KNOW ABOUT

BATTERY

The battery installed in your car as original equipment is covered under the BUMPER TO BUMPER PLUS COVERAGE.

CORROSION (RUST-THROUGH) COVERAGE

The CORROSION COVERAGE applies to perforation due to corrosion only. Perforation means a Rust-Through condition, such as an actual hole in a sheet metal panel. Cosmetic or surface corrosion (resulting from stone chips or scratches in the paint, for example) would not be repaired under this coverage.

AFTER-MANUFACTURE "RUSTPROOFING"

Your vehicle was designed and built to resist corrosion. Application of additional rust inhibiting materials is not necessary or required under the 6 Year/100,000 Mile CORROSION COVERAGE.

Some after-manufacture rustproofing may create a potential environment which reduces the corrosion resistance designed and built into your vehicle. Depending upon application technique, some after-manufacture rustproofing could result in damage or failure of some electrical or mechanical systems of your vehicle. Repairs to correct damage or malfunctions caused by after-manufacture rustproofing are not covered under any of your GM new vehicle warranties.

THINGS YOU SHOULD KNOW ABOUT

PRE-DELIVERY SERVICE

Defects in or damage to the vehicle (including its mechanical and electrical components as well as the sheet metal, paint, trim, or other appearance items of the vehicle) may occur at the factory during assembly or while the vehicle is being transported to the dealer. Normally, any defect or damage occurring during assembly is detected and corrected at the factory during the inspection process. In addition, dealers are obligated to inspect each vehicle before delivery. They repair any uncorrected factory defects or damage and any transit damage which they detect before the vehicle is delivered to you.

Any defects still present at the time the vehicle is delivered to you are covered by the warranty. If you find any such defects when you take delivery, please advise your dealer without delay. For further details concerning any repairs which the dealership may have made prior to your taking delivery of your vehicle, please ask your dealer.

VEHICLE MILEAGE AT DELIVERY

Some mileage may have been put on your vehicle during testing at the assembly plant, during shipping, or while at the dealership. The dealership records this mileage on the inside of the front cover of this warranty booklet at delivery. To ensure you receive the full benefit of the coverages described in this booklet during the applicable warranty periods, this mileage is added to the mileage limits specified in the New Car Limited Warranty and the Emission Control Systems Warranties.

COMPARISON OF NEW CAR WARRANTIES

Sample Coverage	General Motors	Ford	Chrysler
BASIC Warranty, Duration-time/miles, whichever occurs first	3 years/50,000 miles, after 1 year/12,000 miles, $100 deductible	1 year or 12,000 miles	1 year or 12,000 miles
POWERTRAIN Warranty Duration-time/miles, whichever occurs first	3 Years/50,000 miles, after 1 year/12,000 miles $100 deductible	6 years/60,000 miles, $100 deductible	7 years/70,000 miles, $100 deductible
EMISSIONS, 5 years/ 50,000 miles limited	Yes	Yes	Yes
TIRES-warranted by tire manu-facturer	Yes	Yes	Yes
BATTERY-	3 years/50,000 miles, after 1 year/12,000 miles, $100 deductible complete	3 years/50,000 miles pro rata, until 1 year/ 12,000 miles	1 year/12,000 miles

Appendix F

Sample Coverage	Honda	Volkswagen	Toyota
BASIC Warranty, Duration-time/miles, whichever occurs first	3 years or 36,000 miles	2 years or 24,000 miles	3 years or 36,000 miles
POWERTRAIN Warranty Duration-time/miles, whichever occurs first	3 years or 36,000 miles	2 years or 24,000 miles	3 years or 36,000 miles
EMISSIONS, 5 years/ 50,000 miles limited	Yes	Yes	Yes
TIRES-warranted by tire manu-facturer	Yes	Yes	Yes
BATTERY-	3 years/36,000 miles limited	2 years/24,000 miles	3 years/36,000 miles pro rata, until 1 years/ 12,000 miles complete

APPENDIX G

STATE LEMON LAW SUMMARY

STATE	VEHICLES COVERED	LEMON CRITERIA	NOTIFICATION REQUIRED
Alaska	All except tractors, farm or off-road vehicles.	3 unsuccessful repairs or 30 business days (manufacturer has another 30 calendar days to repair after notice) within the shorter of 1 year or warranty	Written notice by certified mail to manufacturer and dealer (or repair agent) that problem has not been corrected in reasonable number of attempts and refund or replacement demanded within 60 days.
Arizona	All under 10,000 lbs. except living portion of motor homes.	4 unsuccessful repairs or 30 calendar days within shorter of 1 year or warranty	Written notice and opportunity to repair to manufacturer.
California*	All except motorcycles, motor homes or off-road vehicles.	4 unsuccessful repairs or 31 calendar days within shorter of 1 year/12,000 miles	Direct notice to manufacturer of need for repair.
Colorado	Private passenger motor vehicles except motor homes and those with fewer than 4 wheels.	4 unsuccessful repairs or 30 business days within shorter of 1 year or warranty	Certified mail written notice and opportunity to repair to manufacturer.
Connecticut*	Passenger vehicles.	4 unsuccessful repairs or 30 calendar days within shorter of 2 years/18,000 miles or 2 repairs of problem likely to cause serious bodily injury within shorter of one year or warranty.	Report to manufacturer, agent or authorized dealer. Written notice to manufacturer only if required in owner's manual or warranty.
Delaware	All except motorcycles and living facilities of motor homes.	4 unsuccessful repairs or 31 calendar days within shorter of 1 year or warranty.	Written notice and opportunity to repair to manufacturer.
District of Columbia*	All except buses, motorcycles, motor homes and RVs.	4 unsuccessful repairs or 30 calendar days or one unsuccessful repair of a safety-related defect, within shorter of 2 years/18,000 miles.	Report to manufacturer, agent or authorized dealer.

STATE	VEHICLES COVERED	LEMON CRITERIA	NOTIFICATION REQUIRED
Florida*	All except off-road vehicles, motorcycles and mopeds.	4 unsuccessful repairs or 30 working days within shorter of 1 year or 12,000 miles.	After 3 unsuccessful repair attempts or 20 days out-of-service, written notice by registered, express or certified mail, return receipt requested. Manufacturer has 14 business days to repair after delivery to designated dealer.
Hawaii*	All	3 unsuccessful repairs or 30 business days within warranty on repaired components	Written notice and opportunity to repair to manufacturer.
Illinois	All passenger cars except motor homes and van camper.	4 unsuccessful repairs or 30 business days within shorter of 1 year/12,000 miles.	Written notice and opportunity to repair to manufacturer.
Indiana	All registered with gross vehicle weight less than 10,000 lbs., primarily for use on public roads, except RVs, farm equipment, motorcycles, mopeds and off-road vehicles.	4 unsuccessful repairs or 31 business days within shorter of 18 months/18,000 miles.	Written notice to dealer and manufacturer.
Iowa	Cars and pickups.	4 unsuccessful repairs or 30 calendar days within shorter of 1 year or warranty.	Direct notice and opportunity to repair to manufacturer.
Kansas	All under 12,000 lbs., except parts added or modified by converters.	4 unsuccessful repairs or 30 calendar days or 10 total repairs within shorter of 1 year or warranty.	Actual notice to manufacturer.
Kentucky	All except conversion vans, motor homes, motorcycles, mopeds, farm machines and those with more than two axles.	4 unsuccessful repairs or 30 calendar days within shorter of 1 year/12,000 miles.	Written notice to manufacturer.

STATE	VEHICLES COVERED	LEMON CRITERIA	NOTIFICATION REQUIRED
Louisiana	All under 10,000 lbs., except those used only for commercial purposes.	4 unsuccessful repairs or 30 calendar days within shorter of 1 year or warranty.	Report to manufacturer or authorized dealer.
Maine	All except commercial vehicles over 8,500 pounds.	3 unsuccessful repairs of 15 business days within shorter of 2 years/18,000 miles.	Written notice to manufacturer or authorized dealer only if required in warranty or owner's manual. Manufacturer has 7 business days after receipt to repair.
Maryland	Passenger vehicles and trucks with 3/4 ton or less rated capacity, except motor homes.	4 unsuccessful repairs or 30 days or 1 unsuccessful repair of failure of braking or steering system within shorter of 15 months/15,000 miles.	Certified mail notice, return receipt requested and opportunity to repair to manufacturer or factory branch.
Massachusetts*	All except motor homes and off-road or commercial vehicles.	3 unsuccessful repairs or 15 business days within shorter of 1 year/15,000 miles	Certified mail notice, return receipt requested to manufacturer's regional office who has 7 additional business days to repair.
Michigan	Passenger vehicles except motor home, buses, motorcycles and large trucks.	4 unsuccessful repairs or 30 calendar days within shorter of 1 year or warranty.	Certified mail notice, return receipt requested, to manufacturer who has 5 business days to repair after delivery.
Minnesota	Passenger cars, pickups, vans and chassis of RVs.	4 unsuccessful repairs or 30 business days or 1 unsuccessful repair of total braking or steering loss likely to cause accident within shorter of 2 years or warranty.	Written notice and opportunity to repair to manufacturer, agent or authorized dealer.

STATE	VEHICLES COVERED	LEMON CRITERIA	NOTIFICATION REQUIRED
Mississippi	All except off-road vehicles, motorcycles, mopeds and portions added by motor home manufacturers.	3 unsuccessful repairs or 15 business days within shorter of 1 year or shorter of 1 year or warranty.	Written notice to manufacturer who has 10 business days to repair after delivery to designated dealer.
Missouri	All except commercial and off-road vehicles, mopeds and motorcycles. Includes the chassis, engine and powertrain of RVs.	4 unsuccessful repairs or 30 business days within shorter of 1 year or warranty.	Written notice to manufacturer who has 10 calendar days to repair after delivery to designated dealer.
Montana	All except motor homes, motorcycles and trucks over 10,000 pounds.	4 unsuccessful repairs or 30 business days after notice within shorter of 2 years/18,000 miles.	Written notice and opportunity to repair to manufacturer.
Nebraska	All except motor homes.	4 unsuccessful repairs or 40 days within shorter of 1 year or warranty.	Certified mail notice and opportunity to repair to manufacturer.
Nevada	All except off-road vehicles and motor homes.	4 unsuccessful repairs or 30 calendar days within shorter of 1 year or warranty.	Written notice to manufacturer.
New Hampshire	All under 9,000 pounds except tractor, off highway RVs and mopeds.	4 unsuccessful repairs or 30 business days within shorter of 1 year or warranty.	Report to manufacturer, distributor, agent or authorized dealer.
New Jersey	All passenger vehicles and motorcycles except living portion of motor homes.	3 unsuccessful repairs or 20 business days within shorter of 2 years/18,000 miles.	Certified mail notice, return receipt requested to manufacturer who has 10 days to repair.
New Mexico	Passenger vehicles under 10,000 pounds.	4 unsuccessful repairs or 30 business days within shorter of 1 year or warranty.	Written notice and opportunity to repair to manufacturer.

STATE	VEHICLES COVERED	LEMON CRITERIA	NOTIFICATION REQUIRED
New York*	Passenger vehicles except motorcycles, off-road vehicles, and living portion of motor home.	4 unsuccessful repairs or 30 days within shorter of 2 years/18,000 miles.	Report to manufacturer, agent or authorized dealer.
North Carolina	All motor vehicles under 10,000 pounds.	4 unsuccessful repairs for problem that occurred within shorter of 24 months/24,000 miles or warranty or 20 business days during any 12 month period of warranty.	Written notice and opportunity to repair (not more than 15 calendar days) to manufacturer only if required in warranty or owner's manual.
North Dakota**	Passenger vehicles and trucks under 10,000 lbs.	4 unsuccessful repairs or 30 business days within shorter of 1 year or warranty.	Direct notice and opportunity to repair to manufacturer.
Ohio	Passenger cars and noncommercial motor vehicles except RVs and living facilities or motor homes.	3 unsuccessful repairs or 30 days, 8 total repairs or 1 unsuccessful repair of problem likely to cause serious bodily injury within shorter of 1 year/18,000 miles.	Report to manufacturer if agent or authorized dealer.
Oklahoma	All under 10,000 lbs. except living facilities of motor homes.	4 unsuccessful repairs or 45 calendar days within shorter of 1 year or warranty.	Written notice and opportunity to repair to manufacturer.
Oregon	All passenger vehicles except motorcycles.	4 unsuccessful repairs or 30 business days within shorter of 1 year/12,000 miles.	Direct written notice and opportunity to repair to manufacturer.
Pennsylvania	All except motorcycles, motor homes and off-road vehicles.	3 unsuccessful repairs or 30 calendar days for problem that first occurred within shorter of warranty or 1 year/12,000 miles.	Delivery to authorized service and repair facility. If delivery impossible, written notice to manufacturer or its repair facility obligates them to pay for delivery.

STATE	VEHICLES COVERED	LEMON CRITERIA	NOTIFICATION REQUIRED
Rhode Island	Autos, trucks, or vans under 10,000 lbs. except motorized campers.	4 unsuccessful repairs or 30 calendar days within shorter of 1 year/15,000 miles.	Report to authorized dealer or manufacturer who has 7 additional days to repair.
South Carolina	All passenger vehicles except living portion of RVs, trucks over 6,000 pounds, and off-road vehicles.	3 unsuccessful repairs or 30 days within shorter of 1 year/12,000 miles.	Written notice and opportunity to repair (not more than 10 business days) to manufacturer only if manufacturer informed consumer of such at time of sale.
Tennessee	All motor vehicles under 10,000 pounds except motorbikes, lawn mowers, garden tractors and RVs and off-road vehicles.	4 unsuccessful repairs of problem reported within shorter of 1 year or warranty or 30 business days within shorter of 1 year or warranty.	Certified mail notice to manufacturer. If 4 unsuccessful repairs or 30 days exhausted before notice manufacturer has additional 10 days to repair.
Texas*	All.	4 unsuccessful repairs or 30 days within shorter of 1 year or warranty.	Written notice and opportunity to repair to manufacturer.
Utah	All under 12,000 lbs. except motorcycles, tractors, motor and mobile homes.	4 unsuccessful repairs or 30 business days within shorter of 1 year or warranty.	Report to manufacturer, agent or authorized dealer.
Vermont*	All passenger vehicles except tractors, motorized highway or road-making equipment, snowmobiles, motorcycles, mopeds, trucks over 6,000 lbs., or living portions of RVs. *Includes leased cars.*	3 unsuccessful repairs or 30 calendar days within warranty on repaired component. Manufacturer has 1 more opportunity to repair within 30 days after notice.	Notice to manufacturer (on provided forms) of 3 unsuccessful repairs or 30 days starts arbitration process.

STATE	VEHICLES COVERED	LEMON CRITERIA	NOTIFICATION REQUIRED
Virginia	Passenger cars, pickup or panel trucks, motorcycles, mopeds and chassis of motor homes.	4 unsuccessful repairs or 30 calendar days within 1 year.	Written notice to manufacturer of need for repair. If 4 unsuccessful repairs or 30 days already exhausted before this notice, manufacturer has 1 more repair attempt not to exceed 15 days.
Washington	All motor vehicles except motorcycles, trucks with more than 19,000 pounds GVWR, and living portions of motor homes.	4 unsuccessful repairs, 30 calendar days (15 during warranty period), 2 repairs for serious safety defects, first reported within shorter of warranty or 24 months/24,000 miles.	Written notice to manufacturer.
West Virginia	All passenger automobiles, including pickup trucks, vans and chassis of motor homes.	3 unsuccessful repairs or 30 calendar days or 1 unsuccessful repair of problem likely to cause death or serious bodily injury within shorter of 1 year or warranty.	Written notice and opportunity to repair to manufacturer.
Wisconsin	All except mopeds and semitrailers. *Includes leased cars.*	4 unsuccessful repairs or 30 days within shorter of 1 year or warranty.	Report to manufacturer or any authorized dealer.
Wyoming	All under 10,000 lbs.	3 unsuccessful repairs or 30 business days within 1 year.	Direct written notice and opportunity to repair to manufacturer.

*A state-run alternative dispute resolution program is available.

**WARNING: Consumers who seek a refund or replacement under the North Dakota lemon law may lose other important legal rights against the dealer and manufacturer.

APPENDIX H

SAMPLE SMALL CLAIMS COURT COMPLAINT

DISTRICT COURT OF MARYLAND FOR _____

DC-CV-1 (REV 9/84)

LOCATED AT (COURT ADDRESS)

COMPLAINT □ $1,000 and under □ over $1,000

Clerk: Please docket this case in an action of □ contract

The particulars of this case are

CASE NO.	TRIAL DATE
CV	

(YOUR STATEMENT OF CLAIM BRIEFLY, AND NOT IN GREAT DETAIL, WHAT THE CLAIM IS FOR, GIVING DATE OR DATES, AND PLACE OF OCCURRENCE, ALSO STATE THE AMOUNT FOR WHICH YOU ARE SUING OR FILING.)

PARTIES

Plaintiff:

(YOUR FULL NAME)
(YOUR PRESENT ADDRESS)

(See Continuation Sheet)

The Plaintiff claims:

□ $_____ plus interest of $_____ and attorney's fees of $_____ plus court costs.

Signature of Attorney: _____

VS.

Defendant (s): | Return

1
(PERSON OR FIRM YOU ARE SUING AND THEIR ADDRESS)

Signature of Plaintiff: (YOUR SIGNATURE)

Telephone No.: (YOUR DAYTIME PHONE)

□ Other:

and demands judgment for relief.

2
(ADDITIONAL PERSONS OR FIRM YOU ARE SUING AND THEIR ADDRESS)

APPLICATION AND AFFIDAVIT IN SUPPORT OF JUDGMENT

There are attached the documents indicated which contain sufficient detail as to liability and damage to apprise the Defendant clearly of the claim against the Defendant, including the amount of any interest claimed.

□ Properly authenticated copy of any note, security agreement upon which claim is based □ Itemized statement of account □ Interest Work Sheet

□ Vouchers □ Check □ Other written document □ _____ □ Verified itemized repair bill or estimate

3

I HEREBY CERTIFY: That I am the □ Plaintiff □ _____ of the plaintiff herein and am competent
(Owner/Partner/Agent/Officer)
to testify to the matters stated herein, which are made on my personal knowledge; that there is justly due and owing by the Defendant to the Plaintiff the sum set forth in the Complaint.

□ That (SHORTER STATEMENT OF ABOVE CLAIM)
(Here state any facts upon which the Plaintiff claim is based.)

4

I solemnly affirm under the penalties of perjury and upon personal knowledge that the contents of the above Complaint are true and I am competent to testify to these matters. The Defendant is not now in the military service, as defined in the Soldier's and Sailor's Civil Relief Act of 1940 with amendments, nor has been in such service within thirty days hereof.

ATTORNEYS

For Plaintiff - Name & Address

(THIS SPACE IS PROVIDED FOR ATTORNEYS, IF ONE IS USED.)

(YOUR SIGNATURE

Date | Signature of Affiant

WRIT OF SUMMONS

You are summoned to appear for trial in the District Court of Maryland at the above location and on the date and time shown below. If you intend to be present, you must file Notice of Intention to Defend no later than 15 days after you receive this Complaint. Judgment by default or relief sought may be granted if you fail to file.

Serve by □ sheriff □ restricted delivery mail

Fees for service enclosed.

□ Return to Plaintiff for service.

(LEAVE BLANK)

Trial Date | Time | Clerk | Date

DEFENDANT: SIGN NOTICE OF INTENTION TO DEFEND AND RETURN TO COURT IF YOU WILL APPEAR FOR TRIAL.
COURT COPY

TRIAL DATE NOTICE

****

(LEAVE BLANK)
Plaintiff VS. Defendant

NOTICE TO PLAINTIFF

Rule 3-306 provides that prior to entry of final judgment the Plaintiff shall inform the court of any reduction in the amount of the claim by virtue of any payment made after the case is filed.

Address of Plaintiff or Attorney

City, State, Zip

Therefore, if Affidavit Judgment has been requested in this case, and if no defense to the claim is made, the Plaintiff may be entitled to judgment on or after the trial date, upon filing with the court information as to any payments or credits, and the amount claimed at the date judgment is to be entered.

Case No. | Trial Date

APPENDIX I

STATE SMALL CLAIMS COURT DIRECTORY

State	Type of Court	Claim Limit	Informal Procedure?	Lawyers Allowed?	Appeals	Dispute Resolution?
Alabama*	Small Claims Docket in District Court	$1,000	Yes	Yes	Either party within 14 days to Circuit Court for new trial	No
Alaska*	Small Claims	$5,000	Yes	Yes	Either party if over $50 on law not facts	No
Arizona	Justice Court Small Claims Division	$500	No	Yes if both parties agree in writing	No	Commission on the Courts: Task Force on Dispute Resolution
Arkansas	Urban: Municipal Court Small Claims Division Rural: Justice of the Peace	$300	Yes	No small claims; Yes Justice of the Peace	Either party within 30 days to Circuit Court for new trial	No
California	Small Claims Division in Municipal or Justice Court	$1,500	Yes	No	Defendant within 20 days to Superior Court for new trial	Dispute Resolution Advisory Council

State	Type of Court	Claim Limit	Informal Procedure?	Lawyers Allowed?	Appeals	Dispute Resolution?
Colorado	County Court Small Claims Division	$1,000	Yes	Depends	Either party within 15 days to District Court on law not facts	Council of Mediators and Mediation Organizations
Connecticut	Small Claims in Superior Court	$1,000	Yes	Yes	No	No
Delaware	Justice of the Peace (no small claims system)	$2,500	Yes	Yes	Either party within 15 days to Superior Court for new trial if over $5	Mediation Unit
District of Columbia	Superior Court Small Claims and Conciliation Branch	$2,000	Yes	Yes	Either party within 3 days to Court of Appeals on law not facts	No
Florida	Summary Procedure in County Court	$2,500	Yes	Yes	Motion for new trial within 10 days; either party within 30 days to Circuit Court on law not facts	Dispute Resolution Center
Georgia	Magistrate Court	$2,500	Depends	Yes	To Superior Court for new trial	No

State	Type of Court	Claim Limit	Informal Procedure?	Lawyers Allowed?	Appeals	Dispute Resolution?
Hawaii*	Small Claims Division in District Court	$2,500	Yes	Yes	No	Program on Alternative Dispute Resolution
Idaho	Small Claims Department of Magistrate's Division in District Court	$2,000	Yes	No	Either party within 30 days to Attorney Magistrate for new trial	No
Illinois	Small Claims in Circuit Court	$2,500 small claims; $1,000 Cook County "pro se"	Yes	Yes except Cook County pro se branch	Either party within 30 days to Appellate Court on law not facts	No
Indiana	Small Claims Court; Small Claims Docket in Circuit Court, Superior Court, and County Court	$3,000	Yes	Yes	Yes	No
Iowa	Small Claims in Docket District Court	$2,000	Yes	Yes	Either party within 20 days to District Court	Advisory Committee on Dispute Resolution

State	Type of Court	Claim Limit	Informal Procedure?	Lawyers Allowed?	Appeals	Dispute Resolution?
Kansas	Small Claims in District Court	$1,000	Yes	No	Either party within 10 days to District Court for new trial	No
Kentucky*	Small Claims Division in District Court	$1,000	Yes	Yes	Either party within 10 days to Circuit Court on law not facts	No
Louisiana	Urban: City Court Small Claims Divisions. Rural: Justice of the Peace	$2,000 Small Claims; $1,200 Justice of the Peace	Yes	Yes	No for Small Claims; Either party within 15 days to District Court for new trial if Justice of the Peace	No
Maine	Small Claims in District Court	$1,400	Yes	Yes	Either party within 10 days to Superior Court on law not facts	No
Maryland	Small Claims Action in District Court	$1,000	Yes	Yes	Either party within 30 days to Circuit Court for new trial	No

State	Type of Court	Claim Limit	Informal Procedure?	Lawyers Allowed?	Appeals	Dispute Resolution?
Massachusetts	Small Claims Court (Boston-Municipal Court; Elsewhere-District Court)	$1,500	Yes	Yes	Defendant within 10 days to Superior Court for new trial; $100 bond required	Mediation Service
Michigan	Small Claims Division in District Court	$1,500	Yes	No	Depends	No
Minnesota	Conciliation Court in County Court	$2,000	Yes	Need Court approval	Within 10 days to County Court for new trial	University Affiliated Dispute Resolution Advisory Council
Mississippi	Justice Court	$1,000	Yes	Yes	Either party within 10 days to Circuit Court for new trial	No
Missouri	Small Claims Court in Circuit Court	$1,000	Depends	Yes	Either party within 10 days for new trial	No

State	Type of Court	Claim Limit	Informal Procedure?	Lawyers Allowed?	Appeals	Dispute Resolution?
Montana*	Small Claims Court in Justice Court and District Court	$1,500	Yes	No	Either party within 30 days if District Court for new trial or 10 days if Justice Court on law not facts	No
Nebraska	Small Claims Court in County or Municipal Court	$1,500	Yes	No	Either party within 30 days to District Court for new trial	No
Nevada	Small Claims in Justice Court	$1,500	Yes	Yes	Either party within 5 days to District Court on law not facts	No
New Hampshire*	Small Claims Actions in District or Municipal Court	$1,500	Yes	Yes	Either party within 30 days to Supreme Court on law not facts	No

319

Appendix I

State	Type of Court	Claim Limit	Informal Procedure?	Lawyers Allowed?	Appeals	Dispute Resolution?
New Jersey	Small Claims Section which is Special Civil Part of Law Division of Superior Court	$1,000	Yes	Yes	Either party within 45 days to Appellate Division of Superior Court on law not facts	Center for Public Dispute Resolution
New Mexico	Urban: Metropolitan Court; Rural: Magistrate's Court	$2,000 Magistrate's Court; $5,000 Metropolitan Court	Yes	No	Either party within 15 days to District Court	No
New York	Small Claims in Civil Court, District Court & Justice Court	$1,500	Yes	Yes	Defendant within 30 days to County Court Appellate Division on law not facts	Community Dispute Resolution Center
North Carolina	Small Claims Actions in District Court	$1,500	No	Yes	Either party within 10 days to District Court for new trial	Mediation Network of North Carolina
North Dakota	Small Claims Court	$2,000	Yes	Yes	No	No

State	Type of Court	Claim Limit	Informal Procedure?	Lawyers Allowed?	Appeals	Dispute Resolution?
Ohio	Small Claims in Municipal and County Courts	$1,000	Yes	Yes	Within 30 days to Court of Appeals	Peace and Conflict Management Commission
Oklahoma	Small Claims in District Court	$1,500	Yes	Yes	Either party within 30 days to Supreme Court on law not facts	Dispute Resolution Advisory Council
Oregon	Small Claims Department in District or Justice Courts	$1,500	Yes	Need judge's consent	District Court: No Justice Court: Defendant within 10 days to Circuit Court for new trial	Dispute Resolution Advisory Council
Pennsylvania	Philadelphia: Municipal Court; Elsewhere: District or Justice Court	$5,000 Municipal Court; $4,000 District or Justice Court	No	Yes	Either party within 30 days to Court of Common Pleas for new trial	Council of Mediators
Puerto Rico	District Court	$500	Yes	Yes	Either party within 10 days to Superior Court on law not facts	No

State	Type of Court	Claim Limit	Informal Procedure?	Lawyers Allowed?	Appeals	Dispute Resolution?
Rhode Island	Small Claims in District Court	$1,000	Yes	Yes	Defendant within 2 days to Superior Court for new trial	No
South Carolina	Magistrate's Court (no small claims procedure)	$1,000	Yes	Yes	To County or Circuit Court on law not facts; Within 5 days motion for new trial	No
South Dakota	Small Claims Procedure in Circuit or Magistrate's Court	$2,000	No	Yes	No	No
Tennessee	Court of General Sessions (no small claims procedure)	$10,000. $15,000 if County population over 700,000	Yes	Yes	Either party to Circuit Court for new trial	No
Texas	Small Claims Court in Justice Court	$1,000	Yes	Yes	Either party within 10 days to County Court for new trial if over $20	ADP Committee of the State Bar of Texas
Utah	Small Claims in Circuit or Justice Court	$1,000	Yes	Yes	Defendant within 5 days to District Court for new trial	No

State	Type of Court	Claim Limit	Informal Procedure?	Lawyers Allowed?	Appeals	Dispute Resolution?
Vermont	Small Claims Procedure in District Court	$2,000	Yes	Yes	Either party within 30 days to Superior Court on law not facts	No
Virginia	General District (no small claims procedure)	$7,000	Yes	Yes	Either party within 10 days to Circuit Court for new trial if over $50	Alternative Paths to Justice Task Force; Special Joint Com. on ADP
Washington	Small Claims Dept. of District Courts	$2,000	Yes	No	Defendant only, must be more than $100	No
West Virginia	Magistrate's Court	$3,000	No	Yes	Either party within 20 days to Circuit Court for new trial	No
Wisconsin	Small Claims in Circuit Court	$1,000	Yes	Yes	Either party within 45 days to Court of Appeals on law not facts	No
Wyoming	County Court or Justice of the Peace Court Code	$750	Yes	Yes	Either party within 10 days to District Court on law not facts	No

*State publishes guide; see court clerk

323

APPENDIX J

SMALL CLAIMS COURT GUIDES

1. *Collecting the Money*
   Counsel for Courts
     Excellence
   1024 Vermont Avenue, N.W.
   Suite 510
   Washington, D.C. 20005

2. *Everybody's Guide to Small
     Claims*
   by Ralph Warner (1987)
   Nolo Press
   950 Parker St.
   Berkeley, CA 94710

3. *Guide to Small Claims*
   Montgomery County Office
     of Consumer Affairs
   100 Maryland Ave.
   Rockville, MD 20850

4. *Inexpensive Justice: Self-
     representation in the Small
     Claims Court*
   by Robert L. Spurrier, Jr.
     (1983)
   Associated Faculty Press, Inc.
   New York, NY

5. *Small Claims Court*
   HALT
   Memberships Department
   1319 F St. N.W.
   Suite 300
   Washington, D.C. 20004
   send $6.95

A P P E N D I X   K

HISTORY OF PROTEST LAW: PICKETING WITHIN THE LAW

Businesses which want to stop the picketing usually go to a court seeking an injunction. This is a court order prohibiting some specific activity either on a temporary or permanent basis. The forbidden activity is supposed to be unjustly injurious to the party requesting the injunction. State courts commonly enjoin violent picketing, mass picketing, obstructing entrance to or egress from public and private property. In addition, peaceful picketing which is either conducted for an unlawful purpose or fraudulently misrepresents the facts may be enjoined.

In the past, courts were liberal in granting injunctions to dealers and manufacturers. A 1937 court enjoined a man from displaying his automobile near the dealer's place of business. It was decorated with lemons and signs reading "Don't believe what they say, this car is no good; I have tried to have it fixed and they will do nothing about it," and "This was no good when I got it; don't be a sucker, this car is no good but it looks all right." [*Menard v. Houle*, 298 Mass 546, 11 N.E.2d 436 (1937).] The court said this was an unjustified and wrongful attack causing damage to the plaintiff's business. The following year, a court equated the use of similar signs on a car with attempts at physical obstruction to interfere with the dealer's business, and granted an injunction. *Saxon Motor Sales, Inc. v. Torino*, 166 Misc 863, 2 NYS2d 885 (1938). In *Carter v. Knapp Motor Co.*, 243 Ala 600, 11 So2d 383 (1943), an Alabama court stopped a man from exhibiting the car on which he had painted a white elephant, characterizing the act as a wrongful interference with lawful business.

Beginning in 1950, an emerging social concern with consumer rights began to surface in the courts. In *McMorries v. Hudson Sales Corp.*, 233 S.W.2d 938 (Tex. Civ. App. 1950) a dissatisfied consumer painted his car and parked it near various Hudson dealers. The signs boasted "Frame out of line when purchased new, Hudson refuses to make good," and "Another dissatisfied Hudson owner." Although the manufacturer initially won an injunction, a higher court reversed the order, stressing that in the absence of any proof that the statements were untrue or represented an attempt at intimidation or coercion, the injunction was a violation of First Amendment rights.

Courts now tend to examine picketing along the lines of classical cases on the rights of free speech under the Constitution. This is clearly set forth by a Washington State court:

> [W]herever one has a lawful right to express an opinion on the street, on the platform and in the press, such person has the same right without abridgment to express it on the picket line. . . . Peaceful picketing is a manifestation of the exercise of freedom of speech and it can be restrained only upon those grounds and conditions which warrant restraint in any other case involving freedom of speech.

State ex rel. Lumber and Sawmill Workers v. Superior Ct., 24 Wash.2d 314, 164 P.2d 662, 669, 672 (1945). See also *United States v. Grace*, 461 U.S. 171, 176 (1983), which says that "peaceful picketing and leaflets are expressive activities involving 'speech' protected by the first amendment."

At present courts analyze the breadth and effect of the limits on picketing to determine whether injunctions are proper. While picketing and parading and the use of the streets for such purpose is subject to reasonable time, manner and place regulation, such activity may not be wholly denied. *Shuttleworth v. Birmingham*, 394 U.S. 147 (1969). Thus injunctions which serve to completely prohibit communication of the consumer's views and experiences, rather than simply restricting the means and time of this expression, are unconstitutional. In overturning an injunction against consumer picketing, a Wisconsin Federal District Judge said the following about the group's peaceful, educational picketing in *Concerned Consumers League v. O'Neill*, 371 F. Supp. 644, 648–49 (1974):

> They clearly have an interest in matters which affect their roles as consumers, and peaceful activities . . . which inform them about

such matters are protected by the First Amendment. . . . The method of expression used . . . in this case is probably the most effective way, if not the only way, to inform unsophisticated consumers, i.e., by direct contact at the particular place of business.

Although courts in the past often granted injunctions when they felt the picketers were attempting to coerce business people, this aspect of favoritism for business interest is also undergoing a change. In dissolving a preliminary injunction against picketing an auto dealer, a Pennsylvania court held that "all picketing is to some degree 'coercive' if it is successful," and "peaceful attempts to persuade the public not to deal with a merchant [except for defamation] does [sic.] not constitute an unlawful act." *Book Chevrolet v. Alliance for Consumer Protection*, (Ct. of Common Pleas, Allegheny Cty., PA, (Jan. 21, 1971). Another court which refused to grant an injunction said that it still would refuse to do so even if the statements were intended to have a coercive impact and even if they were untrue. *Stansbury v. Beckstrom* (1973 Tex Civ App) 491 SW2d 947. Finally, it has been established that "so long as the means are peaceful, the communication need not meet standards of acceptability." *Organization For A Better Austin v. Keefe*, 402 U.S. 415, 419 (1971).

Many consumer organizations are set up to help supply members with sympathetic participants for picketing activity. The right to enlist the aid of outsiders was clearly established by the court in *Individual Retail Food Store Owners Assn. v. Penn Treaty Food Stores Assn.*, 33 Pa D & C 100, 111 (1938), which stated:

[I]t is immaterial that the pickets are hired by defendants and have no personal interest in the dispute. The hired advocate is not novel, and the hired picket may likewise walk in the stead of his employer and do the same things the latter might lawfully do.

The written and oral assertions made while picketing are subject to careful scrutiny. In *Hajek v. Bill Mowbray Motors, Inc.*, 647 S.W.2d 253 (Tex. Sup. Ct. 1983), the dealer sued a disgruntled consumer for libel and temporary injunction because the consumer painted messages on his car stating the Mowbray Motors sold him a "lemon" and then drove the car in the community. The Texas Supreme Court stated that the painted message "evoked no threat of danger to anyone and, therefore, may not be subjected to the prior restraint of a temporary injunction." The court further expressed that "[d]efamation alone is not a sufficient justification for restraining an individual's right to speak freely." Although a court cannot enjoin picketing merely because false statements are made, if a dealer feels your allegations are untrue and defamatory, he may successfully sue for libel or slander. If you are honest there is no need to be intimidated by such lawsuits. Truth is a defense in suits for libel or slander (defamation) in the great majority of jurisdictions. Restatement (Second) of Torts section 581A (1977); W. Prosser, Law of Torts section 116 (4th ed. (1971). This means that if you can prove the statements were true, you should not lose the case.

APPENDIX L

CONSUMER'S NEW VEHICLE ORDER FORM
CONDITIONS OF THE AGREEMENT

(Rewritten to preserve some basic consumer rights)

1. If vehicle ordered by purchaser cannot be delivered or tendered for delivery to purchaser within 15 days of delivery date specified hereon, purchaser reserves the right to cancel this order. Dealer shall be liable in event of cancellation for the return in full of deposit, in amount specified hereon.
2. If purchaser revokes order before delivery to purchaser of vehicle ordered, dealer reserves the right to retain deposit.
3. Price of new vehicle ordered is governed by this order. Any increase by dealer in price of vehicle ordered over the price specified hereon shall create in the buyer the right to obtain any vehicle offered for sale by dealer at the price stated hereon. Purchaser shall not be required to pay dealer more than price agreed upon as specified hereon, except for the cost of options or features ordered by purchaser after the signing of this order.
4. Vehicle offered in trade (hereinafter "trade-in") shall be delivered within 30 days of the date of this order or within 30 days of trade-in delivery date, if such date is specified, but in no case later than date new car is accepted by purchaser. If trade-in is not so delivered, dealer reserves the right to reappraise the trade-in. If trade-in is not delivered to dealer in substantially the same condition as when it was appraised, dealer may reappraise the trade-in. If trade-in allowance is substantially reduced by dealer after initial appraisal for any reason, purchaser may terminate this

order, and in the event of such termination, dealer shall retain advance deposit or $50, whichever is less.

5. In the event purchaser terminates this order before delivery of the new vehicle, but after dealer has sold trade-in, dealer may retain as a sales commission 8 percent of trade-in allowance specified in this order, plus reasonable itemized costs for repairs to the trade-in, but in no case shall the total of sales commission and repair costs exceed 35 percent of said trade-in allowance.

In the event purchaser rightfully revokes or terminates this order after the delivery of the new vehicle to purchaser, but after trade-in has been resold, purchaser shall receive from dealer 100 percent of resale price of trade-in.

6. Purchaser certifies he is over 18 years of age and under no legal disability and has right to dispose of trade-in, if any, and to assign to dealer certificate of title to said trade-in.

7. Dealer may cancel this order if purchaser fails to take delivery of ordered vehicle and make settlement (payment, or arrangements for time payments) within 15 days of the time dealer notifies purchaser of readiness of ordered vehicle for delivery, in person, by telephone, or in writing to address of purchaser specified hereon. In the event purchaser fails to make such settlement, dealer reserves the right to retain deposit.

8. Above and beyond all warranty protection provided to purchaser, dealer agrees to remedy all defects or malfunctions in new vehicle reported to dealer within 90 days of date or original retail delivery, at no charge to purchaser, unless the need for such repair is the result of misuse or racing of new vehicle, accident, fire or other casualty (unless the accident, fire, or other casualty is itself the result of a factory defect).

If within 10 days of date purchaser tenders vehicle to dealer for repair and provides dealer with written notice of defects or malfunctions in new vehicle, dealer has not corrected all such defects or malfunctions to the satisfaction of purchaser, purchaser reserves the right to have such corrections made at location of his choice, and if purchaser exercises this right, dealer agrees to reimburse purchaser for reasonable, itemized costs incurred in obtaining necessary repairs at location other than dealer's.

If the purchase of vehicle is a credit transaction, buyer may withhold payments to dealer or to any third party to whom the dealer referred the buyer, or who furnished forms to the dealer, or has taken paper from the dealer, until such defects have been remedied and outside repairman is paid in full.

9. If defects which substantially impair the safety or operating condition of said vehicle are not corrected to purchaser's satisfaction, purchaser reserves the right to revoke his acceptance of new vehicle in accordance with the provisions of the Uniform Commercial Code and/or other applicable laws.

If purchaser so revokes his acceptance of the vehicle, dealer shall refund within 10 days to purchaser all payments plus any interest payments made by purchaser for said vehicle, regardless of to whom paid. Such refund shall become payable upon delivery of vehicle to dealer's premises, and shall be adjusted only to the extent of (a) cost of repairing damages to vehicle or vehicle equipment resulting from purchaser's abuse or negligence, or from accident, fire, or other casualty not themselves caused by a manufacturing or dealer-repair defect, and (b) cost of replacing parts or equipment removed from vehicle if any after initial retail delivery.

10. In the event purchaser revokes acceptance of said vehicle under section nine of this agreement, all obligations of purchaser to third parties to whom the dealer referred the buyer, or who furnished forms to the dealer, or has taken paper from the dealer, for payments on said vehicle shall terminate on written notice to such third party of such revocation. Except that purchaser shall remain liable to such third party for any amounts due to third party prior to date third party receives notice of such revocation, Dealer hereby agrees to assume any and all obligations to such third parties in excess of amount due to such third parties prior to date third party receives notice of such revocation.

11. If within three weeks of the date of delivery of new vehicle to purchaser, vehicle is rendered inoperable and cannot be removed under its own power because of a defect in said vehicle, unless shown by dealer to have resulted from accident or negligence or abuse on the part of purchaser, purchaser may revoke his acceptance of said vehicle, regardless of any efforts on the part of dealer to cure such defects. In such event, dealer agrees to refund all payment made for such vehicle in full upon return of vehicle to his premises.

12. Nothing herein shall be construed in any way as limiting, waiving, or otherwise affecting rights of purchaser under any warranties, express or implied, created by the operation of the law or otherwise, pursuant to or as an incident of this agreement.
13. Nothing herein shall be construed in any way as limiting, waiving, or otherwise affecting the rights of the dealer to secure from the manufacturer appropriate reimbursement for expenses incurred by dealer in curing or attempting to cure defects or malfunctions attributable to manufacturer workmanship or manufacturer materials.
14. Any controversy or claim, except personal injury claims, arising out of or relating to this agreement, the breach thereof, or the goods affected hereby, whether such claim is founded in tort or in contract, shall be settled by arbitration under the rules of the American Arbitration Association, provided, however, that upon any such arbitratation, the arbitrator(s) not vary or modify any of the provisions of this agreement. If any award is made to purchaser, dealer shall pay arbitration costs.

CONSUMER'S NEW VEHICLE WARRANTY

FIRST WARRANTY

(Name of Manufacturer and Dealer) warrant this (year and make of vehicle) to be fit for normal and anticipated uses for 7 years or 70,000 miles, whichever shall first occur.

SECOND WARRANTY

(Name of Manufacturer and Dealer) also warrant this new (year and make of vehicle) to be free from defects in material, workmanship, design and assembly for the duration of its useful life.

LIMITATION

Repair or replacement of any part which fails as a result of noncompliance by owner with the schedule of maintenance specified by the manufacturer in the owner's manual for the (year and make of vehicle) shall not be covered by these warranties.

THIRD WARRANTY (Not Subject to Above Limitation)

In addition, during the first 90 days following the delivery of the new vehicle to purchaser, the manufacturer will provide, free of charge, at any (name of make) dealer, any adjustments and services required to maintain the vehicle in reasonable working order (unless the need for them is clearly the result of accident, vandalism, fire or other casualty, misuse, or racing) including, but not limited to:

- lubrication as needed
- wheel balancing, wheel alignment, and removal of all vibrations in the suspension
- headlight alignment
- cleaning of fuel, cooling, and brake systems
- addition of engine coolants, power steering, brake and air-conditioning fluids and engine oil
- tightening of nuts, bolts and fittings
- adjustment to fuel injection, carburetors, valves, belts, transmission, clutch and brake systems, hood, deck and door-closing mechanisms
- repair or replacement of soft trim and external appearance items damaged by normal exposure

LOANER CAR

If the vehicle needs warranty repair work and "same day" (morning to evening) service cannot be completed as promised or if warranty repairs require that the vehicle be kept overnight, the dealer will provide purchaser with a free loaner vehicle equivalent to the consumer's vehicle until the vehicle is repaired.

MANUFACTURER'S PREDELIVERY INSPECTION

SUBARU.

Vehicle Identification Number:	Dealer Code:
Dealer Stock Number:	
Owner's Name:	Delivery Date:
Owner's Address: Street	

City:	State:	Zip:	Phone:

RECOMMENDED DEALER PREPARATION CHECKLIST—SALES DEPARTMENT

BEFORE CUSTOMER ARRIVES

☐ Complete all owner forms and paperwork

☐ Inspect Car
  —Neatness
  —Proper Equipment
  —Fluid Levels

☐ Road test car and check equipment operation

☐ Complete the selling dealer information

IN CUSTOMER'S PRESENCE

☐ Demonstrate to the customer the location of dipsticks, fluid levels, spare tire, jack, driver's controls, instruments, and switches

☐ Explain the three key system

☐ Introduce customer to a service department representative

☐ Demonstrate to the customer the operation of features, accessories, options, and controls

☐ Orientation drive with customer

☐ Give your customer the owner information kit (owner's manual, warranty and service booklet)

☐ Explain the service and maintenance schedule

☐ Review warranty booklet

☐ Explain that the vehicle warranty expires 12 months from the delivery date reported to Subaru of America

☐ Review Added Security® available from Subaru of America or other extended service contract options

_____ _____ _____
Salesperson's S.S. #   Salesperson's Signature   Date

The salesperson has taken the time to give me the above explanations and demonstrations.
I have received a Subaru Warranty and Service Booklet which contains the written warranties covering the vehicle described above.
I certify that my name and address and the date of delivery as shown above are true and correct.

_____ _____
Owner's Signature   Date

MSA 5T87460 (9/86)

Appendix N

SUBARU.

DEALER PREPARATION CHECKLIST—SERVICE DEPARTMENT

Vehicle Identification Number: All Models	Dealer Code:

BEFORE ROAD TEST

Engine and Transmission
- ☐ Check all fluid levels
- ☐ Check alternator/power steering (W/A)/air conditioning (W/A) belt(s)

Emission Control Components
- ☐ Operating in accordance with manufacturer's specifications

Electrical System
- ☐ Connect clock power lead (W/A)
- ☐ Program trip computer by depressing clock alarm, arrive simultaneously (W/A)
- ☐ Horn
- ☐ Install antenna mast (W/A)
- ☐ Radio/speaker operation (W/A)
- ☐ Windshield wipers/washer (rear window W/A)
- ☐ Rear window defogger/indicator
- ☐ Emergency brake/indicator
- ☐ Alternator/oil pressure/brake warning lights/check engine light (W/A) ECS indicator (W/A)
- ☐ Turn signals/indicator
- ☐ Brake lights/dome lights
- ☐ Headlights/high beam indicator
- ☐ Back-up lights
- ☐ Parking/license plate light(s) side markers

Chassis and Body
- ☐ Tire pressure including spare
- ☐ Toe-in
- ☐ Brake fluid reservoir level
- ☐ Brake lines and hoses
- ☐ Steering linkage
- ☐ Seat adjustment/operation
- ☐ Power door locks (W/A)
- ☐ Seat belt latches/warning system
- ☐ Wheel nut torque
- ☐ Door locks/latches/hinges

- ☐ Steering locks
- ☐ Brake pedal height/FREE play
- ☐ Window washer fluids
- ☐ Operation of tilt steering column (W/A) telescoping column (W/A)
- ☐ Hood, trunk, tailgate and fuel door latches/operation
- ☐ Remove plastic seat protector
- ☐ Install wheel caps
- ☐ Power steering fluid (W/A)
- ☐ Sunroof operation (W/A)
- ☐ Operation of air suspension (W A)

DURING ROAD TEST

Engine and Transmission
- ☐ Engine/performance
- ☐ Clutch/gear on automatic shifting (including 4WD) (W/A)
- ☐ Check turbo indicator light on gauge (turbo vehicles only)

Chassis and Body
- ☐ Foot brake/handbrake
- ☐ Steering
- ☐ Heater/defroster/air conditioner (W/A)
- ☐ Hillholder (W/A)

Electrical System and Instruments
- ☐ Instrument operation
- ☐ Power window and mirrors (W/A)
- ☐ Operation of cruise control (W/A)

AFTER ROAD TEST

Engine and Transmission
- ☐ Transaxle fluid levels
- ☐ Engine oil levels
- ☐ Oil/fuel/coolant leaks
- ☐ Ignition timing
- ☐ Idle speed/FICD (W/A)

I certify that the SUBARU identified by the vehicle serial number shown above has received a Pre-Delivery check as prescribed by the Importer, prior to retail delivery to the owner, and all items requiring correction or adjustment have been corrected or adjusted to specifications shown in the Subaru Shop Manual.

ABBREVIATIONS: W/A —Where applicable
4WD—Four wheel drive

INSTRUCTIONS: Prepare in duplicate—no carbon paper required. *white* copy to owner—*duplicate* copy to dealer file.

_____ _____

Technician or Supervisor   Date

_____
S.S. #

This list does not include any cosmetic or appearance item preparation, which services are not required by Subaru and vary from dealer to dealer. The suggested retail price for performing such services appears on the window sticker in most states.

DO-IT-YOURSELF MAINTENANCE GUIDES

Check your favorite bookstore or local library for the following:

AUTO REPAIR FOR DUMMIES
By Deanna Sclar.
McGraw Hill, $14.95.

BASIC AUTO REPAIR MANUAL
By Spence Murray.
Petersen Publishing Co., $3.95.

HOW TO GET YOUR CAR REPAIRED WITHOUT GETTING GYPPED
By Margaret Bresnahan Carlson
Harper & Row Publishers, 1973.

HOW TO KEEP YOUR VOLKSWAGEN ALIVE
By John Muir.
John Muir Publications, $17.95.

HOW TO MAKE YOUR CAR LAST ALMOST FOREVER
By Jack Gillis.
Perigee Books, $6.95.

LAST CHANCE GARAGE
By Brad Sears and William Scheller.
Harper and Row, $8.61.

Appendix O

699 WAYS TO IMPROVE THE PERFORMANCE OF YOUR CAR
By Harry Alexandrowicz.
Sterling Publishing Co., $13.29.

THE ARMCHAIR MECHANIC
By Jack Gillis and Tom Kelly.
Perennial Library, $8.95.

THE GREAT AMERICAN AUTO REPAIR ROBBERY
By Donald A. Randall & Arthur P. Glickman.
Charterhouse, 1972.

WEEKEND MECHANIC'S HANDBOOK
By Paul Weissler.
Arco Publishing, $11.95.

APPENDIX P

FEDERAL GOVERNMENT ADDRESSES

The White House
1600 Pennsylvania Ave., NW
Washington, DC 20500
(202) 456–1414
    White House Office of Consumer Affairs

Agencies:

Department of Energy
1000 Independence Ave., SW
Washington, DC 20585
(202) 586–5000

Department of Transportation
National Highway Traffic Safety Administration
400 Seventh St., SW
Washington, DC 20590
TOLL-FREE HOTLINE (800) 424–9393/Washington, DC
                call 366–0123
          TTY (800) 424–9153/Washington, DC
                call 755–8919
  Administrator (202) 366–1836
  Director, Office of Defects Investigation (202) 366–2850

Environmental Protection Agency
401 M St., SW
Washington, DC 20460
(202) 382–2090
Office of Mobile Sources (202) 382–7645

Federal Trade Commission
Bureau of Consumer Protection
6th and Pennsylvania Ave., NW
Washington, DC 20580
(202) 326–2000

Congressional Committees:

Committee on Commerce, Science, and Transportation
U.S. Senate
Washington, DC 20510
(202) 224—5115
       Consumer Subcommittee (202) 224–0415

Committee on Energy and Commerce
U.S. House of Representatives
Washington, DC 20515
(202) 225–2927
       Subcommittees on: Commerce, Consumer Protection,
                 and Competitiveness (202) 226–3160
                 Telecommunications and Finance
                 (202) 226–2424

Individual Members of Congress:

Senator: The Honorable (full name)
       U.S. Senate
       Washington, DC 20510

Representative: The Honorable (full name)
       U.S. House of Representatives
       Washington, DC 20515

Call (202) 224–3121 (Capitol switchboard) and ask for your senator or representative.

APPENDIX Q

NEW/USED CAR BUYING GUIDES

"Consumer Complaint Resource and Referral Guide." Available for $5 from the State of California Consumer Affairs Office, 1020 N Street, Room 547, Sacramento, CA 95814.

"Consumer Protection Under the Federal Odometer Law." For a free copy, write National Highway Traffic Safety Administration, U.S. Department of Transportation, Office of Public Affairs and Consumer Services, Washington, D.C. 20590.

"Consumer Reports Magazine" Annual Auto Issue (April of every year). Lists "Frequency of repair records," based on readers' replies to CU's Annual Questionnaire, as well as other valuable information. Available from newsstands or by subscription. To order call: 1–800–234–1645.

Consumer Reports Annual Buying Guide (December of every year). Rates prior model year and provides frequency of repair charts. Available in bookstores or newsstands. To order call: 1–800–234–1645.

Consumer Reports Guide to Used Cars. Sums up Consumers Union's advice on which models to consider and which to avoid, where to buy and how to inspect a used car. To order call: 1–800–242–7737 ($8.00).

Available from Consumer Information Center, Pueblo, Colorado 81009:

"Buying a Used Car" ($.50)
"New Car Buying Guide" ($.50)

Available from your local bookstore or library:

The Used Car Book
by Jack Gillis: Tells consumers what to look for and what to avoid by rating hundreds of used cars. Offers tips on getting a good deal on your purchase and repairs. (Harper & Row)

The Car Book
by Jack Gillis. Annual guide to new car safety, fuel economy, maintenance and insurance costs; organized by make and model. (Harper & Row)

Don't Get Taken Every Time: The Insider's Guide to Buying or Leasing Your Next Car or Truck
by Remar Sutton. Former auto dealer and sales manager gives advice on getting the best car for the best price. (Penguin)

A P P E N D I X   R

CENTER FOR AUTO SAFETY
MEMBERSHIP

The Center for Auto Safety is the only consumer group working fulltime to stop lemons and improve auto safety and quality. For car buyers stuck with lemons, the Center is the best "lemon-aid" available.

The Center for Auto Safety depends on your support in our fight for consumers against the giant car companies. Annual membership contributions of $15 or more are fully tax deductible. As a Center member, you will receive our "Lemon Times" newsletter telling you about the latest "lemon crop" and our efforts to weed them out.

CENTER FOR AUTO SAFETY   MEMBERSHIP FORM

Yes! I strongly support the work of the Center for Auto Safety to stop lemons and to make our cars and highways safer. Be sure to keep me informed of the Center's actions through your quarterly newsletter, The Lemon Times.

☐ Enclosed is my annual membership contribution of $15—less than the price of an oil change.

☐ I want to give an additional contribution.
   Enclosed is ☐ $25   ☐ $50   ☐ $100   ☐ other $ _____.

Your contribution is tax-deductible.

Name: _____

Address: _____

_____

2001 S St., NW • Washington, D.C. • 20009

I N D E X